Published by T&T Clark
A Continuum imprint
The Tower Building, 11 York Road, London SE1 7NX
80 Maiden Lane, Suite 704, New York, NY 10038

www.continuumbooks.com

Copyright © Philomena Cullen, Bernard Hoose and Gerard Mannion and contributors, 2007

British Library Cataloguing-in-Publication Data
A catalogue record for this book is available from the British Library

Typset by RefineCatch Limited, Bungay, Suffolk
Printed on acid-free paper in Great Britain by Athenaeum Press Ltd.

ISBN–10: HB: 0–567–04541–2
         PB: 0–567–04542–0
ISBN–13: HB: 978–0–567–04541–6
         PB: 978–0–567–04542–3

Catholic Social Justice

D0494007

Catholic Social Justice

Theological and Practical Exploratio

Edited by
Philomena Cullen, Bernard Hoose
and Gerard Mannion

continuum

Contents

Contents

Acknowledgements

Our first debt in any collection of essays of this sort is to the contributors of this volume. Without their support, talent and generosity this book would not have come to be. A sincere thank you for your passion for social justice and for your willingness to support the charity, Caritas-social action.

We also acknowledge the advice and guidance of the members of Caritas-social action's Theological Commission on Social Spirituality, led by Bishop Christopher Budd, where the enthusiasm and inspiration for this book was born and honed. Support has also been forthcoming from the Caritas Internationalis federation and in particular from its general secretary Duncan MacLaren, whose encouragement has been invaluable.

Finally we would like to thank Georgina Brindley at Continuum for believing in this project and for bearing with us so patiently during the writing process.

Grateful acknowledgement is made to the following for permission to reprint previously published material. Hans Küng's chapter was previously published in his book *A Global Ethic for Global Politics and Economics* (London: SCM Press, 1997), translated by John Bowden from the German *Weltethos für Weltpolitik und Weltwirtschaft*, published by Piper Verlag GmbH Munich, 1997. It is reproduced here with kind permission from the author. Duncan B. Forrester's chapter was previously published in Italian as 'La giustizia sociale nel pensiero protestante', in Giancarlo Mazzocchi and Andrea Villani (eds), *Etica, Economia, Principi di Giustizia* (Milano: FrancoAngeli, 2001), pp. 304–17. It is again reproduced here with kind permission from the author.

Every effort has been made to obtain relevant permissions for material cited. If any such permissions have been overlooked the publisher will seek to rectify this situation as soon as possible.

Preface

Duncan MacLaren (Secretary General, Caritas Internationalis)

This book is an important contribution to the social justice cause within the Catholic Church from a member of the Caritas Confederation in England and Wales: Caritas-social action. It is important because it makes the link between faith and praxis, between the search for truth that is at the heart of all good theology and a spirituality founded on the encounter of God in all human experience in order to inform and nurture action to transform the world, especially the world of the poor, the excluded and the marginalized.

It is this mixture of contemplation, reflection and action that distinguishes the Christian activist in social justice matters from others. It is our specificity. Without the elements of theological reflection and spiritual nourishment, our actions for justice can easily become ideological, knee-jerk or even trivial. Timothy Radcliffe OP, the former Master of the Dominican Order, wrote once:

> Contemplation is not the discovery of God through retreat from the world . . . It is opening our eyes to discover God waiting for us in the most unpromising situations. The discipline of the contemplative life liberates us from the banal and trivial way of looking at things and at each other which is characteristic of the world of consumerism. We learn to see properly, to see in the dark, and above all to see compassionately, as God sees us. The contemplative must dare to be vulnerable to the pain and suffering of this world and to 'allow ourselves to be touched by what happens to us and the world around, in the belief that in this way we come upon the traces of the God of salvation and liberation'.[1]

This book is especially pertinent at this time in history when the social, the collective and the public realm are characterized by neo-liberals as the enemies of prosperity, thus endangering the welfare state; where conservative axioms about taxation, security, unfair trade and warmongering are too often taken as acceptable international norms, thus militating against any sense of distributive justice and a just peace; and where conflict, especially identity conflict between one ethnic or religious group and another within one country, still ravages many parts of our world, causing more extreme poverty and division within the human family. The answer to the world's woes is not a mindless activism to change things but one that is profoundly based on our understanding of what it is to be human. That search can only be done for Christians through theological reflection, prayer and spiritual direction. This book of essays assists us marvellously in this, our Christian journey towards greater social justice.

Note

1. Timothy Radcliffe OP, 'Foreword', in Eric Borgman, *Dominican Spirituality: An Exploration* (London: Continuum: 2001), p. vii.

Foreword

Bishop Christopher Budd

In 1995 the Catholic Bishops' Conference of England and Wales set up a new organization called the Catholic Agency for Social Concern (CASC). The scope of the new agency was to be:

- an umbrella and focus for Catholic social welfare agencies and other groups in the Church in England and Wales which were involved in any way with social concern;
- a catalyst for education and the promotion of Catholic social teaching (CST);
- an agency for advocacy in relationship to the UK and the EU;
- an agency encouraging research and development.

The new agency developed steadily towards the Jubilee Year 2000. It engaged in some specialist subjects like the report on Women in Prison (2000). This was in pursuit of one of its four basic aims – research. It took longer to encourage the main diocesan agencies to come on board and be actively involved.

In 2003, CASC came together with the Catholic Child Welfare Committee and the Social Welfare Committee of the Bishops' Conference, to form Caritas-social action. By this time most of the diocesan agencies had become involved, strong advocacy links had developed with a variety of national non-governmental organizations who shared our domestic social justice concerns and with groups within Parliament (both inter-party and ecumenical), and an active theological reflection group had been put in place. This faith-reflection activity that we called 'social spirituality' has given birth to the present volume.

The importance of faith reflection and its interaction with human reasoning is endorsed by the words of Pope Benedict XVI in his first Encyclical Letter, *Deus Caritas Est*:

Faith by its specific nature is an encounter with the living God – an encounter opening up new horizons extending beyond the sphere or reason. But it is also a purifying force for reason itself. From God's standpoint faith liberates reason from its blind spots and therefore helps it to be ever more fully itself. Faith enables reason to do its work effectively and to see its proper object more clearly. This is where Catholic social doctrine has its place: it has no intention of giving the Church power over the State. Even less is it an attempt to impose on those who do not share the faith ways of thinking and modes of conduct proper to faith. Its aim is simply to help purify reason and to contribute, here and now, to the acknowledgement and attainment of what is just.[1]

The teaching of the Church about social matters, and there has been a lot over the last 100 years, is not purely an exercise in relevance. It lies much deeper – the Kingdom of God is not just in the future in a place well outside the present era, but is in our midst. Its presence requires us to reveal it and to make it manifest. Both the social teaching of the Church, and its implementation in and by the Church, are a part of the process through which the presence of the Kingdom is shown. In this way the Church is not seeking to impose justice for her own advantage. She is the servant of social affairs.

The love of God poured into our hearts is not just about the transformation of individuals. It affects our corporate reality and forms the communities of faith to which we belong. There is no human being who does not enjoy the inviolable dignity proper to human beings and who is not called into some form of community.

We often hear the phrase, 'the dignity of the human person', and yet we can often be at a loss to unpack what it means. The dignity of the human person is rooted in his/her relationship with God (we call this creation) and their sharing in the profound mystery of God. The mystery of God (shared in by all human beings) means that our attitude to another person has some measure of awe about it – an acceptance of the other person as other than me and worthy of worshipful respect. God's otherness is total and that elicits the response of worship. I cannot treat another human being as a commodity that I can use as I wish. All human beings, no matter how self-sufficient or vulnerable, require others to treat them with due respect and to promote their well-being.

The essays in this volume are an attempt to spell out and analyse what this dignity of the human person means in different areas of our communal life. Community is quite complex because its members are related in different ways within it. The complexity of these relationships between people means that we need clear principles and sometimes more detailed rules and regulations to ensure that human beings can flourish.

The chapters in this book represent an effort, coordinated by Caritas-social action, to fulfil the Church's task in consolidating reason as it engages in social reflection and the ordering of civil society, both local, national and international. As the present Pope has said so clearly, the

Church has no ambition to take over state power. She has in history done that, often because Church and State became identified with each other or unhelpfully confused. The body of social teaching which has been developed by the Church over the centuries, and particularly in the last 100 years, can be likened to the comments of a critical friend, and sometimes, because of an alien ideology, a critical opponent (e.g. Communism). The essays in this volume stand in that tradition.

Caritas and all Catholic agencies will, in pursuing the preferential option for the poor, concentrate much of their activity on people who are, in one way or another, vulnerable and often in need of special protection and advocacy. It is not a question of those who can do a good turn to those who cannot, but an acknowledgement that we are brothers and sisters to each other and that nobody, no matter how frail, can fall outside the loving concern of all of us. To run the risk of refusing human community to anyone is something that faith and justice cannot tolerate. Nobody, no matter what they have done or how frail they are, falls outside the scope of concern and justice and therefore of the community of faith.

The phrase 'social spirituality' may sound a little odd. Spirituality is a broad term and refers to the way we think, feel and try to live. Its main point of reference is generally individuals or groups of individuals. It does not necessarily and exclusively relate to faith, although faith normally expresses itself in some form of spirituality or way of thinking and living.

Social spirituality refers to the importance of making the rich tradition of the Church's social teaching a main focus of the way we think and live. It will form and shape our instinctive responses and sensitivities.

In particular, it will ensure that we think 'persons'! It is chilling to think that the first stage of developing contempt towards individuals or groups is to dehumanize them in our thought (we saw this horrifically during the Nazi era in Europe). The next step is easy because we can dispose of them, as we will. If our way of thinking and living is totally coloured and shaped by an acknowledgement of the personal dignity of all human beings, we are developing a social spirituality.

Another feature of social spirituality is our willingness to be humble in the presence of other ways of looking at our reality. This does not mean that we agree with everything that is being proposed. It does mean that we listen to what others are saying and try to understand them. We may then become critics of their views, but we do so having shown respect for the people who promote a different view or teaching.

Ultimately the Church has to be busy about the things of the Kingdom. Kingdom truths are her concern both in what she teaches and in the way she tries to live. In both she needs to make manifest that Kingdom which is already present and yet yearns for its final form to be revealed and established at the end of time. Her concern for the welfare of people here and now is a part of making visible that Kingdom. Not to do so would be a major failure in her commitment to her Lord. The overall message of the Incarnation is that God is concerned for all people. We the Church are custodians of that message and we need to be vocal about it and active in using it to influence the arrangement of our societies.

A concluding word from Pope Benedict summarizes what the volume is about:

> We have seen that the formation of just structures is not directly the duty of the Church, but belongs to the world of politics, the sphere of the autonomous use of reason. The Church has an indirect duty here, in that she is called to contribute to the purification of reason and to the reawakening of those moral forces without which just structures are neither established nor prove effective in the long run.[2]

This book is a serious contribution to that endeavour.

Notes

1. Pope Benedict XVI, encyclical letter *Deus Caritas Est* (Libreria Editrice Vaticana, 2006), §28a, para. 3.
2. Ibid., §29, para. 1.

Contributors' Biographies

Tissa Balasuriya

Fr Tissa Balasuriya is a member of the Oblates of Mary Immaculate and one of Sri Lanka's most esteemed theologians. His studies ranged from history to economics and politics, to theology and then sociology. These studies took him from Sri Lanka to Rome, to Oxford and finally Paris. He served as Rector of Colombo's Aquinas Institute and as Asian Chaplain to the International Catholic Student Movement. He has been a leading pioneer in the fields of Asian liberation theology, theology of religions, Christian mission in a pluralist society, ecological theology, in ecumenical and interfaith dialogue and in Christian responsibility for justice and peace. In 1971, he established the *Centre for Society and Religion* in Colombo which encapsulates the heart of Christian social spirituality and Catholic social justice in the work that it does – from educational classes to research projects, to reconciliation work across Sri Lanka's divided communities, to the work of its international conference centre and orphanage north of Colombo. A founding member of the Association of Third World Theologians (EATWOT), he edited its journal for 17 years (*Voices from the Third World*). Excommunicated for a year following a controversial assessment of his books by the Vatican's Congregation for the Doctrine of the Faith, he was reconciled to full communion following his recitation of *The Credo of the People of God*, written by Pope Paul VI. He has published extensively over several decades including *Jesus and Human Liberation* (Quest Series, 1976), *Planetary Theology* (Orbis, 1984), *God Has No Favourites* (Orbis, 1988), *Mary and Human Liberation* (Geoffrey Chapman, 1997) and *The Eucharist and Human Liberation* (Maryknoll, NY: Orbis Books, 1979).

John Battle MP

John Battle has been Member of Parliament for Leeds West since 1987. He was appointed as a Minister of State at the Department of Trade and Industry following Labour's 1997 election victory, and from 1999 to 2001 was Minister of State at the Foreign Office. He is currently the Prime Minister's Envoy to the Faith Communities as well as a Member of the

International Development Select Committee. He is also Chair of All-Party Parliamentary Groups on Poverty and on Overseas Development. Before becoming an MP, John Battle was National Coordinator for Church Action on Poverty from 1983.

Sheila Cassidy

Sheila Cassidy retired from hospital work in 2002 after 40 years in the NHS. Although known to many as the young doctor tortured under the Pinochet regime, she spent her 30 post-Chile years working with cancer patients in both a hospital and hospice setting. She now works part time as a psychotherapist and spends many happy hours sitting on the edge of Plymouth Sound with her two beloved chows, Anchor and Molly. She is the author of seven books and has just published a new book, *Made for Laughter* (Darton, Longman and Todd), an autobiography including both the Chile experience and the years that followed.

Philomena Cullen

Philomena Cullen was the social policy coordinator of Caritas-social action in England and Wales. Trained in theology, philosophy and social studies, she is also a qualified social worker. She was educated at New College, Oxford and at Durham University. Her social work experience includes posts with the Vincentians in Dublin, Ireland and with *Save the Children* in London, UK. She has been responsible for numerous policy documents for Caritas and was behind the formation of its Theology Commission in 2004. She is currently undertaking doctoral research in the area of feminist theology.

Duncan B. Forrester

Duncan B. Forrester was ordained as a presbyter of the Church of South India in 1962. As a Church of Scotland missionary he taught politics at Madras Christian College for eight years. After a period as chaplain and lecturer in politics and religious studies at the University of Sussex, he was appointed in 1978 to the chair of Christian ethics and practical theology in New College, University of Edinburgh. He was Principal of New College from 1986–96, and Dean of the Faculty of Divinity from 1996–2000. He established and was first Director of the Centre for Theology and Public Issues. He retired in 2001. His recent publications include *The True Church and Morality: Reflections on Ecclesiology and Ethics* (WCC, 1997), *Christian Justice and Public Policy* (Cambridge University Press, 1997), *Truthful Action: Explorations in Practical Theology* (T&T Clark, 2000), *On Human Worth: A Christian Vindication of Equality* (SCM Press, 2001), *Theological Fragments: Explorations in Unsystematic Theology* (Continuum, 2005) and *Apocalypse Now? Reflections on Faith in a Time of Terror* (Ashgate, 2005).

Bernard Hoose

Bernard Hoose lectures in Christian ethics at Heythrop College, University of London and has taught at various seminaries. He has published widely in the field of moral theology and Christian ethics. His work is well known on both sides of the Atlantic. He was a student at the Gregorian University in Rome, where he obtained degrees in philosophy and theology as well as a licentiate and a doctorate in moral theology. Dr Hoose is perhaps best known for his writings in the sphere of fundamental moral theology – most notably his contributions to the international debate on proportionalism. He has also made significant contributions to debate on various other issues, including the punishment of criminals, authority, truth and human gene therapy. His publications include *Proportionalism: The American Debate and Its European Roots* (Washington DC: Georgetown University Press, 1987) and *Received Wisdom? Reviewing the Role of Tradition in Christian Ethics* (London: Geoffrey Chapman, 1994). He is editor of *Christian Ethics: An Introduction* (London: Cassell, 1998), *Authority in the Roman Catholic Church* (Aldershot: Ashgate, 2002) and *Authority in Roman Catholicism* (Chelmsford: Matthew James, 2002). He presently serves on the Theology Commission of Caritas-Social Action.

Jayne Hoose

Jayne Hoose is formerly a senior lecturer at Canterbury Christ Church University, she studied moral theology at King's College, London and currently works as a freelance writer and lecturer. She has published a range of articles, book chapters and books in the two disciplines of leisure and moral theology, including two internationally recognized books: *An Introduction to Leisure Studies* and *Conscience in World Religions*.

Hans Küng

Hans Küng is a Catholic priest, an eminent Swiss theologian and a prolific author. Küng studied theology and philosophy at the Pontifical Gregorian University in Rome and was ordained in 1954. He then continued his education in various European cities, including the Sorbonne in Paris. In 1960 Küng was appointed professor of theology at Eberhard Karls University, Tübingen, Germany where he taught until his retirement (*Emeritierung*) in 1996. Just like his colleague Joseph Ratzinger (now Pope Benedict XVI), in 1962 he was appointed *peritus* by Pope John XXIII, serving as an expert theological adviser to members of the Second Vatican Council until its conclusion in 1965. His ecclesiological works soon began to attract the investigative attention of the Vatican's Congregation for the Doctrine of the Faith (CDF). In particular, his books *The Church* (1967; English translation, London: Search, 1968)) and *Infallible? An Inquiry* (1971; English translation, rev. edn, London, SCM, 1994), aroused questions concerning his 'orthodoxy'. Over the years, he has continued to teach and conduct research on a variety of subjects, from Christian faith and life to dialogue with world religions; from the philosophical question of God's existence to the possibility of a 'global ethic'. Nonetheless, ecclesiology and church reform have never been far from his mind. His uneasy relations with the Vatican came to a head when he published a short text, *The Church – Maintained in Truth*, in 1979 (English translation, London, SCM, 1980). In it he extolled the virtues of a teaching authority of the Church which could admit it was fallible and live and learn by its failings. The CDF (Congregation for the Doctrine of the Faith) issued a declaration on 18 December, that same year, stating that the book proved Küng had 'departed from the integral truth of the Catholic Faith' and went on to assert that Küng could no longer be considered a Catholic theologian, nor function as one in his teaching. Much controversy followed and many theologians rallied to Küng's defence. Suffice to say, Küng has tried to remain faithful to his principles and has continued to speak out against what he considers to be the Curial authorities' betrayal of the hope of Vatican II in the decades since that council. In the early 1990s Küng initiated a project called *Weltethos* (Global Ethic), which is an attempt at describing what the world religions have in common (rather than what separates them) and at drawing up a minimal code of rules of behaviour everyone can accept. Since 1995 he has been President of the Foundation for a Global Ethic (*Stiftung Weltethos*). His vision of a global ethic was embodied in the document for which he wrote the initial draft, *Towards a Global Ethic: An Initial Declaration*. This Declaration was signed at the 1993 Parliament of the World's Religions by many religious and spiritual leaders from around the world. Later Küng's project would culminate into the UN's 'Dialogue among Civilizations'.

Gerard Mannion

Gerard Mannion is associate professor of ecclesiology and ethics at Liverpool Hope University where he is Director of the Centre for the Study of Contemporary Ecclesiology and co-director of the Applied Ethics Initiative. The Archbishop Derek Worlock Research Fellow for 2006–07, he previously taught at Church Colleges of the Universities of Leeds and Oxford and was a 2004 Coolidge Fellow at Union Theological Seminary, New York. Educated at King's College, Cambridge and New College, Oxford, his publications include *Schopenhauer, Religion and Morality* (Ashgate, 2003), *Readings in Church Authority: Gifts and Challenges for Contemporary Catholicism* (co-editor) (Ashgate, 2003) and *Ecclesiology and Postmodernity: Questions for the Church in our Times* (Collegeville, Liturgical Press, 2007). He is the co-editor of two forthcoming volumes, *The Routledge Companion to the Christian Church*, 2007 (with Lewis Mudge) and *The Ratzinger Reader* (with Lieven Boeve). Mannion is also presently chair of the Ecclesiological Investigations International Research Network, and founding co-chair of the Ecclesiological Investigations Program Unit of the American Academy of Religion.

Judith A. Merkle

Judith A. Merkle SNDdeN (Sisters of Notre Dame de Namur) is an associate professor of religious studies at Niagara University, New York. She is the author of *From the Heart of the Church: The Catholic Social Tradition* (Liturgical Press, 2004) as well as other books and articles on religious life in contemporary society, justice and peace and Christian ethics. She is a member of the Sisters of Notre Dame de Namur, an international religious community of women within the Catholic Church.

Peter C. Phan

Peter C. Phan has earned three doctorates, one (STD, Doctor of Sacred Theology) from the Pontifical Salesian University, Rome and the other two (PhD and DD) from the University of London. He has written and edited some 20 books and over 300 essays on various aspects of theology. Currently he holds the Ignacio Ellacuria Chair in Catholic Social Thought at Georgetown University.

Jim Richards

Jim Richards is Chief Executive of the Catholic Children's Society (Westminster). He has worked in the probation service and local authorities. He is a trustee of NCVCCO (National Council of Voluntary Child Care Organisations) and the Cardinal Hume Centre and is a member of his diocesan child protection commission. He is also a deacon in the Catholic Church.

Noel Timms

After graduating in medieval history Noel Timms practised as a social worker in family service units and trained as a psychiatric social worker. His career as a university lecturer eventually took him to chairs in social work studies at the universities of Bradford, Newcastle and Leicester. Taking early retirement enabled him to care for his wife in her years of Alzheimer's disease. It also enabled him to complete work on European Values and on the Queen's Working Group, Birmingham, on Authority and Governance in the Catholic Church. He has edited and written widely on social work, social problems and social philosophy. He has recently completed a part-time MA in Catholic Theology and has just registered for a certificate course in Islamic Studies.

Sir Stephen Wall

Stephen Wall was born in January 1947 and educated at Douai School and Selwyn College, Cambridge. Stephen Wall joined the Diplomatic Service in 1968, and had a career there that spanned 35 years. Among his appointments was Private Secretary to three successive Foreign Secretaries (Geoffrey Howe, John Major and Douglas Hurd), and from 1991 to 1993 he was Private Secretary to the Prime Minister, John Major, responsible for Foreign Policy and Defence. Stephen Wall also served as British Ambassador to Portugal from 1993 to 1995. He was the Permanent Representative to the European Union from 1995–2000. From 2000–2004 he was the Head of the European Secretariat in the Cabinet Office in London and EU adviser to the Prime Minister, Tony Blair. From June 2004–June 2005 he was principal adviser to the Roman Catholic Archbishop of Westminster, Cardinal Cormac Murphy-O'Connor.

Introduction

Caritas in Theory and Practice

Philomena Cullen, Bernard Hoose and Gerard Mannion

The rationale for this volume of essays on Catholic social justice is a conviction that the contemporary implications of the oft-stated comment that the Church does not simply have, but *is*, a social mission, now call for fresh perspectives for the twenty-first century. Different times and rapidly changing contexts and societies present new and different problems and challenges to human communities. Throughout the Christian Church people recognize and acknowledge this. The *World Council of Churches*, as well as numerous national ecumenical and denominational bodies, and church-linked charities and NGOs across many countries, have devoted much time and effort to revisiting the fundamental questions and priorities concerning Christian social justice and social spirituality in the contemporary era.

Roman Catholics have sought to do likewise and, over 40 years since the promulgation of the *Pastoral Constitution on the Church in the Modern World*, Catholics across the globe are seeking to respond to these new social realities. Indeed, the official Roman Catholic Church body in this area, the Pontifical Council for Justice and Peace, launched its substantial *Compendium of the Social Doctrine of the Church* in October 2004. This document proclaims that 'the transformation of the world is essential in our age too'. New courses and modules in aspects of Catholic, Christian and religious social ethics are becoming increasingly popular. Governments are engaging in ongoing debates and developing new partnerships with faith-based communities across the globe. Questions of the relations between religion and public life enjoy their highest media profile in many decades. So the Catholic Church, like other religious communities, is striving to discern the contemporary situation, as well as to look to the future and ascertain how to ensure that values pertaining to the building of the Kingdom of love and justice impact upon our local, societal and international communities. In short, social justice is very much on the contemporary church agenda.

There are, of course, vigorous debates to be had in all of this discernment of the demands of justice in our time and different contexts. Topics such as how the Church identifies its social priorities today (how the Church allocates its resources; how it shapes, facilitates and governs its practices; how it relates to and seeks to influence civil and secular society) all demand attention. Furthermore, in today's post 9/11 climate, the emerging relationship between religion and State is a matter of intense public interest. What does it mean, anyway, to be in the world but not of the world in our postmodern context?

It is such pressing and complex questions of this kind that have motivated the social justice agency of the Catholic Bishops' Conference in England and Wales, Caritas-social action, to produce this book. Caritas-social action has launched a range of initiatives in recent years to ensure that the Catholic Church in England and Wales plays as full a part as possible in the fight for social justice. The agency was in part formed to help coordinate the efforts of the thousands of individuals and organizations involved in Catholic social, caring and advocacy work in the UK, as well as to help shape the Church's response to the domestic social justice agenda. Knowing that it is important to render the gospel more and more present by applying it to our particular situations and times, Caritas-social action established a major Theological Commission on Social Spirituality. This was launched in March 2004 at the British House of Commons. A group of church people, academics and practitioners, concerned with exploring the contemporary interface between theology, social justice and social spirituality, were thus assembled, and this volume emerged as one of the early projects undertaken by this group. Caritas has adopted as its own the motto, 'Providing Support, Creating Hope, Uniting in Faith'. This book seeks to explore the dimensions of each such aspiration.

This volume draws together perspectives from an esteemed international collection of scholars and practitioners in the field of Christian social ethics. All of the essays address the Roman Catholic tradition in social ethics and social spirituality, but some chapters also address the ecumenical and Protestant traditions, as well. The book is concerned to nurture ecumenical and interreligious dialogue on social justice, as well as to foster dialogue with all people of goodwill.

Hence the title '*Catholic* Social Justice' must be understood in the broadest sense of the term. Thus, for example, Professor Duncan Forrester's esteemed contribution is every bit as Catholic a reflection upon social justice as those from Roman Catholic contributors. Forrester's work has spanned several decades and has been at the forefront, often in a pioneering fashion, of Christian ethics – especially social and political ethics – as well as of ecclesiology and of moral, political, practical, contextual, ecumenical and, finally, of course, *public* theology. Forrester defines the latter as a theology which 'attends to the Bible and the tradition of faith at the same time as it attempts to discern the signs of the times and understand what is going on in the light of the gospel'.[1]

In his recent essay, 'Working in the Quarry', he believes that public theology must always avoid the twin evils of inward-looking aloofness and exclusivism just as it must shun over-accommodation to the point of the disappearance of what Christianity has to offer that is enduring and distinctive (and one takes him to mean it has something to offer that is the former, *because* it is the latter). He speaks of rekindling our utopian energies and steadfastly defends the role of, indeed the *need* for, theology in public debate. 'What we need is a theology which makes a difference, a theology that heals, reconciles, helps, challenges. Perhaps we need more theologians who are angry, and determined to make a difference . . .'[2] One would struggle to find a better definition of true social catholicity for our times.

All of the 14 chapters represent an exploration of contemporary social justice concerns from a range of diverse perspectives. The authors write from different backgrounds, geographical locations and professional milieux. Yet what will be clear to readers is that, regardless of the different theological, social scientific, philosophical and ecclesiological perspectives articulated here, the myriad voices are united by a common unswerving commitment to social justice – that the Catholic faith *is* social spirituality.

The original vision for the book was for a lively and interdisciplinary bridging of theoretical and practical theology that would discern the signs of our times within the UK context, in particular, but which would also touch upon key debates in the US and European contexts, as well as dealing with matters of pressing concern in the wider global Church. The volume seeks to identify and explore a number of questions pertinent to all Christians, and, given the organization that has commissioned the volume and the background of most contributors, it will appeal especially to those within the Roman Catholic tradition who are concerned with a spirituality that does justice. In short it is a book about Christian social justice and charity – Caritas in theory and in practice. Only for ease of reference and to enable readers better to focus their attention and to explore particular dimensions of social spirituality have the theological and practical explorations of Catholic social justice been artificially divided into two parts in the book

Part I of the book focuses upon theological explorations in social justice and social spirituality. The British Catholic moral theologian, Bernard Hoose, begins by firmly setting personal spirituality within a social context. He attacks the notion of privatized spirituality, arguing instead that it is within and through relationships with other people that we can, and should, speak of spirituality, of relationship with the Holy Spirit. Expanding on this theme, Peter C. Phan, one of the world's foremost scholars in Catholic social teaching, examines the social dimension of Christian spirituality in a global perspective. Tackling the complex phenomenon known as globalization and the seemingly opposing need of Christian spirituality to be deeply rooted in local cultures, he explores some of the urgent socio-political and economic challenges Christian spirituality must grapple with today. The Sri Lankan theologian Tissa Balasuriya reminds us that, over long periods of its history, the Church fostered unjust structures of society through its alliance with Western Christian colonizers. Reflecting on Pope Benedict XVI's encyclical, *Deus Caritas Est*, he suggests that justice as a requirement of love has been somewhat overlooked here as well. Next, the Scottish theologian, Duncan Forrester, offers some reflections on social justice in Protestant thought and, while noting the similarities between Catholic and Protestant traditions, also appraises the differences, most notably the more diverse and episodic nature of Protestant justice thinking, which can contribute creatively to the confusing debate on justice that is taking place in the UK public policy arena today. Then Judith Merkle, the American theologian and Sister of Notre Dame de Namur, takes up the challenge of defining the nature of faith that seeks to do justice in this new millennium. She argues that our new context reframes the old question, what is worth my effort? She goes on to suggest that while the search for faith to do justice is never resolved, our faith continues to offer us a way beyond the paralysis that many feel before this question. The Irish theologian, Gerard Mannion, turns his attention to the world of work and offers some insights as to how theology in general and Catholic social teaching in particular might help us all to flourish through truly being, rather than through spending the majority of our lives merely working in ways and conditions that are detrimental to life itself, and hence to our relationship with God and with one another. Finally in Part I, in a complementary essay, the British polymath scholar and moral theologian, Jayne Hoose, looks at the leisure phenomenon and constructs a 'theology of leisure' which could help free us from some of those long-held bonds of productivity and status gained through work.

Part II of the book is more practically oriented and examines a number of topical themes about the practice of social spirituality in today's world. Former civil servant Sir Stephen Wall reflects on his experience of the changed nature of being a Catholic advocate today and believes that carrying our faith into public life requires us to choose whether to rest on the absolute truth of the Church's teaching or to use the tools of a democratic society, including compromise, to reach our justice goals. The British politician, John Battle MP, ponders what it means to hear the cry of the poor today, and argues for a renewed, positive valuing of politics as the means of acting out the 'preferential option' for the poor. Such a project of a change of consciousness as the task for the new millennium is mirrored in the next chapter by theologian Hans Küng. He likewise asserts that within the worlds of business and management there exists an opportunity to build a new sense of responsibility and a responsible economics which seeks to achieve the precarious balance between ideals and realities and which can combine economic strategies with ethical convictions to make clearer the outlines of a more peaceful, just and humane world. Two subsequent chapters, by social work professionals Jim Richards and Philomena Cullen, shift the focus on to our familial relationships. Jim Richards explores the opportunities and tensions within the concept and practice of children's rights and asserts that, while giving clear rights to children is the best way of protecting them, they must always be applied within the context of a child's life, that is, as a member of a family. Philomena Cullen believes that social justice is served when we move beyond damaging romanticizations of the family to acknowledge that our family life and forms are not fixed but open to change and development. She encourages us to avoid the 'idolatry of the family' and instead construct open, fluid families that are characterized by equality and mutuality and responsive to the needs of all our brothers and sisters. Exploring the quality of our interpersonal relationships further, the international writer and psychoanalyst Sheila Cassidy writes about empathy as the key to Christian care in many different settings. 'The ability to enter the other's world as if it were your own' leads to a depth of understanding and compassion which makes the Christian call to loving-kindness a necessity rather than an option. To conclude our reflections, the British social policy professor Noel Timms raises questions about the reception and development of Catholic social teaching. He challenges the sources of such teaching, notes the ambiguity of discernment of the signs of the times and leaves us pondering whether Catholic social teaching can and should be developed.

We believe that this is a rich and challenging volume of reflection on contemporary social justice issues both within and beyond the Catholic tradition. All of those scholars and activists involved with and interested in contemporary debates surrounding the interrelationship between theology, social justice and social spirituality should be able to find food for thought here. It is our hope, as modest editors of this volume, that it will inspire readers in their own credible witness, in thought and by action, of the Christian call to social justice.

Notes

1. Cited in *Public Theology for the Twenty-First Century: Essays in Honour of Duncan B. Forrester*, ed. William F. Storrar and Andrew R. Morton (London, T&T Clark, 2004), p. 1.
2. Ibid., p. 436.

Part I

Theological Explorations in Social Justice and Social Spirituality

Chapter 1

Spirituality and Morality in a Social Context

Bernard Hoose

It is important for us to grow in self-knowledge and thus gain greater awareness of the Spirit who lives within us. One way to achieve this is through prayer. Another is through relationships with other people. Without this two-pronged approach, we run the risk of making matters worse rather than better when we set out to help our fellow humans. If we adopt it, however, we can be instruments of the most positive of all powers.

Spirituality is often spoken about in the context of individuals alone with God, a well-known example being that of St John of the Cross, who was inspired to write his *Spiritual Canticle* in the silence and solitude of his prison cell. We humans, however, are, by our very nature, relational creatures – in relationship with other human beings as well as with God. We need to be in relationships:

> Growth in human beings is like the growth of plants and of trees. We need to be rooted in earth, nourished by this earth and by the sun, water and air in order to grow and reach fulfilment, to bear fruit and give new life. If this 'earth' is a place of language and culture, it is essentially made up of people, people to whom we are bonded, committed people who love and appreciate us, people who call us forth to healthy relationships, openness, and love. Without other human beings, we close up in fear.
>
> Our personalities deepen and grow as we live in openness and respect for others, when weakness is listened to and the weak are empowered, that is to say, when people are helped to be truly them-selves, to own their lives and discover their capacity to give life to others. Fear closes us down; love opens us up.[1]

Within and through relationships with other people we can, and should, speak of spirituality, of relationship with the Holy Spirit. A major problem is that we all experience some difficulty in becoming truly ourselves, in

9

learning to own our lives and in discovering 'our capacity to give life to others'. If we spend a little time examining one or two ways of making progress with regard to these matters, however, we may achieve some insight into spirituality in relationships. A familiar passage from the Old Testament would seem to be as good a place as any to begin our examination. The passage I have in mind is that in which the prophet Ezekiel describes a vision he has had of a valley full of bones. In accordance with instructions from God, he prophesies to the bones that God will make breath enter them, give them flesh and make them live. When they do come to life, God tells Ezekiel that the bones are the house of Israel, and Ezekiel is then instructed to prophesy thus to the Israelites:

> I am going to open your graves and bring you back to the land of Israel. Then you, my people, will know that I am the Lord, when I open your graves and bring you up from them. I will put my Spirit in you and you will live, and I will settle you in your own land. (Ezek. 37.12–14)

The Hebrew word translated here as 'Spirit' is '*ruah*', which could also be translated as 'breath'. In the Israelite vision of things, humans had the breath of God within them. In the Book of Genesis we read that Adam was moulded from the earth. God breathed life into him (Gen. 2.7). He lived, as did Abraham and all the others who came after him, because the breath of God was in him. People died when the *ruah*, or breath, left them. The prophecy of Ezekiel quoted above was delivered against the background of a conviction that the inhabitants of Israel were, in a certain sense, not fully alive. There was a felt need of a new infusion of the breath of God so that people might live, but, clearly, something more than mere biological existence is implied here. Earlier in Ezekiel we read: 'I shall give you a new heart, and put a new spirit in you; I shall remove the heart of stone from your bodies and give you a heart of flesh instead' (Ezek. 36.26). In ancient Israel, the Hebrew equivalent of the word 'heart' denoted not merely the centre of the emotions. It was the centre or core of one's personality. The reference to a new heart here seems to indicate some sort of new birth. It seems likely that an immediate sense that most of Ezekiel's Israelite readers might have picked up from the prophecy resulting from the vision of the bones would have concerned a return to their homeland, from which they had been exiled for a considerable period. After the resurrection of Jesus, however, a richer meaning emerged. The breath of God is the Holy Spirit, who comes to live in the core of one's personality. Present-day theologians who write about conscience often make the observation that, in the Hebrew books of the Old Testament, the word 'heart' is the nearest equivalent to our term 'conscience'. It is not surprising, therefore, that, in the *Constitution on the Church in the Modern World* of the Second Vatican

10

Council, conscience is described thus: 'His conscience is man's most secret core, and his sanctuary. There he is alone with God whose voice echoes in his depths.'[2]

The reader will have observed that all that has been said so far could fit into the description of spirituality that was outlined in the first sentence of this chapter. We could still be talking about a person alone with God. It seems absurd, however, to think of the individual and the social aspects of spirituality as existing in isolation from each other. We would expect them to throw light on one another, and indeed they do. It seems sensible, therefore, to pursue the individual theme a little further before entering into discussion of the more social aspects. A generally accepted authority in this sphere is St Teresa of Avila, who, in her most famous work, describes the soul as a castle made from a diamond or a transparent crystal, in which there are many rooms. Some are above, some below, some on the sides and some in the centre. In the midst of them is the principal chamber 'in which God and the soul hold their most secret intercourse'.[3] She then goes on to describe the journey of the soul through the various rooms of the castle (which is, of course, the soul itself), and eventually into the principal chamber. First of all, however, one needs actually to enter the castle:

> Now let us return to our beautiful and charming castle and discover how to enter it. This appears incongruous: if this castle is the soul, clearly no one can have to enter it, for it is the person himself: one might as well tell someone to go into a room he is already in! There are, however, very different ways of being in this castle; many souls live in the courtyard of the building where the sentinels stand, neither caring to enter farther, nor to know who dwells in that most delightful place, what is in it and what rooms it contains.[4]

Much of what Teresa has to say in the rest of this remarkable book is, in some ways, as much about growing in self-knowledge as it is about growing in one's relationship with God. She writes that, insofar as she is able to understand such things, 'the gate by which to enter the castle is prayer and meditation'.[5] For our purposes, however, it is interesting to note that Teresa could hardly be described as a loner. In her writings she mentions numerous relationships with people of both sexes, and it is clear that some of these relationships were of great importance to her. It seems certain that they played a role in her growth in self-knowledge. To suggest this is in no way to underestimate the role of prayer. It does, however, point to the role that relationships can play in helping us to become aware of the fact that such beautiful castles exist.

Social spirituality

The Holy Spirit who dwells in the core of one's personality is the Spirit of Love (agape). St Paul admonishes the Corinthians: 'Let everything you do be done in love' (1 Cor. 16.14). Everything they do will be transformed if they tap into the Spirit who is in their personalities. Astonishing transformations are possible. Looking at things in this way, it is easy to see how the gospel of love can be transmitted and how the transformed person can continue the work of Christ, as Christians are supposed to do. An encounter with such a person would surely be sacramental. In our ordinary daily life, however, it seems that most people's encounters with Christians are not anything like as amazing as this short discussion might lead one to expect. Many, in fact, report having had rather unpleasant experiences when they met Christians. Although deeply impressed by what he read of Jesus, for instance, Mahatma Gandhi seems to have been decidedly unimpressed by most of the Christians he came across, although he did encounter some exceptions to the rule. He saw Jesus as 'one of the greatest teachers humanity has ever had'.[6] The teacher and most of those who claimed to be his disciples, however, appeared to be in very different categories. Remarking upon what had happened in his own country, Gandhi noted that 'the effect of Christianity upon India in general must be judged by the life lived in our midst by the average Christian and its effect upon us'. He was sorry to have to record his opinion 'that it has been disastrous'.[7] If, however, the Holy Spirit is to be found within a particular person, let us say Margaret, how is it possible that those who meet her are left unimpressed? One partial explanation of this can be found in the notion of the 'already but not yet' of salvation that theologians often talk about nowadays. What this means basically is that, although the salvific work of Christ has already taken place, we do not, in this life, experience all the consequences of it. The Kingdom is already here, but we do not see its total fulfilment in this life. We still live in sin-filled situations, and we are still inclined to make bad choices. It is difficult to hear the promptings of the Spirit in the midst of all the atrocious clamouring that surrounds us.

What has just been said about the 'already but not yet' of salvation might be thought by some to be, in many ways, a sufficient explanation of our apparent lack of success at being 'walking sacraments'. There is, however, some usefulness in analysing one particular facet of the 'not yet'. What I propose is that we reflect a little upon the problem of the false identity – or, perhaps more accurately, the numerous false identities – that we adopt. Throughout our lives there are enormous pressures upon us to conform to what we believe other people will find acceptable. In many spheres of life, a process of conforming is, of course, to some extent beneficial. An example is found in table manners. Our parents and other adults taught us to eat as they did. If we had not changed the eating practices we had when we first began feeding ourselves we would now be in the habit of regularly making those at table with us feel rather ill. Similarly, we can easily see that rather precise conformity in the pronunciation of foreign languages that we learn is certainly advantageous if we want to be understood when speaking those languages. Some of our other attempts at conformity, however, are ill-conceived, unnecessary and/or badly executed. We learn, for instance, how to portray ourselves in ways that we think will make us acceptable, and perhaps even attractive, to others. As the years pass, this process of conformity becomes extremely complicated. What we think will satisfy the taste of one group of people does not, we believe, match up to the requirements of others. We thus learn to adopt a variety of masks for different occasions and different sets of people – friends, parents, prospective mates, teachers, employers and so on.

Of course, a felt need to conform is not the only motivating force in play. It is useful, in this regard, to call to mind what St Teresa says about the soul living in its own courtyard, 'neither caring to enter farther, nor to know who dwells in that most delightful place, what is in it and what rooms it contains' People become set in their earthly ways. 'It appears impossible for them to retire into their own hearts; accustomed as they are to be with the reptiles and other creatures which live outside the castle, they have come at last to imitate their habits.'[8] We are all, of course, affected by sin, and the habits we have learned from the metaphorical 'reptiles and other creatures' include activities that involve a fair amount of manipulation of other people. We may thus see, for instance, that benefits for ourselves are likely to result from instilling fear in some people, extracting admiration from a second group and provoking pity in a third. What is worth noting for our purposes here is the fact that, as is the case with conforming, all of these processes involve not just attempted manipulation of other people, but also a certain wearing of masks – a good deal of pretence. One of the problems with this process is that it complicates the task of finding out who we really are. This is a huge problem both for us and for those we meet. The Holy Spirit may live in me, but who and where am I?

It is not that one has been completely transformed into a monster (or, indeed, a series of monsters) of one's own making. There are traces of authenticity, and, hopefully, more than that, but there is also an awful lot that is unauthentic. Overcoming it is difficult, but relationships can play a major role. Participating in intimate relationships is one of the ways in which we learn to drop the masks. In deep friendships and good marriages, people love and are loved. The awareness of being loved enables one slowly to relax into one's real self. The masks gradually melt away. More and more of the real Margaret (or Richard) is revealed to the other, and, indeed, to Margaret herself. In such a process the presence of the Holy Spirit too is in some way revealed because the Holy Spirit is in the real Margaret and in her partner in intimacy. Their relationship can thus be described as, in a very real sense,

13

sacramental. It may prove hard to replicate this degree of openness in her relationships with other people, but some improvement in Margaret's dealings with those outside her intimate circle is at least possible. There too some self-revelation may come about. Margaret may also discover a new sensitivity to the self-revelations of others with whom she works, plays, or whom she simply encounters on a train journey. Gradually she may come to see that the Holy Spirit is all around her, as well as in her.

This process of coming to see the Holy Spirit through coming to know oneself and others in relationships and, of course, through prayer brings one face to face, not only with beauty, but also with some uncomfortable home truths. Margaret may, for instance, have to confront the fact that she has some prejudices which she has hitherto denied in conversation with others on numerous occasions. At some level she has, until now, believed her own denials, but now she sees more clearly. She may discover, to her dismay, for instance, that she has been making ungrounded assumptions about people of certain races, people of a different sexual orientation, people of a different class and/or people with certain illnesses. Such assumptions or prejudices may have made it very difficult for her to relate in any meaningful way with certain groups or classes of people. Any help she has hitherto offered such people when they have been in difficulties may have been seriously compromised. Work of a social nature which is not accompanied by development in self-knowledge and in spiritual growth in the people doing that work is likely to be defective in other ways too.

This does not necessarily mean that no good can result from it. It does indicate, however, that things could be much better. Unfortunately, moreover, there are occasions when it does indeed seem to be the case that more evil than good results from work done ostensibly for others. Without a process of growing in self-knowledge, as well as a developing awareness of the presence of the Holy Spirit in themselves and in others, people who get involved in struggles for justice, for instance, run the risk of making the world a more unjust place than it was before they got involved.[9] A desire to help others should spring from love. Often, however, unruly passions are at the heart of our enthusiasm for a cause.

Thus we may find that a particular person who calls himself a pro-life campaigner is merely an anti-abortionist. Although many of those with whom he campaigns and works are inspired to very positive action, he is energized only by the more negative aspects of the struggle in which he is involved. While he is convincing himself that he is motivated only by love, all that others see when they meet him is an avenger. His lack of self-awareness permits him to believe that he is an evangelist of sorts, and his success in attracting others to join in the fight only serves to strengthen the illusion. His enthusiasm is indeed intoxicating for other people, but what he preaches is not the Gospel. Such fanaticism leads to conflict through the allure of hatred, not spiritual conversion through an encounter with love. There can be little wonder that it occasionally leads to murder.

Our lack of self-knowledge can contribute to many other kinds of disastrous consequences when we are engaged in what we falsely judge to be improving the lot of other people. People who have never admitted to themselves their own feeling of needing to be needed, for instance, are likely to find it hard to let their dependants go, so that they can flourish in their own ways. Any parents, social workers, teachers or spiritual directors who are in this category may find themselves encouraging their charges to continue in dependence upon them, instead of setting them free.

In close association with the need to be needed is the thirst for power and status. Most of us have heard Lord Acton's famous aphorism about power tending to corrupt and absolute power corrupting absolutely. In much discussion about it, there is a tendency to concentrate on the kind of power exercised by people in positions of high office. The corrupting effects of even quite small amounts of power, however, can be remarkable. Even in the caring professions and charitable organizations it seems not unusual for people to compete for the admiration of others and to strive hard to get things done in their way, without properly taking into consideration the views of colleagues. It seems also not uncommon for such people to tell others, and themselves, that what motivates them is the desire to help their fellows. The desire to help may, of course, be a motivating factor. In many cases, however, it may not be the principal one, and a good deal of harm can result when the thirst for power and status plays too significant a role. Most, if not all of us, have probably fallen down in some way or other, at some stage in our lives, in this regard – perhaps on numerous occasions. Again, many of us were made aware of what was happening only when someone else pointed it out to us. None of this should astonish us. If we live behind masks and dwell, at least part of the time, in the courtyard of our own personalities, it is only to be expected that we might fail to face up to the existence of dangerous games that we are playing.

The tendency for human beings to spend a large part of their lives in their personal courtyards and consort with 'the reptiles' was not new, of course, even in the days of Teresa of Avila. In our daily lives we encounter the multiple effects of millennia of unauthentic activity. This may help to explain some difficulties noted in the recent debate about the suggestion of some situation ethicists that, where moral problems are concerned, all we need is love. In any situation, they say, love will tell us what we need to do. Some years ago I considered the appeal of such a notion:

> In spite of its obvious attraction . . . no theory of this kind gets an easy ride from most moral theologians nowadays. One reason for this is undoubtedly the history of Christianity, which abounds in examples of apparently saintly (and therefore loving) people who simply got things

15

very wrong in the ethical sphere on occasions, in spite of the fact that they obviously believed the contrary. Critics of situation ethics thus say that we need more than a vague guarantee of love's guidance. And yet, in spite of the vagueness, one has a nagging feeling that love really ought to be enough. After all, even when the sophisticated arguments have been presented, is it still not the case that an all-embracing commandment really is found in the call to love God and neighbor? Perhaps the truth of the matter is that, in each situation, we really are instructed very precisely by love, but simply do not clearly hear what love is saying. Such an explanation would fit in with 'the already but not yet' theories of redemption. We are already saved, but the effects of corruption are not yet quite overcome.[10]

The effects of corruption, moreover, are in all our cultures and in various structures and systems with which we have to deal in our society, wherever we may be. We live, then, in what we might describe as situations of sin. Many of the problematic systems and structures were in place, perhaps, before we were born. They have always seemed normal to us. For that reason it may be that we have never raised any questions about them. Examples of the kinds of catastrophic effects that can arise from such situations, however, can be seen by glancing at history books. It seems that, in earlier times, numerous people who had a highly developed spirituality were blind to what strike us (in our very different situations) as glaring moral problems. Thus we find that such people supported unjustifiable crusades and the persecution of those they regarded as heretics, whilst apparently not noticing the injustice of slavery. Our blind spots are quite different from theirs, and they vary from one place to another. Fairly common ones in Western societies, however, can easily be listed: we may fail to notice the need for hospitality – in various settings; we may not notice that institutions to which we belong or in which we work have structures that promote racism or sexism, even though we ourselves are neither racist nor sexist; we may not see that our 'normal' way of living our lives helps to maintain the gulf between rich and poor. The list could easily be lengthened, and perhaps there are numerous problems that not a single one of us can see at this stage in time.

None of what has just been said, however, detracts from what was said earlier in this chapter. If anything, it merely accentuates the importance of prayer and relationships. Both activities bring us up against truth, and, if we are eager to find the truth, we have to be prepared to discover where our blind spots, ignorance, prejudices and misjudgements are to be found. One truth of the matter is that we are always part of the problem. In facing up to that fact we can begin to move beyond that courtyard which St Teresa mentions, stop imitating the reptiles and make a small contribution to some solutions.

Notes

1. Jean Vanier, *Becoming Human* (London: Darton, Longman and Todd, 2001), p. 68.
2. *Gaudium et Spes*, §16. *Vatican Council II: The Conciliar and Post Conciliar Documents*, ed. Austin Flannery (Northport: Costello Publishing, 1975), p. 916.
3. Teresa of Avila, *The Interior Castle*, 'The First Mansions', ch. 1, 4 (London: HarperCollins, 1995) p. 6.
4. Ibid., ch. 1, 7, p. 7.
5. Ibid., ch. 1, 9 p. 8.
6. *The Mind of Mahatma Gandhi*, ed. R.K. Prabhu and U.R. Rao (Ahmedabad: Navajivan Publishing, 1946), p. 98.
7. Ibid.
8. *The Interior Castle*, 'The First Mansions', ch. 1, 8, pp. 7–8.
9. It does not follow, of course, that non-Christians are doomed to failure in this respect. One can be aware of love and transcendent goodness without even having heard of the Holy Spirit
10. Bernard Hoose, 'Natural Law, Acts and Persons', in Todd A. Salzman (ed.), *Method and Catholic Moral Theology: The Ongoing Reconstruction* (Omaha: Creighton University Press, 1999), pp. 44–67, here pp. 44–5.

Chapter 2

Christian Social Spirituality: A Global Perspective

Peter C. Phan

The focus of this essay is the social dimension of Christian spirituality in a global perspective. Two aspects of Christian spirituality are explored, namely its sociality and its globality. The former is an intrinsic element of Christian anthropology and ethics, the latter a new perspective imposed by the complex phenomenon known as globalization and the seemingly opposite need of Christian spirituality to be deeply rooted in local cultures.[1] The chapter begins with a brief description of some urgent socio-political and economic challenges that globalization presents to Christian spirituality today. Next, an outline of Christian social spirituality, especially from the Roman Catholic tradition, is presented. Finally, this Christian social spirituality is made more concrete by being located in the situation of Asia and the social teachings of the Asian bishops and theologians.

Christian Spirituality in the Globalized World

A balanced Christian spirituality – as the Irish theologian Donal Dorr has convincingly argued on the basis of the prophet Micah's triple injunction to act justly, love tenderly and walk humbly with God (Mic. 6.8) – must be personal (religious conversion to God), interpersonal (moral conversion to face-to-face relationships with other people) and public (political conversion to the 'poor').[2] These three conversions are not parallel, much less alternative, paths to God. Rather, they are inextricably intertwined with each other such that one without the other two would fail to achieve its goal. Furthermore, Christian spirituality in all its three dimensions must be lived out in the current socio-political, economic and cultural context, which today is encapsulated in the word 'globalization'.

Globalization

There is already a vast literature on globalization in its economic, political and cultural aspects.[3] While some historians still question whether globalization with the implied dissolution of the system of nation-states is occurring or will ever occur, most agree that vast changes in societies and the world economy have been taking place, at least since the sixteenth century, as the result of dramatically increased international trade and cultural exchange, and that globalization is a useful shorthand for this phenomenon. Arjun Appadurai identifies five areas where this global connectivity has occurred: 'ethnoscapes' (movements of people, including tourists, business travellers, legal and illegal immigrants and refugees); 'finanscapes' (global flows of money and capital, thanks to currency markets, stock exchanges and commodity markets); 'ideoscapes' (the global spread of ideas and ideologies); 'mediascapes' (global instant communication through the mass media, especially the Internet); and 'technoscapes' (the spread of technologies around the globe).[4]

As with any movement of this scope, there are both supporters and opponents. Pro-globalists highlight the benefits of globalization and cite hard statistics to support their contentions: since the 1950s, the percentage of people in developing countries living below US$1 per day (adjusted for inflation and purchasing power) has been reduced to half; life expectancy has almost doubled and child mortality has decreased in the developing countries since the Second World War; democracy has increased dramatically throughout the world since 1900; worldwide, per capita food supplies have grown since the 1960s; global literacy has improved significantly since 1950, especially among women; and availability of life necessities such as electricity, car, radio, telephone, television and clean water has increased. In sum, globalization with its capitalist economy, free trade, global political institutions and cultural exchange is said to bring about a more efficient allocation of resources, lower prices, better employment, higher output and democracy.[5]

Anti-globalists, on the other hand, reject this rosy depiction of globalization, which they claim is more accurately characterized as 'corporate globalism'. They are made up of a variety of groups and movements with diverse, even opposing, ideologies: left-wing parties, right-wing state nationalists, religious fundamentalists, national liberation movements, environmentalists, peasant unionists, anti-racism organizations, progressive church groups, and so on. Despite their different agenda, anti-globalists argue that globalization has not taken the interests of poorer nations and the welfare of workers into account. Rather, unrestricted free trade benefits the so-called 'core states' – those of the First World, with higher-skill, capital-intensive production and with military superiority – rather than the so-called 'semi-periphery' and 'periphery' countries, that is, long-independent states outside the West and poor, recently independent colonies (especially in Africa, Latin America and Asia) respectively, which focus on low-skill, labour-intensive production and extraction of raw materials and have weak military power. In their view, globalization promotes a corporatist agenda at the expense of the poor, imposes credit-based economies with an unsustainable growth of debt as a result and is an instrument of neo-imperialism and neo-colonialism.[6]

Any fair assessment of globalization must of course recognize both its benefits and its deleterious effects, the former no doubt exaggerated by pro-globalists and the latter by anti-globalists. It is of course not the competence of Christians qua Christians to render a judgement on globalization as a process of internationalizing trade, capital, labour forces and technology. But it must be admitted that such an economic, political and cultural process is by no means morally neutral. On the contrary, it is driven by certain assumptions about the meaning of human life and activities, especially the economic ones that have profound ethical and spiritual implications for the Church's mission of fostering peace, justice and the integrity of creation.

Challenges of globalization to Christian social spirituality

To live the social dimension of Christian spirituality responsibly in our globalized world, Christians must have an adequate grasp of the destructive effects, intended and otherwise, of globalization. Without pretension to completeness, the following can be noted.[7] First, *the ever-expanding gap between the rich and the poor*. Even though virtually all countries may stand to benefit from globalization, as pro-globalists claim, so far the strongest gains, and this is admitted even by pro-globalists, have been made by the 'core' countries and, to a lesser extent, by only some of the 'semi-periphery' and 'periphery' ones. Consequently, the gap *between* the rich and the poor countries and between the wealthy and the destitute *within* each country is becoming ever wider. While the inevitable fact that there are rich and poor people does not constitute social injustice, that there is dehumanizing poverty alongside extravagant wealth and that this wealth and the luxurious lifestyle it provides to a small group of humanity are obtained at the expense of impoverished men, women and children – who constitute the majority of the world population – is a morally scandalous exploitation.

Second, *international debt*. As a result of the economic policies of the wealthy nations and their banks, especially the International Money Fund, many countries, particularly in Africa and Latin America, are saddled with crushing debts, with the unpaid interest added to the original loans. Loans were made to fund misguided 'development' programmes that benefit more the donor countries of the First World and the corrupt dictators of the receiving countries than the poor people themselves whom the loans were designed to help. Ironically, it is the poor who most often have to shoulder the burden of the debt repayment.

Third, *ecological destruction*. Through globalization the First World is exporting its severe pollution problems to the poorer countries. Un-scrupulous multinational companies have dumped toxic industrial waste and even radioactive materials in the Third World where laws against pollution are non-existent or less stringent. Furthermore, large cutting down of the tropical rainforests and the rapid erosion of land due to overgrazing are producing the 'greenhouse effect' which raises the earth's temperature and causes massive floods and hurricanes. These ecological disasters harm not only humans but also the earth's flora and fauna.

Fourth, *chronic unemployment*. Globalization exports the Western methods of mass production, automation and computerization. While these technological advances have reduced the drudgery of heavy manual labour, they have also produced what has been called 'structural unemployment,' that is, large-scale chronic and inevitable unemployment inherent in the use of high technology and in the economic system itself. Furthermore, corporations are not loath to move their factories or outsourcing jobs to countries where production costs are lowest, thus causing unemployment in former places of manufacturing.

Fifth, *increase in immigrants and refugees*. Scarcity of jobs and food shortages, in addition to war and racial/ethnic and religious persecutions, have caused massive immigration in many countries of the Third World. These refugees, political and economic, suffer immense physical and emotional damage, even when settled in countries that are willing to accept them.

Sixth, and perhaps most importantly, globalization exports *the Western model of economic development*, that is, producing material goods as cheaply and efficiently as possible and selling them for maximum financial profits. Such a purely economic analysis does not take into account the costs in ecological destruction, structural unemployment and human misery. Furthermore, the highly consumerist lifestyle of the First World is not sustainable with the earth's resources were it to be reproduced in the Third World. Consequently, an alternative model of development must be devised, to be adopted by both the First World and the Third World, one that rejects the ideology of limitless 'growth' and omnivorous consumption, cares for human and ecological resources and promotes other human values in addition to the economic ones.

Other social challenges

The six challenges mentioned above, which are directly tied with globalization, are of course not the only ones that concern Christians today. Other social issues, listed here without detailed comment, continue to confront Christian social spirituality; they include racism, sexism, political oppression, human rights violation, abortion, the arms race and, lately, stateless terrorism. The question is raised as to what Christians can and should do as part of their social spirituality to remove or at least reduce the negative effects of these challenges on both individuals and society.

Contours of Contemporary Christian Social Spirituality

Christian spirituality

Spirituality as a way of living has three connotations. In its broadest sense, (1) spirituality refers to the human capacity for self-transcendence in acts of knowledge and love of realities other than oneself. More narrowly, (2) it refers to the religious dimension of life by which one is in touch with a more-than-human, transcendent reality, however interpreted and named (e.g., the Empty, the Holy, the Ultimate, or God). More strictly still, (3) it indicates a particular way of living one's relationship with this transcendent reality, through specific beliefs, rituals, prayers, moral behaviours and community participation (e.g., Hindu, Buddhist, Jewish, Christian, Muslim, and so on). It is important to note that there is no generic spirituality, untethered from a historical and particular tradition and community. Even when one attempts to construct one's own spirituality, one can only do so by drawing upon various elements of pre-existing spiritual traditions.

Needless to say, Christian spirituality embodies all these three connotations, i.e., human self-transcendence towards the Ultimate Other carried out within a particular religious tradition. More precisely, it is a particular way of relating to the Holy and Ultimate Being revealed as 'Abba/Father' by Jesus of Nazareth in his ministry, death and resurrection, a relationship mediated by Jesus himself and actualized by the power of the Holy Spirit, who has been poured out upon the community of Jesus' followers called Church. In other words, Christian spirituality is theocentric (relationship with God), Christic (mediated by and modelled after Christ), pneumatological (empowered by the Spirit) and ecclesial (realized in and through the Church).

Christian social spirituality

As pointed out above, Christian spirituality is at once and inextricably personal, interpersonal and political. Here, our focus is only on the political dimension, and the question is what a Christian as an individual and the Church as a community of believers can and should do to meet the challenges of globalization to promote peace, justice and the integrity of creation. Within Roman Catholicism, this question has been the subject of extensive reflection in recent decades, especially by liberation theologians of various stripes and by popes, especially John Paul II. From these sources a rough sketch of Christian social spirituality may be drawn which would include at least the following elements.[8]

Unconditional and total commitment to the reign of God
At the heart of Christian social spirituality lies a total commitment to the

service of the Kingdom of God or the Kingdom of Heaven which Jesus proclaimed and inaugurated. The Kingdom of Heaven, that is, God's rule in and through Jesus, is, however, no mere transcendent and spiritual reality in the post-mortem, empyreal realm. God's gracious sharing of God's triune life with us brings about not only forgiveness of sins and reconciliation with God but also truth, justice, peace and the integrity of creation. Furthermore, this gift of socio-political, economic and ecological well-being is at the same time a task; it is, to play on German words, both *Gabe* (gift) and *Aufgabe* (task). It demands that we dedicate ourselves to making, by means of collective action, God's gifts into a universal historical reality, especially for those who have been deprived of them by oppressive, unjust and exploitative systems.

This single-minded and total commitment to the reign of God is *the* essential and distinctive feature of Christian social spirituality in general and of liberation spirituality in particular. It informs the way Christian social spirituality understands the ministry of the historical Jesus, the Trinity and the Incarnation.

Understanding the Jesus of history, the Trinity, the Incarnation anew

It is well known that liberation theologians are interested in discovering the 'true Jesus' of history. However, their concern is not to retrieve the *ipsissima verba et gesta Jesu* (Jesus' very words and deeds), as is done in various 'quests for the historical Jesus', most recently, in the Jesus Seminar, by nature an uncertain and inconclusive enterprise. Rather, it is to discover the *ipsissima intentio Jesu* (Jesus' very 'cause'): that to which he dedicated his entire ministry and on account of which he was killed, his all-consuming passion and exclusive obsession. Contemporary biblical scholarship has shown beyond dispute that Jesus' cause is nothing other than the Kingdom of God – the Kingdom of truth, justice, peace, love, forgiveness, reconciliation, grace and ecological harmony – which he proclaimed and brought to all, particularly to those the Bible calls the 'poor'.[9]

The task of social spirituality is not to demythologize Jesus from the dogmatic incrustations of the 'Christ of faith' but, in Jon Sobrino's pregnant expression, to 'de-manipulate' Jesus from the vested interests of the rich and the powerful, to rescue him from contamination by idolatry and from the injustices committed throughout history in his very name, and to restore the centrality of the reign of God to his life and ministry. It will then be clear that the goal of Jesus' ministry is neither to preach about himself nor to found a religious organization but to proclaim God, and not just any God, such as the inaccessible Unmoved Mover dwelling in the empyreal realm, but the God of the reign and the reign of God in history.

Christian social spirituality also professes faith in the triune God, but it sees the problem of faith today to consist not so much in atheism as in idolatry. The real issue for Christian social spirituality is not whether God *exists* but whether the God one worships is the *true* God, a masked idol or the God who reveals himself as the Father of Jesus and the Sender of the Spirit and whose reign is one of truth and justice and peace, especially for the poor and the marginalized. This triune God, constituted by the three divine Persons in absolute equality, perfect communion and mutual love, is Christianity's social agenda in a nutshell. Like the all-embracing Trinity in Andrej Rublev's famous icon, Christians welcome all, especially those deprived of human dignity, to the table of life, peace, justice and love.

Because social spirituality by its very nature is rooted in history, it puts a premium on the doctrine of the Incarnation. However, while affirming Jesus' real humanity over against monophysitism and docetism, social spirituality does not understand the Incarnation to refer simply to the once-upon-a-time physical conception and birth of the Word of God from Mary. Rather it takes this divine enfleshment to mean that in Jesus God has truly become history and therefore can be encountered only within history; that God has 'emptied' Godself and therefore can be encountered only in those who have been 'emptied' of their humanity; that God has assumed a particular culture, i.e., the Jewish one, and therefore can be encountered only in the particularities of each culture; and that God has become a Jew in colonized Palestine and therefore can be encountered only within the struggle for the political freedom, human rights and economic well-being of victims of new forms of colonialism.

Honesty about and fidelity to reality
One fundamental implication of a full-throated acceptance of the Jesus of history, of the God of the reign and of the Incarnation for Christian social spirituality is what Jon Sobrino calls 'honesty about the real' and 'fidelity to the real'.[10] By the former, Sobrino means an objective and adequate knowledge of the socio-political and economic condition of the majority of people and to recognize it for what it is: namely, human life today is being assaulted by systematic impoverishment and institutionalized violence. Without this honesty to the real, any attempt to live a Christian social spirituality is a castle built on sands. By the latter Sobrino means the willingness to accept the risks to life and limb for being honest about reality and for trying to transform this negative reality into one of truth, justice and peace.

Because of the need to be honest about and faithful to reality, Christian social spirituality insists on the use of the methodology of Pierre Cardijn's Young Christian Workers movement, i.e., 'see–judge–act'.[11] It is imperative to 'see' reality clearly and accurately, and not be blinded by personal bias or collective ideology. In terms of social spirituality, it is necessary to see poverty with the eyes of the poor and to understand injustice and oppression from the perspective of the victims. Consequently, it is a vital part of contemporary Christian social spirituality to grasp fully, by means of a thorough social analysis, the nature of globalization as an economic, socio-political and cultural process and its deleterious impact upon the poor.

Following and imitating the Jesus of the reign of God

Christian spirituality, whatever its form or orientation, is in essence a following (*sequela*) or imitation (*imitatio*) or discipleship of Jesus. But the crucial question is: which Jesus? As mentioned above, Christian social spirituality focuses on the Jesus of the reign of God. Pedro Casaldáliga, Bishop of São Felix, Brazil, and José-Maria Vigil, a Spanish-born and naturalized Nicaraguan theologian, have drawn a detailed portrait of this Jesus which includes the following features: Jesus who reveals the true God; who is deeply human; who is devoted to the cause of the poor; who proclaims the God of the reign; who is poor among the poor; who subverts the established order; who inaugurated and realized the reign of God; who denounced the forces opposed to such reign; who is free and promotes freedom in others; who brings abundant life; who is compassionate; who welcomes people of different faiths; who defends the full dignity of women; who does not avoid conflicts for the sake of God's reign; who is persecuted and martyred, and who is the way, the truth and the life of God's reign.[12] Christian social spirituality aims at appropriating the teachings and deeds of such a Jesus in one's life.

Option for the poor

Following the Jesus of the reign of God requires what liberation theologians term the 'option for the poor'. Such an 'option', which is not exclusive but preferential, is not inspired by the Marxist notion of class struggle but is rooted in the action of the triune God who throughout history has always taken the side of the oppressed and the poor and empowered them to reclaim their freedom. As Casaldáliga and Vigil assert, 'the option for the poor becomes a "mark" of the true church, of discipleship of Jesus, of Christian spirituality.'[13]

An essential element of social spirituality, this option for the poor is no mere theological posturing but rather entails attitudinal changes and concrete actions: removing oneself from the privileged and dominant classes, real sharing of day-to-day life with the poor, taking up the cause of the poor and the oppressed in active solidarity that respects them as agents of their own liberation.[14]

Persecution and martyrdom

In a world where power and wealth are often acquired through violence and exploitation, this fundamental option will sooner or later bring Christians engaged in social spirituality into a deadly conflict with the rich and the powerful whose political domination is challenged and economic interests are threatened by such an option. It is not that social spirituality seeks class conflicts; rather these *inevitably* arise as the result of Christians doing in their time what Jesus did in his, to assist those who are oppressed and impoverished to gain liberation from the powers that exploited and dominated them. Indeed, Jesus repeatedly warned his followers that they would suffer persecution and even death at the hands of their family members, political leaders and religious authorities, as he himself did. His predictions were amply borne out throughout history, and recently, in many parts of the world where Christians – lay as well as clerical – were maimed and murdered.

Martyrdom has become once again the mark of Christian discipleship and authentic social spirituality. Sobrino has persuasively argued that persecution is not only a historical inevitability for a Church that wants to remain faithful to Jesus' mission to and for the poor but also 'an a priori theological necessity'[15] insofar as it is rooted in the persecution that Jesus suffered because of his service to the reign of God. Hence, it is necessary for a Christian social spirituality to develop a 'spirituality of persecution', not as something peripheral and secondary but as its central element, by which 'the possibility and reality of persecution in some form and in some degree be taken seriously as an essential ingredient of the Christian life'.[16] In this readiness to accept persecution as a historical inevitability and a theological necessity, the three 'theological' virtues of faith, hope and love acquire a new maturity and depth. It is in persecution that faith encounters the silence of God the Father, as Jesus did on the Cross; hope meets its ultimate test and passes it, as Jesus entrusted his life to his Father at the moment of his death; and love finds its supreme fulfilment, since there is no greater love than laying down one's life for one's friends.

Sobrino goes on to show that persecution and martyrdom enrich Christian life with five new spirits: a spirit of *fortitude* with which one bears the burdens of witnessing to the Gospel; the spirit of *impoverishment* by which one patiently accepts the fact that one must lose one's life in order to find it; the spirit of *creativity* with which one devises new ways to live and reflect on the Christian life; the spirit of *solidarity* by which one grows in the awareness that one is not saved alone but always with others; and the spirit of *joy* because one knows that martyrdom makes one more like Jesus and the Church more faithful.[17]

Contemplation in liberation

As air for birds and water for fish, prayer is the absolute *sine qua non* for any spirituality, Christian or otherwise. But within social spirituality, prayer acquires a new dimension. If in the past prayer was done for the most part in the church, the monastery, the desert or the private study, today there is a consensus in social spirituality that, while these locales still retain their importance, prayer must be done in liberative action and vice versa. In the past it was felt necessary to withdraw from the world in order to contemplate and commune with God. Today the world is seen as the proper arena for contemplation and prayer, and action in favour of justice and peace and the integrity of creation is an intrinsic part of and even a form of prayer and contemplation.

This contemplation in liberation and liberation in contemplation, which is another key hallmark of contemporary social spirituality, reconfigure both where we meet God today and what kind of God we meet. As to the locale of the divine–human encounter, there is no longer a separation between the sacred and the profane, between the temple and the marketplace, between Church and world, between salvation and liberation. Indeed, the place from which God is contemplated and in which God is encountered is no other than the everyday life with its evolving history and its diverse and even conflicting kinds of economic systems, political regimes, social structures, cultural traditions and religious beliefs and practices. Furthermore, because the vantage point from which contemplation and prayer are done is the underside of history, the God contemplated and prayed to is no other than the Father of Jesus, the God of the reign of truth and life, justice and peace, grace and freedom.

This unity between contemplation and liberative action is not an excuse to neglect setting aside a certain amount of time every day (e.g., at least half an hour) for prayer on the specious grounds that 'everything is prayer'. Casaldáliga and Vigil issue a useful warning against the temptation of activism without a serious dedication to prayer and contemplation: 'It is true that all Christian action genuinely carried out in faith, "in a state of prayer", is in some sense a living of prayer, but it is not comparable to prayer itself. Charity is charity, service is service, and prayer is prayer.'[18]

Political holiness

One widely used expression to characterize the new Christian social spirituality with its emphasis on contemplation in liberation is 'political holiness'. Admittedly, such holiness is traditional in the sense that it is nourished by the liturgy and the sacraments, strengthened by prayer and contemplation and seasoned by the practice of virtues and asceticism. However, 'political holiness' is a helpful shorthand to highlight the new features of Christian social spirituality in the global context and to give primacy to certain virtues that have been neglected and downplayed in traditional spirituality. To summarize what has been said so far of Christian social spirituality, political spirituality, like that of Jesus himself, is oriented to the Kingdom of God, lived out not away from but within history and the world, animated by the preferential option for the poor and a willing acceptance of persecution and even martyrdom and actualized within the unity of contemplation and liberation.

As a consequence, political holiness fosters a set of virtues and practices that were either neglected or even derogated by traditional spirituality. For example, whereas traditional spirituality uniformly regards anger as a vice to be controlled, political spirituality sees it as a necessary and beneficial emotional reaction to systemic and organized injustice and oppression. This anger is the opposite of indifference and lack of courage. Rather than a vice to be avoided, this moral indignation is a force impelling compassion for the victims and action to help them regain their humanity. As Casaldáliga and Vigil note:

> . . . it affects us, shakes us and moves us, imperatively. We feel questioned by it, in the depths of our being. We see it bringing an inescapable challenge: we know we cannot compromise with, tolerate, live with or agree to injustice, because to do so would be to betray what is innermost and deepest in ourselves.[19]

Political holiness also prizes certain virtues often ignored in the past. For example, whereas obedience, humility, meekness, chastity, mortification, renunciation and what Nietzsche derides as unmanly Christianity are often extolled in traditional spirituality and asceticism (not always untainted by sadism or masochism), political holiness, while not denigrating these virtues, promotes a greater appreciation for more 'active' and 'social' virtues and practices directed towards the building of a just and peaceful world. There is a greater awareness of the 'structural evils' and 'social sins', in addition to personal sins. Hence, conversion is not only a turning away from evil actions and an immoral way of life, a transformation of the heart, but also a commitment to the struggle for the cause of Jesus, that is, to the removal of unjust and oppressive structures and the establishment of a peaceful and just society. Of course, social spirituality recognizes the necessity of both conversions, transformation of the heart and structural change, since they are mutually conditioned. A conversion of the heart without a commitment to social transformation runs the risk of individualism and escapism; on the other hand, efforts at social change without a conversion of the heart are doomed to failure and prone to despair, especially when success is not immediate.

In this context, another virtue is given primacy, namely, hope, which, of the three theological virtues, is the most neglected. Yet, in social spirituality, hope, especially hope in the resurrection, is the primary virtue: 'Political holiness is a holiness of active hope, which is able to overcome the defeatism of the poor in the face of the status quo, the established powers, the regrouping of capitalism and imperialism, in the face of the wave of neo-liberalism, the thrust of capitalism against labour, North against South. It is a holiness capable of enduring the hours of darkness for the poor, upholding the asceticism of hope against all hope.'[20] Of course, such hope must be backed up by vigorous and effective action in favour of social justice; otherwise, Karl Marx's dismissal of religion in general, and of Christianity in

28

particular, as the opium of the people would prove uncomfortably close to the truth.

Back to globalization: a spirituality for our time

It is by now clear that in an age such as ours a social spirituality as outlined above is more urgent than ever. When the gap between the rich and the poor is ever expanding; when the burdens of the debts that the Third World owes to the First World are being borne by the poor; when the ecology is being destroyed for economic development; when unemployment is chronic and built into the economic system; when more and more immigrants and refugees have to leave their homes for survival; and when the Western consumerist model of economic development is being imposed on other parts of the world, and all of this in the name of globalization, then Christians have to ask: Is there a way of being human, Christian and Church that leads to a more just, equitable, peaceful and harmonious society?

From the Christian point of view, one way is to make the heart and soul of Jesus' life and ministry, namely, the Kingdom of God, the central focus of one's life. In so doing, one must see–judge–act. Reality – and here, globalization – must be seen, that is, carefully investigated in all its dimensions, both positive and negative, and this investigation must be carried out from the perspective of the victims, and not only of the beneficiaries, of globalization. Next, a judgement must be rendered on this reality, in the light of the reign of God. The reign of God, and nothing else, serves as the all-encompassing and decisive criterion. Finally, one must act, individually and collectively, to remove the unjust and oppressive structures and establish a society and a Church that approximate as closely as possible to the utopia of the reign of God. In this action, one follows Jesus as his disciple, in solidarity with the poor and the marginalized, accepting persecution and death as the inevitable price of one's service to God's reign, and hoping and trusting in the resurrection of Jesus, which is the first-fruits and the guarantee of our own resurrection, especially of those who are most impoverished, oppressed, exploited among us.

Social Spirituality: An Asian Perspective

One of the remarkable developments in contemporary theology is the rapid spread of liberation theology, and with it, Christian social spirituality, throughout the globe. It seems as if where globalization reaches, there liberation theology and social spirituality arrive too, as an antidote to the deleterious effects of globalization on its victims because of their class, gender and race.[21] The previous pages have shown how social spirituality developed in Latin America.[22] In Africa, too, social spirituality has received sustained attention.[23] While a study of social spirituality in the global perspective must take into account its developments in all the continents, in the remaining pages, because of space limitation, focus will be given to the Asian context.[24]

Asia's spiritual quest

It is no exaggeration to say that Asia, understood here to include East Asia (the Far East), West Asia (the Middle East), South Asia and North Asia (Central Asia), embodies a long-standing and dynamic spiritual quest. After all, it is the cradle of all of the world's major religions (e.g., Hinduism, Buddhism, Judaism, Christianity and Islam), many other spiritual traditions (e.g., Daoism, Confucianism, Zoroastrianism, Jainism, Sikhism and Shinto-ism), innumerable tribal and indigenous religions and an untold number of new religious movements and sects. Despite its bewildering diversity and multiplicity, the Asian spiritual quest is characterized by certain common cultural and religious values, which Pope John Paul II describes succinctly:

> The people of Asia take pride in their religious and cultural values, such as love of silence and contemplation, simplicity, harmony, detachment, non-violence, the spirit of hard work, discipline, frugal living, the thirst for learning and philosophical inquiry. They hold dear the values of respect for life, compassion for all beings, closeness to nature, filial piety towards parents, elders and ancestors, and a highly developed sense of community . . . Asian people are known for their spirit of religious tolerance and peaceful coexistence . . . Asia has often demonstrated a remarkable capacity for accommodation and a natural openness to the mutual enrichment of peoples in the midst of a plurality of religions and cultures . . . Many people, especially the young, experience a deep thirst for spiritual values, as the rise of new religious movements clearly demonstrates.[25]

As a consequence, Christian social spirituality must be developed in dialogue with Asia's deep religiousness.

Secondly, Asia is also steeped in extreme and dehumanizing poverty. This poverty is not an accidental phenomenon but the result of systemic exploitation perpetrated by colonialism in the past and globalization today.[26] The Church in Asia, as Sri Lankan theologian Aloysius Pieris has repeatedly insisted, must be baptized in the Jordan of Asian multi-religiousness and in the Calvary of Asian poverty.[27] A third characteristic of Asian Christianity is its numerical minority (some three per cent of the Asian population) and this suggests a focus on mission and evangelization as the primary task of the Church. A Christian social spirituality must address these three concerns.

Spirituality in dialogue with Asian religions

Because Asia is the birthplace of most if not all religions, and because Christians form but a tiny minority of the Asian population, Asian Christians, more than their fellow believers in any other part of the world, cannot live their Spirit-empowered lives apart from non-Christian religions.[28] At first, most missionaries, both Catholic and Protestant, were pessimistic about the spiritual values of these religious ways of life. But the goodness of non-Christians (some of them are holier than Christians!), with whom very often Christians share their daily life intimately as family members, gives the lie to the Church's pre-Vatican II teaching that heathens are condemned to hell, that Christianity is the only acceptable way to God and that non-Christian religions are infested with superstition and depravity. Clearly, non-Christians are good and holy not in spite of but *because* of the beliefs and practices of their religions. From the Christian perspective, these elements of truth and grace must be regarded as fruits of the Spirit, who is the gift of God and the Risen Christ, but who is active outside of, albeit not independently from, the visible sphere of action of Jesus and the Church, in ways known to God alone.

But if this is true, then the Asian-Christian spiritual quest must be carried out in sincere and humble dialogue with other religions to learn from, among other things, their sacred Scriptures, doctrinal teachings, moral and spiritual practices, prayers and devotions and monastic and mystical traditions. It is to the credit of the Society of Jesus that many of their members were the first missionaries in Asia to develop a Christian spirituality in dialogue with Asian cultures and religions. Jesuits such as Francis Xavier and Alessandro Valignano in Japan, Matteo Ricci in China, Roberto de Nobili in India and Alexandre de Rhodes in Vietnam, notwithstanding whatever deficiencies of their accommodationist policies from the perspective of today's contextual theology, were visionary pioneers who paved the way, often at great personal cost, to a Christian spirituality enriched by other religious traditions and in turn enriching them through interfaith dialogue.

In more recent times, bold and even controversial efforts have been made to incorporate monastic and spiritual practices of non-Christian religions into Christian spirituality. In India, French priest Jules Monchanin (who took the name of Prama Arabi Ananda), French Benedictine Henri Le Saux (also known as Abishiktananda), English Benedictine Dom Bede Griffiths, Belgian Cistercian monk Francis Mahieu and Indian Jesuit Ignatius Hirudayam, to cite only the better-known ones, have been active in incorporating into their Christian experience of God as Trinity the Hindu advaitic quest for God as *sat* (being), *cit* (truth) and bliss (*ananda*). Moreover, through their Ashram Movement, they have assimilated into Christian worship and monasticism the Hindu sacred scriptures, religious symbols, ascetic practices, meditation technique, religious songs and dance, sacred art, clothing and postures.

In Japan, the resource for spiritual enrichment has been mainly Zen Buddhism. Not surprisingly, the first efforts at dialogue with Zen were made by the Quakers. Among Catholics, Jesuits Hugo M. Enomiya-Lassalle, Kakichi Kadowaki and William Johnston, and Dominican priest Oshida, have been instrumental in enriching Christian spirituality with the Zen meditation practices. Dialogue with Buddhism, especially in its Theravada branch, has been carried out extensively in Thailand and Sri Lanka. Dialogue with Islam is active in certain parts of India and in Indonesia. In countries heavily influenced by Confucianism such as China, Taiwan, Vietnam and Korea, Christian spirituality has recently incorporated the rituals of the cult of ancestors after it had been severely condemned by the Church for several centuries.

From a practical point of view, interfaith dialogue as a part of the Asian–Christian spiritual quest is a genuine opening of persons of different faiths to one another with a view to sharing and being enriched by another faith and serves a multiplicity of functions. It helps overcome fear of the other, removes misunderstandings of and prejudices against other religions, promotes collaboration with others in areas of life beyond religion and enhances the understanding and practice of one's own faith.

The Pontifical Council for Interreligious Dialogue of the Roman Catholic Church and the Federation of Asian Bishops' Conferences have suggested four modes in which interfaith dialogue can be carried out. First, the dialogue of *life* consists in sharing daily life together, which fosters mutual understanding, neighbourly assistance and cordial friendship among adherents of different religions. Second, the dialogue of *collaborative action* brings believers of different faiths to work together to promote justice, human rights, peace, human development and ecological well-being. Third, the dialogue of *theological reflection* enables a deeper understanding of and enrichment by the beliefs and practices of religions other than one's own. Lastly, the dialogue of *spiritual experience*, which is the deepest and most transformative, brings people together to *pray*, each in the way of his or her tradition, and later, possibly, to pray *together*, in a common way.

Spirituality as discipleship to Jesus: service to the reign of God

As with Latin American spirituality, Asian-Christian spirituality takes discipleship and imitation of Jesus as its central focus.[29] The question then arises as to which Jesus would appeal to Asian cultural and religious sensibilities. There are, of course, many and diverse Asian Christologies, and the participants at the Asian Synod suggested several images of Jesus. Among them were 'Jesus Christ as the Teacher of Wisdom, the Healer, the Liberator, the Spiritual Guide, the Enlightened One, the Compassionate

Friend of the Poor, the Good Samaritan, the Good Shepherd, the Obedient One'.[30] Running through these diverse Christologies and linking them together is the view that at the heart of Jesus' ministry stands the Kingdom of God of which he, the Eschatological Prophet, is the personal embodiment. It was in the service of this reign of justice, peace, forgiveness, reconciliation and love that he was crucified. Christian spirituality insofar as it is an imitation of Christ must therefore take the form of service to God's reign.[31]

But what form of service to God's reign is most appropriate to the spiritual quest in Asia? The answer is determined by the socio-political and economic contexts of the continent. While some countries such as Japan, South Korea, Singapore, Taiwan and Hong Kong have a well-developed economy, they form but a small portion of the Asian population. By contrast, several Asian countries are among the poorest nations on earth, and the majority of Asians are oppressed people who for centuries have been kept economically, culturally and politically on the margins of society. Of special concern are women's oppression within a patriarchal and androcentric culture, abortion of female foetuses, marginalization of the outcasts and the tribal or indigenous people, the exploitation of migrant and child labour and sex tourism. Though Western colonialism has ended, its deleterious legacy is now being extended by neo-colonialism through economic globalization. Politically, Asia is a complex array of ideologies ranging from democracy to military dictatorship and Communism.

In this economic and socio-political context, Asian spirituality as *imitatio Christi* must take the form of a preferential option for the poor, which is a distinctive hallmark of Latin American spirituality and which has been appropriated by the Asian churches. Spirituality as service to the Kingdom of God occupies a central place in Asian theologies of liberation, such as the theologies of Choan-Seng Song, Tissa Balasuryia, Aloysius Pieris, Michael Amaladoss, Samuel Rayan, Felix Wilfred, R.S. Sugirtharajah, Carlos H. Abesamis, Aruna Gnanadason; *minjung* theology (Korea); homeland theology (Taiwan); the theology of struggle (the Philippines); *dalit* theology (India); and Asian feminist theology (Virginia Fabella, Chung Hyun Kyung, Mary John Mananzan, Kwok Pui-lan, Elizabeth Tapia). This kind of spirituality allows Asians to overcome the pronounced individualism of their religions and ethics and to view the spiritual quest as necessarily comprising the quest for social justice. It requires Asian Christians to make the 'preferential option for the poor', join with those who are oppressed in their struggle for human rights and freedom and name and fight against the forces that enslave their fellow Asians (e.g., Communism, neo-capitalism, sex tourism, human labour trafficking, ecological destruction, and so on). Finally, spirituality as service to the reign of God directs Asian eyes away from the golden age located in the mythic past and turns them towards the *eschaton*, which is the Risen Christ himself, who will 'come again' to judge the living and the dead and to bring the reign of God to ultimate fulfilment.

Spirituality as an ecclesial quest: realizing the Church's mission

The third dimension of Christian spirituality is its ecclesiality. By this is meant that spirituality is not a private and solitary pursuit for the salvation of one's soul or the mystical union of the 'one with the One'. Rather it is a communal quest carried out in the bosom of the Church, together with the other members of the body of Christ, by means of the Church's resources such as the Bible and the sacraments. Thus, Asian-Christian spirituality is fundamentally biblical, sacramental and liturgical.

Furthermore, because it is ecclesial, Asian spirituality is also missionary, since the Church, as Vatican II has affirmed, is missionary by nature.[32] But what is meant by mission in Asia is different from what was understood in pre-Vatican II theology of missions (*missio ad gentes*), which was predicated upon two basic concepts, i.e., salvation of souls and planting the Church. Mission as saving souls is inspired primarily by Mt. 18.19–20. Jesus' command to go and make disciples of all nations, baptize them in the name of the Father and the Son and the Holy Spirit and teach them to observe all that he has commanded is taken to mean proclaiming, through words and deeds, the Good News of God's salvation to the heathens and converting them to the Christian religion. Salvation is exclusively that of the soul, for which conversion and baptism are absolute requirements. Missions are made urgent by the doctrine of original sin according to which all humans are born as enemies of God and by the belief that very few indeed will be saved. All non-Christian religions are condemned as idolatry and superstition or at least as powerless human attempts at self-salvation. On the other hand, mission as church-planting (*plantatio ecclesiae*) is inspired by Lk. 14.23. In this parable the master orders his servants to go out to the roads and country lanes and bring everybody to the banquet so that his house may be full. Conversion and baptism are the first steps towards the final goal of mission, i.e., establishing the Church, with all its institutional and sacramental structures. This model is operative mostly in mainline churches, especially the Roman Catholic Church.

By contrast, it is customary today to distinguish between 'mission' and 'missions'. By *mission* is meant God the Father's own 'mission' or activities in history through Jesus and in the power of the Holy Spirit (*missio Dei*). This mission actualizes in time and space the eternal relations among the divine Persons in the Trinity itself. It is the mission of the Church only insofar as the Church is empowered to participate in it. *Missions* refers to the various forms and activities by which the Church carries out God's mission at a particular place and time. Today there is a keen awareness that missions are not restricted to certain individuals, i.e., missionaries, but are incumbent upon *all* Christians. 'Missions' here are understood as serving God's kingdom of truth, love and justice. This model is rooted in Luke 4.18–19, which speaks of Jesus' mission of preaching the Good News to the poor, releasing the captives, giving sight to the blind, setting the oppressed free and proclaiming the favourable year of the Lord. Salvation is understood not in spiritualistic and individualistic terms (as salvation of souls) nor in ecclesiastical terms (as planting the Church) but as comprising, as we have seen above, the social, political, economic and cosmic dimensions of human existence.

Furthermore, while not denying the necessity of witness, proclamation, baptism and church planting, this model of mission focuses on finding the most effective way to carry out God's mission amidst cultural diversity, religious pluralism and massive poverty. This modality is dialogue, based on the mystery of God's incarnation. The modes of dialogue, as has been mentioned above, are four: common life, action, theological exchange and religious experience. Furthermore, this dialogue is carried out in three areas, as the Federation of Asian Bishops' Conferences has repeatedly emphasized, namely, liberation, inculturation and interreligious dialogue.

So far we have shown how interfaith dialogue and liberation are constitutive dimensions of Asian-Christian spirituality. But inculturation is no less essential for Asian-Christian spirituality.[33] By it is meant the double movement of bringing the gospel into a particular culture and using the categories of a particular culture to express and live the gospel, a process by which the local culture and the gospel are enriched and transformed. The Asian bishops have stressed that the primary agent of the inculturation of the Christian faith in Asia is the Holy Spirit, and that the persons responsible for this process are not experts but the local church. Inculturation must be carried out in all aspects of church life, including theology, liturgy, preaching, catechesis and styles of spirituality. The intrinsic connection between inculturation and spirituality is evident in the fact that the test of true inculturation is 'whether people become more committed to their Christian faith because they perceive it more clearly with the eyes of their own culture'.[34]

Because of this missionary character of Asian spirituality, in addition to the well-known spiritualities of various schools and religious orders imported from the West (e.g., Benedictine, Franciscan, Dominican, Carmelite, Jesuit, and so on), there has been an interesting development in the Asian churches, namely, the founding of Asian missionary societies with their own distinctive spiritualities that reflect the Asian cultures and religious traditions. These missionary societies of apostolic life focus on mission to non-Christians (*ad gentes*), in foreign countries (*ad exteros*) and for life (*ad vitam*). Notable among these are the Mission Society of the Philippines, the Missionary Society of St Thomas the Apostle (India), the Catholic Foreign Mission Society of Korea, the Missionary Society of

Heralds of Good News (India), the Missionary Society of Thailand and the Lorenzo Ruiz Mission Society (the Philippines).[35]

A final characteristic of this missionary spirituality is its emphasis on the laity since, given the vast, not yet evangelized Asian territories and the insufficient number of clergy and Religious, the laity, both women and men, especially catechists, are assuming an increasing role in church missions. This lay character of Asian spirituality also gives a preponderant place to popular devotions (in addition to liturgy and sacraments), especially devotion to Mary and the saints.

Mission as well as spirituality is contemplative action and active contemplation. Mission is convincing only if it is steeped in spirituality. In Pope John Paul II's words, 'In Asia, home to great religions where individuals and entire peoples are thirsting for the divine, the Church is called to be a praying Church, deeply spiritual even as she engages in immediate human and social concerns. All Christians need a true missionary spirituality of prayer and contemplation.'[36] Such a spirituality is nothing more than life lived under the power of the Spirit (interreligious dialogue), in imitation of Christ (liberation) and for the sake of the Church's mission (inculturation). Such spirituality by nature is also social spirituality.

Notes

1. The term 'globalization' has been coined by the eminent theorist of globalization Roland Robertson to express this double movement, i.e., globalization and localization. See his *Globalization: Social Theory and Global Cultures* (London and Thousand Oaks, CA: Sage, 1992).
2. See Donal Dorr, *Spirituality and Justice* (Maryknoll, NY: Orbis Books, 1984), pp. 8–18.
3. For a helpful study of globalization from the Catholic perspective, see *Globalization and Catholic Social Thought: Present Crisis, Future Hope*, ed. John A. Coleman and William F. Ryan (Maryknoll, NY: Orbis Books, 2005) and the entire vol. 2, no. 1 of *Journal of Catholic Social Thought* (Winter, 2005), pp. 1–276. For very helpful reflections on globalization and bibliography, see the Globalization Website at Emory University, Atlanta, Georgia, USA: http://www.sociology.emory.edu/globalization.
4. See Arjun Appadurai, 'Disjuncture and Difference in the Global Economy', *Public Culture* 2/2 (1990), pp. 1–24.
5. John Coleman briefly lists the good effects of globalization: 'The positive effects of globalization include increased consciousness of being one world. Information is also more democratically available, and human rights language now permeates a wider global consciousness.' See *Globalization and Catholic Social Thought*, p. 13.

6. John Coleman lists four negative effects of globalization: insensitivity to human suffering, inattention to ecological sustainability, polarization between and within cultures and the erosion of the abilities of states to provide for societal needs. See *Globalization and Catholic Social Thought*, pp. 13–14.

7. See Donal Dorr, *The Social Justice Agenda: Justice, Ecology, Power and the Church* (Maryknoll, NY: Orbis Books, 1991), pp. 7–41.

8. The following works are to be noted: Gustavo Gutiérrez, *We Drink from Our Own Wells: The Spiritual Journey of a People* (Maryknoll, NY: Orbis Books, 1983); Pedro Casaldáliga and José-María Vigil, *Liberating Spirituality: A Spirituality of Liberation*, trans. Paul Burns and Francis McDonagh (Quezon City, Philippines: Claretian Publications, 1996), with a very helpful bibliography; Jon Sobrino, *Spirituality of Liberation: Toward Political Holiness*, trans. Robert R. Barr (Maryknoll, NY: Orbis Books, 1988); Antonio González, *The Gospel of Faith and Justice*, trans. Joseph Owens (Maryknoll, NY: Orbis Books, 2005). Obviously, Catholic social spirituality is rooted in Catholic social thought. For studies of Catholic social thought, see *One Hundred Years of Catholic Social Thought*, ed. John Coleman (Maryknoll, NY: Orbis Books, 1991); Charles E. Curran, *Catholic Social Teaching 1891–Present: A Historical, Theological, and Ethical Analysis* (Washington, DC: Georgetown University Press, 2002); Judith A. Merkle, *From the Heart of the Church: The Catholic Social Tradition* (Collegeville, MN: Liturgical Press, 2004); Thomas Massaro, *Living Justice: Catholic Social Teaching in Action* (Lanham, MD: Sheed & Ward, 2000); and *Modern Catholic Social Teaching: Commentaries & Interpretations*, ed. Kenneth Himes (Washington, DC: Georgetown University Press, 2005). Of Catholic social thought, John Coleman says that it is made up of eight basic principles: human dignity (based on the fact that humans are made in God's image and are called to be co-creators of society and culture); the human person (as a social, dependent and interdependent being); the common good (the sum total of institutional arrangements that guarantee and promote human flourishing); subsidiarity (higher forms of governance must not co-opt or dissipate the proper roles of local units); solidarity (moral obligations to come to the aid and support of others); the preferential option for the poor (rooted in God's and Jesus' preferential identification with the poor); justice (commutative, distributive and social); and integral humanism (authentic or integral human development). See *Globalization and Catholic Social Thought*, pp. 15–18.

9. For a most recent study on the theme of the Kingdom of God in Jesus' preaching in the context of the quest for the historical Jesus, see James D.G. Dunn, *Jesus Remembered* (Grand Rapids, MI: Eerdmans, 2003), pp. 383–541. Dunn's conclusion is pertinent: 'In short, the evidence

we have points to one and only one clear conclusion: that Jesus was remembered as preaching about the kingdom of God and that this was central to his message and mission' (p. 387). Contemporary biblical scholars whose works are important for the rediscovery of the historical Jesus include, beside those of the 'Jesus Seminar', Raymond Brown, Bruce A. Chilton, Martin Hengel, Gerd Theissen, Larry Hurtado, John Meier, N.T. Wright and Luke Timothy Johnson, among many others.

10. See Jon Sobrino, *Spirituality of Liberation*, pp. 14–19.
11. Clodovis Boff develops this 'see–judge–act' into a full-fledged theological method of socio-analytical, hermeneutical and practical mediations in his *Theology and Praxis: Epistemological Foundations*, trans. Robert Barr (Maryknoll, NY: Orbis Books, 1987). See Peter C. Phan, 'A Common Journey, Different Paths, the Same Destination: Method in Liberation Theologies', in Peter C. Phan, *Christianity with an Asian Face* (Maryknoll, NY: Orbis Books, 2003) pp. 26–46.
12. See Casaldáliga and Vigil, *Liberating Spirituality*, pp. 96–9.
13. Casaldáliga and Vigil, *Liberating Spirituality*, p. 140.
14. Implicit in the option for the poor is the philosophical assumption in social spirituality that action (praxis) and not philosophical reflection (theoria) provides the integral and holistic approach to reality and to God. See Antonio González, *The Gospel of Faith and Justice*, pp. 2–5.
15. See Jon Sobrino, *Spirituality of Liberation*, p. 90.
16. Jon Sobrino, *Spirituality of Liberation*, p. 92.
17. Jon Sobrino, *Spirituality of Liberation*, pp. 96–102.
18. Casaldáliga and Vigil, *Liberating Spirituality*, p. 122.
19. Casaldáliga and Vigil, *Liberating Spirituality*, p. 23.
20. Casaldáliga and Vigil, *Liberating Spirituality*, p. 180.
21. For a recent helpful overview of liberation theology in its global development, see Christopher Rowland (ed.), *The Cambridge Companion to Liberation Theology* (Cambridge: Cambridge University Press, 1999).
22. In addition to the works by Gustavo Gutiérrez, Pedro Casaldáliga, José-María Vigil and Jon Sobrino already cited above, those on spirituality by Leonardo Boff, Clodovis Boff, Juan Luis Segundo, José Comblin, Ignacio Ellacuría, Segundo Galilea, Carlos Mestes, João Batista Libânio, Oscar Romero, Pablo Richard, Ivone Gebara, María Clara Bingemer and a host of younger theologians deserve a close reading. To note that liberation theology has spread throughout the globe is not to deny that in recent times it has suffered an eclipse, due in part to the opposition of Cardinal Joseph Ratzinger, Prefect of the Congregation for the Doctrine of the Faith, now Pope Benedict XVI. However, as Christopher Rowland has rightly noted, 'We are dealing with a movement whose high point as the topic of discussion may now have passed, but whose influence, in a multitude of ways, direct

and indirect, is as strong as ever' (*The Cambridge Companion to Liberation Theology*, p. 248).

23. See, for example, Patrick A. Kalilombe, 'Spirituality in the African Perspective', in Rosino Gibellini (ed.), *Paths of African Theology* (Maryknoll, NY: Orbis Books, 1994), pp. 115–35 and Diane B. Stinton, *Jesus of Africa: Voices of Contemporary African Christology* (Maryknoll, NY: Orbis Books, 2004). Works by other theologians such as Mercy Oduyoye, Bénézet Bujo, Jean-Marc Ela, J.N.K. Mugambi, John S. Pobee, Kwame Bediako, John S. Mbiti, Charles Nyamiti, Peter K. Sarpong, Justin S. Ukpong, François Kabasélé Lumbala and Magesa Laurenti deserve serious study.

24. My chief resources here will be the teachings of the Federation of Asian Bishops' Conferences (FABC) and the Special Assembly of the Synod of Bishops for Asia, which met in Rome on 19 April–14 May 1998 (the Asian Synod for short). The FABC was founded in 1970, on the occasion of Pope Paul VI's visit to Manila, Philippines. Its statutes, approved by the Holy See ad experimentum in 1972, were amended several times and were also approved again ad limina by the Holy See. For the documents of the FABC and its various institutes, see Gaudencio Rosales and C. G. Arévalo (eds), *For All the Peoples of Asia: Federation of Asian Bishops' Conferences. Documents from 1970 to 1991* (New York/Quezon City: Orbis Books/Claretian Publications, 1992), Franz-Josef Eilers (ed.), *For All the Peoples of Asia: Federation of Asian Bishops' Conferences. Documents from 1992 to 1996, vol. 2* (Quezon City: Claretian Publications, 1997), and *idem* (ed.), *For All the Peoples of Asia: Federation of Asian Bishops' Conferences. Documents from 1997 to 2002, vol. 3* (Quezon City: Claretian Publications, 2002). For a history of the FABC, see Edmund Chia, *Thirty Years of FABC: History, Foundation. Context and Theology* (Hong Kong: FABC Papers, 2003).

25. Pope John Paul II's Apostolic Exhortation Ecclesia in Asia, §6. English translation in Peter C. Phan (ed.), *The Asian Synod: Texts and Commentaries* (Maryknoll, NY: Orbis Books, 2002), pp. 286–340.

26. Of globalization, the Asian bishops say:

> While the process of economic globalization has brought certain positive effects, we are aware that it 'has also worked to the detriment of the poor, tending to push poorer countries to the margin of economic and political relations. Many Asian nations are unable to hold their own in a global market economy' (*Ecclesia in Asia*, p. 39). The phenomena of marginalization and exclusion are its direct consequences. It has produced greater inequalities among people. It has enabled only a small portion of the population to improve their standards of living, leaving many to remain in poverty. Another consequence is excessive urbanization,

causing the emergence of huge urban conglomerations and the resultant migration, crime and exploitation of the weaker sections (*For All the Peoples of Asia*, vol. 3, p. 6).

27. See Aloysius Pieris, *An Asian Theology of Liberation* (Maryknoll, NY: Orbis Books, 1988); *Love Meets Wisdom: A Christian Experience of Buddhism* (Maryknoll, NY: Orbis Books, 1988); *Fire and Water: Basic Issues in Asian Buddhism and Christianity* (Maryknoll, NY: Orbis Books, 1996); *God's Reign for God's Poor – A Return to the Jesus Formula: A Critical Evaluation of Contemporary Reformulations of the Mission Manifestation in Roman Catholic Theology in Recent Jesuit Documents* (Kelaniya: Tulana Research Centre, 1999); *Mysticism of Service: A Short Treatise on Spirituality with a Pauline-Ignatian Focus on the Prayer-Life of Christian Activists* (Kelaniya: Tulana Research Centre, 2000).

28. On interreligious dialogue in Asia, see Peter C. Phan, *Being Religious Interreligiously: Asian Perspectives on Interfaith Dialogue* (Maryknoll, NY: Orbis Books, 2005).

29. For a clear and comprehensive presentation of Asian liberation theologies, see Michael Amaladoss, *Life in Freedom: Liberation Theologies from Asia* (Maryknoll, NY: Orbis Books, 1997).

30. *Ecclesia in Asia*, §20.

31. For a challenging study of Asian Christology, see George M. Soares-Prabhu, *The Dharma of Jesus*, ed. Francis Xavier D'Sa (Maryknoll, NY: Orbis Books, 2003).

32. For a magisterial history of Christian missions in Asia, see Samuel Hugh Moffett, *A History of Christianity in Asia; Vol. I: Beginnings to 1500* (Maryknoll, NY: Orbis Books, 1992) and *A History of Christianity in Asia; Vol. II: 1500–1900* (Maryknoll, NY: Orbis Books, 2005).

33. On inculturation in Asia, see Peter C. Phan, *In Our Own Tongues: Perspectives from Asia on Mission and Inculturation* (Maryknoll, NY: Orbis Books, 2003) and James H. Kroeger (ed.), *Inculturation in Asia: Directions, Initiatives, and Options* (Hong Kong: FABC Papers, 2005).

34. *Ecclesia in Asia*, §22.

35. On Asian mission societies, see James H. Kroeger, 'The Asian Churches' Awakening to Mission', in Peter C. Phan (ed.), *The Asian Synod*, pp. 89–211.

36. *Ecclesia in Asia*, §23.

Chapter 3

Benedict XVI's *Deus Caritas Est* and Social Action

Tissa Balasuriya

While appreciating what the Pope has to say about love, the writer opines that justice as a requirement of love has been somewhat sidelined in this encyclical. He reminds us that, over long periods of its history, the Church fostered unjust structures of society, while, at the same time, exercising its mission and ministry of social service and love of neighbour. Even in the twenty-first century, there is a need for the Church to sever its 'unholy alliance' with the dominant Western colonizers. He respectfully suggests that, in a subsequent encyclical, the Pope could address the radical demands of the gospel concerning issues of justice.

God is Love and God is Just – in Church History

Part II of the encyclical deals with charity as a responsibility of the Church and a manifestation of Trinitarian love. In this part the Pope emphasizes the need and obligation of charity that is social service, especially to the needy, rendered in a loving manner. While appreciating this perspective, my comments are on the sidelining of love as requiring justice among persons and in local and global communities.

The Pope mentions the social teaching of the Church historically as charity, and in recent times as demanding social justice. He confesses that:

> historically, the issue of the just ordering of the collectivity had taken a new dimension with the industrialization of society in the nineteenth century . . . It must be admitted that the Church's leadership was slow to realize that the issue of the just structuring of society needed to be approached in a new way.

Part II also deals with the speculative theory of the practice, rather than with the actual historical practice of the theory. The God of theology may be the God of generous forgiving love, but is not the God of Christian history generally presented as de facto siding with the Christians who were often arrogant, violent dominators of others? While acknowledging the importance of what the Pope says, several critical comments can be made about this part of the encyclical. My reflections are in the context of modern European history.

The Early Church

The Pope begins this part with a reflection on the Acts of the Apostles, with the well-known story of charity in the early Church:

> Charity as a responsibility of the Church . . . The awareness of this responsibility has had a constitutive relevance in the Church from the beginning.

> 'All who believed were together and held all things in common; they sold their possessions and goods and distributed them to all, as any had need.'[1] In these words, St Luke provides a kind of definition of the Church, whose constitutive elements include fidelity to the 'teaching of the apostles', 'communion' koinonia, 'breaking of the bread' and 'prayer' . . .

The Pope comments that, even as the Church grew, its: 'essential core remained: within the community of believers there can never be room for a poverty that denies anyone what is needed for a dignified life'.[2]

This is a beautiful story, but the history of the Church is far from bearing witness to the communion, the sharing of prayer and the impact of prayer. The continuation of the story in the Acts is significant. It related how Barnabas 'sold a field he owned, brought the money, and handed it over to the apostles'.

Ananias and Sapphira

Acts continues with the story of Ananias and Sapphira who sold some property of theirs and kept part of the money thus obtained, thereby deceiving the apostles and the Spirit.[3] They underwent an instantaneous miraculous punishment of death. This shows that the early Church too had persons and families who lied to the community and did not share as they professed to do. It may be asked whether this is a precursor of what was to happen historically in regard to the Christian profession of charity and communion, of sharing and fidelity to the teaching of the apostles. In modern times it may resemble the proclamation of development aid by the rich (Christian) countries while continuing to exploit poor people.

Aren't there many Ananiases and Sapphiras today, with even trans-national combinations, that take away the wealth of poor peoples and classes? Are not the workings of the system of international investment and trade today with the neo-liberal capitalistic pressures of the IMF, World Bank and WTO, dominated by the (Christian) USA and Europe, worse than the behaviour of Ananias and Sapphira, though they may profess to be good believers like the honest Barnabas? Perhaps further reflections on the early Church may induce the Pope to comment on these two stories also as prototypes of human weakness even in the community of believers.

The whole story or tragedy of the Crusades, slavery, the torture of witches, the Inquisition and colonization since the early modern period seems to be neglected or bypassed. This could lead some readers to believe that the Pope assumes that Christian charity was sufficient for those periods, especially as he refers to:

the monastic and mendicant orders, and later for the various male and female religious institutes all through the history of the Church. The figures of saints such as Francis of Assisi, Ignatius of Loyola, John of God, Camillus of Lellis, Vincent de Paul, Louise de Marillac, Guiseppe B. Cotolengo, John Bosco, Luigi Orine, Teresa of Calcutta to name but a few – stand out as lasting models of social charity for all people of good will. The saints are the true bearers of light within history, for they are men and women of faith, hope and love.[4]

These saints, almost all male celibates, are great personalities with their different charisms. It can, however, be questioned how far their social charity dealt with issues of social global justice, or even with issues of interpersonal relations. I was fortunate to meet Mother Teresa on three occasions, including once at her convent in Calcutta. On another occasion at a Catholic students' meeting in India, she was asked why she did not work for a fair distribution of the surplus food stocked in India. She replied: 'That is not my mission, I leave it to others.'

It is not possible to realize through more charity a world in which the abundant food available is so distributed that there is no one in need. This requires political will and political decisions. The preaching of the Word, the Eucharist and Christian service must participate in this task, especially when it is the rich and powerful Christian peoples who cause and benefit from such inequality.

In the early Church itself the apostles also had to face the problem of maldistribution of resources. 'Some time later, as the number of disciples kept growing, there was a quarrel between the Greek-speaking Jews and the native Jews. The Greek-speaking Jews claimed that their widows were being neglected in the daily distribution of funds. So the twelve apostles called the whole group of believers together . . .'[5] Thus seven helpers were chosen to handle finances. Even in the exercise of charity there were problems of justice to be resolved by recourse to authority and to the community.

Love requires that all be cared for, and that no one is in need of the essentials for the good life. To realize this in a situation of great inequality at the local and global levels, a coordinated strategic struggle against inequality, often based on long-term robbery and injustice, is required. The present world order is based on centennial exploitation by powers that claimed to be Christian and to be favourably linked to the mission and history of salvation.

Church and State

The just ordering of society and of the State is a central responsibility of politics. As Augustine once said, a state which is not governed according to justice would be just a bunch of thieves. *Remota itaque justitia quid sunt regna nisi magna latrocinia?*[6]

It may be asked: did not Christians coexist with and even legitimize the enormously unjust regimes that have existed throughout many centuries of colonial rule by European powers? From the point of view of the colonized peoples, were they not a bunch of robbers?

> Fundamental to Christianity is the distinction between what belongs to Caesar and what belongs to God (Mt. 22.21), in other words the distinction between Church and State, or as the Second Vatican Council puts it, the autonomy of the temporal sphere . . . The two spheres are distinct, yet always interrelated.[7]

This reply of Jesus to the lawyers who wanted to trap him concerning payment of tax to the Roman rulers did not mean separation of Church and State. His response to the crafty questioners seems to be: since you accept Roman rule, you should pay tax to them. This is not to say that the State is not under God, or not amenable to action by the civil society or religious groups. There is no teaching by Jesus concerning the Church in this context, or elsewhere. In Christian thinking both the Church and the State are under God.

Why was Jesus Killed?

It would be a useful exercise to ask what were the real causes of the death of Jesus. Did he choose to die? Did he die in obedience to the Father – as a sacrificial lamb? Or was he killed by a combination of the high priests and Pharisees and the representatives of the Roman imperial power? Was he not

killed as a presumed traitor to Rome, and an opponent of the official interpretation of religion as a burden on the mass of the poor afflicted people?
The Gospels seem to bear witness to such a view.[8]

Jesus was killed because he was accused of being a threat to the Roman
Empire. 'Above his head they put the written notice of the accusation
against him: "This is Jesus, king of the Jews".'[9] Mark says, 'He (Pilate) knew
very well that the chief priests had handed Jesus over to him because they
were jealous.'[10] 'If you set him free, that means you are not the emperor's
friend! Anyone who claims to be a king is a rebel against the emperor.'[11]
The Gospels reveal that Jesus himself was involved in issues of justice and
politics, and the chief priests used these to accuse him in front of Pilate. His
ministry was much more than one of mere social activity. His witness to the
God of love included teachings and actions that led to his crucifixion. Jesus
died not because of the justice of God, but because of the injustice of the
dominant system and of the rulers and high priests of the time.

The Pope writes of the distinction of the roles of the Church and of the
State: 'A just society must be the achievement of politics, not of the Church.
Yet the promotion of justice through efforts to bring about openness of
mind and will to the demands of the common good is something which
concerns the Church deeply.'[12]

Papal States

The encyclical speaks of the Church, especially the clergy, not being
involved in the affairs of the State, especially in ideological strategies. The
encyclical seems to forget that for over 1,000 years till the mid-nineteenth
century (1870) the popes were the political rulers of the Papal States cover-
ing much of Italy with an army and even engaging in wars for political
power. It was with reluctance that Pope Pius IX acquiesced in the freedom
and independence of Italy in 1870. He became a self-proclaimed prisoner
in the Vatican. The popes continued this protest from 1870 to 1929 as
prisoners in the Vatican, till the Lateran Treaty with Mussolini acknowledged the Vatican as an independent sovereign state in 1929. Interestingly
the Vatican is about the smallest state in the world. It is also the only state
in the world in which a woman cannot be head of State. The papal envoys
or ambassadors are members of the political diplomatic corps in many
nations.

A characteristic of the teaching and life of the Church has been that, while
the Church preached that God is love, and exercised a mission and ministry
of social service and charitable love of neighbour, the Church not only
tolerated the unjust structures of society, but even benefited from them and
fostered them as with the spread of colonialism.

Justice in the World

The encyclical does not give the ministry of justice the essential role it should have in the mission of the Church. The 1971 Synod of Bishops presented justice as an essential constituent of the mission of the Church:

> Action on behalf of justice and participation in the transformation of the world fully appear to us as a constitutive dimension of the preaching of the Gospel, or, in other words, of the Church's mission for the redemption of the human race and its liberation from every oppressive situation.
>
> Unless combated and overcome by social and political action, the influence of the new industrial and technological order favours the concentration of wealth, power and decision-making in the hands of a small public or private controlling group. Economic injustice and lack of social participation keep people from attaining their basic human and civil rights.
>
> 30. In the Old Testament God reveals himself to us as the liberator of the oppressed and the defender of the poor, demanding from people faith in him and justice towards one's neighbour. It is only in the observance of the duties of justice that God is truly recognized as the liberator of the oppressed.
>
> 34. According to the Christian message, therefore, our relationship to our neighbour is bound up with our relationship to God; our response to the love of God, saving us through Christ, is shown to be effective in our love and service of people. Christian love of neighbour and justice cannot be separated. For love implies an absolute demand for justice, namely a recognition of the dignity and rights of one's neighbour. Justice attains its inner fullness only in love. Because every person is truly a visible image of the invisible God and a sibling of Christ, the Christian finds in every person God himself and God's absolute demand for justice and love.
>
> 36. The Church has received from Christ the mission of preaching the Gospel message, which contains a call to people to turn away from sin to the love of the Father, universal kinship and a consequent demand for justice in the world. This is the reason why the Church has the right, indeed the duty, to proclaim justice on the social, national and international level, and to denounce instances of injustice, when the fundamental rights of people and their very salvation demand it.[13]

What is even more questionable in the history of the Church is whether Christians and the Church have de facto been manifesting other centred oblative love. Is the evidence of history not the contrary? While saintly Christians and missionaries have witnessed to charitable service, the Church has been structurally allied to the dominant, exploiting rulers, invaders, colonial rulers and affluent rich. Pope John Paul II apologized over 99 times for such abuses.

Benedict XVI refers to the documents of Catholic social teaching from the 1891 *Rerum Novarum* of Leo XIII to *Centesimus Annus* of 1991. One of their deficiencies is the lack of structural analysis in terms of global social justice. They were all written mainly from a European-dominated world-view. There has been no critical moral evaluation of European colonialism by the central Church authority throughout the 450 years since 1492. Much less has there been a demand for compensation from the exploiters, who were by and large Christian powers.

The writers of the encyclicals were influenced by the dominant ideology and surrounding culture of their times. The same can be said of the late Pope John Paul II who wrote disparagingly concerning Buddhism as negative, and of the present Pope in the Vatican Congregation for the Doctrine of the Faith (CDF) document *Dominus Iesus*. While their scholarship and goodwill are not in doubt, the fact remains that they both lack close live contact with the other religions in an ongoing manner. They have lived their lives almost entirely in a world dominated by white racism, whether under capitalism or Communism. They have had no live-in experience (yet) of other peoples dominated by the West. It may be recalled that even Soviet Communism continued the white Russian colonial domination over Asian peoples of East Asia. Both Popes implicitly accept not only the world of neo-liberal domination but also the global world system of land distribution in which the European peoples have taken over the main habitable areas of the world in the Americas and Oceania.[14]

Structural Lovelessness

The encyclical does not refer to the structured lovelessness that has prevailed in the world system, especially since 1492. The accent on charity and social work does not take the Pope to the analysis of the social structures that regulate the social order. It is such structures as the distribution of wealth and incomes that prevent so many peoples from having their daily bread in a world of plenty and waste. Hence the encyclical does not deal with the root causes of poverty and injustice. Opposition to structured injustice in the society of his day led Jesus to his clashes with the then political and social power elites and eventually to his death. Unfortunately, the preaching and liturgy of the Churches do not bring this aspect to the fore, while emphasizing charity.

It is legitimate to ask respectfully: can Benedict XVI claim that the Catholic Church witnesses to the God of genuine authentic love, when historically the Church, by and large, has not been on the side of reforming and transforming social action for justice, except indirectly by her education and other social service activities? The claims in the encyclical in favour of the Church's social action are hardly credible in our Asian context where there is presently much critical academic and social evaluation of the position of the Church during the past five centuries.

On the contrary – have not the other religions been at the receiving end of Christian downgrading and even violence? This was linked to the Church's traditional interpretation of God's love as benefiting exclusively Christians. While being well versed in Western classical literature, European philosophy and the biblical tradition, the authors of the encyclical do not seem to have close and respectful acquaintance with culture, religious perspectives and millennial search for the divine by other peoples. It may also be asked whether the encyclical takes adequate note of the thinking of feminist scholars, activists and movements in relation to issues in both Part I and Part II. This is a major lacuna in the approach of the teaching hierarchical Church that is systematically male dominated.

The encyclical distinguishes functions in the Church and in a way separates the hierarchy from the laity. The charitable service by the Church is to be organized as an essential activity of the Church, whereas action for justice is said to belong to the political field and is to be undertaken by the laity. The Church (clergy) is given the responsibility of inspiring a rational approach to issues of justice but, it would seem, not of participating in its being practically actualized. It is understandable that the clergy of the Church should not be involved in the running of the State. But the Church should not be identified with the clergy. The laity are also Church, and will be more so in a Church in which the clergy are ageing and decreasing in numbers. Yet the clergy still exercise a major controlling influence in church life. To exempt them from participation in political issues often results in the laity lacking an effective leadership at critical moments in a country's evolution. Thus the bishops in countries like the Philippines and some countries of Africa and Latin America have contributed courageously to the removing of oppressive dictatorial regimes in recent times.

In Jesus' parable of the Good Samaritan, when the priest and the Levite saw the man robbed, stripped, beaten and left half-dead, they walked by on the other side. Evidently they were lacking in the required love of neighbour. This could be a message to the Christian clergy today, even if those two passing by were not Christian priests. Jesus pinpoints the spirituality involved in the concern for the neighbour fallen among robbers.

Several times the Pope refers to the need for the Church not to be linked to political ideologies. 'Christian charitable activity must be independent of parties and ideologies. It is not a means of changing the world ideologically, and it is not at the service of worldly stratagems, but it is a way of making present here and now the love which man always needs.'[15]

However, whether we like it or not, a certain dominant ideology prevails in social relations and situations. Thus, in a time of slavery, the given social order was taken for granted and de facto supported as it was not opposed. St Paul, while wanting slaves to be well treated, teaches slaves to be obedient to their masters. 'Obey your human masters in all things . . . for Christ is the real Master you serve.'[16] Likewise the colonial enterprise was not actively opposed, but was accepted and even supported by Christians and the Church. An explanation of this position could be that hitherto the author/s of the papal encyclicals may not have been adequately sensitive to the impact of the prevailing global social order on the oppressed peoples other than on the working classes of Europe after the Industrial Revolution.

Marxism

The Pope refers several times to Marxism and explains its social thinking that considers social service as preventing social revolution:

> Part of Marxist strategy is the theory of impoverishment: in a situation of unjust power, it is claimed, anyone who engages in charitable initiatives is actually serving that unjust system, making it appear at least to some extent tolerable. This in turn slows down the potential revolution and thus blocks the struggle for a better world.[17]

It is significant that, while the Pope criticizes the Marxist theory and system as really an inhuman philosophy, people of the present are sacrificed to the Moloch of the future. The encyclical does not criticize the prevailing capitalist system and especially the dominant neo-liberalism directly or in such language. Is not the Pope himself taking an ideological position implicitly in favour of the capitalist system and colonialism that dominated the world for centuries and continues to do so?

In a sense Marx, a Jew, was perhaps inspired by the values of the Bible also, and his social analysis contributed to modern Christians being reminded of the demands of social justice. But both Marx and the papal encyclicals overlooked the injustices of European colonialism. By asking the Church (clergy) to abstain from ideological struggles the Pope virtually favours the status quo, as mere charitable social action would not change the unjust global system. The hierarchical leadership should be encouraged to participate in peoples' movements for justice. It may even be asked whether the Churches have shared in the present-day struggle for peace in the world – especially in the face of the blatant violation of human rights in invading Iraq in March 2003. How different the situation would have been if the Christians in the USA, the UK and Australia had been led by their hierarchies to oppose this war non-violently. This would, of course, require the willingness of the faithful to follow or join a hierarchy that would have won their confidence by credible witness on other contemporary issues also.

The thinking in Part II of the encyclical is reminiscent of the strictures on liberation theology that emanated from the Congregation for the Doctrine of the Faith (CDF) when Cardinal Ratzinger was its head. It is noteworthy that the Pope does not speak of the mass movements for human liberation and structural changes in favour of justice in which the Churches of the world have been participating in recent decades. Neither does he mention great champions of social justice, such as Archbishops Oscar Romero and Helder Camara, whom the whole world honours as active contemporary friends of the poor, and brave Christian leaders of their peoples.

The encyclical emphasizes the service of charity as an essential mission of the Church:

> The Church's deepest nature is expressed in her threefold responsibility: of proclaiming the word of God (*kerygma-martyria*), celebrating the sacraments (*leitourgia*), and exercising the ministry of charity (*diakonia*). These duties presuppose each other and are inseparable. For the Church, charity is not a kind of welfare activity which could equally well be left to others, but it is part of her nature, an indispensable expression of her very being.[18]

The link between the celebration of the sacraments and the ministry and action for justice is not noted in the encyclical. On the contrary, it speaks of centuries of Christian liturgical celebration, of service of charity and saints in the mission of charity, but almost totally forgets the centuries of alliance of the Church and Christians with an exploitative social order such as slavery, and colonialism, not to mention feudalism. How were the ministries of the word, of liturgy and *diakonia* or charity, exercised over these centuries, and with what impact on the exploited and needy? How was Mt. 25. 31–44, 'I was hungry and you fed me . . .', implemented by a Church that stressed such views of mission without an emphasis on justice? From my part of the world, one is inclined to ask for whom is the encyclical written, and by whom? Should not the God of *Deus Caritas Est* necessarily imply that God is also the God of justice? Does not the story of the Good Samaritan imply a need to get rid of the robbers who waylay defenceless travellers?

Further Dimensions of 'God is Love'

The love of God for humanity can be revealed, understood and interpreted in many senses. Common to all Christians is the view that God is love and God's one commandment is that a person loves others as one loves oneself.

Personal and collective service as charity to those in need is emphasized in the second part of the encyclical 'God is Love'. The encyclical develops this teaching and the relevant example of Jesus in his life to persons in all manner of need.

Continuing the analysis of love, and God as love, proposed in this encyclical, we can refer to love in the gospel of Jesus in several senses:

(1) Love as the charity of social service. This is beyond the basic love of desire termed *eros*, and is other-centred like the *philia* of friendship and the *agape* of self-giving communion.

(2) Justice that is demanded by love. Justice requires that what is due is given to each one, in distributive and social justice. The encyclical refers to this, somewhat in passing, and does not engage itself in the local and global struggle for justice.

(3) Love as understood in the Beatitudes, as in the Sermon on the Mount This is a deeper level of self-giving that goes beyond the service of charity and the norms of justice. This is a spirituality that is distinctive in the teaching of Jesus and some of the deeper levels of other world religions. It is a spiritual culture and a way of life that has a rare power of transforming persons and communities. It is the development of a soul force that does not impose harm on others but tries to overcome evil and anger by love. It bears the burden of interpersonal relations by suffering in oneself rather than by harming others. It is a message of supreme endurance that bears up suffering imposed by others without harming others.

Jesus on the Cross bears witness to this message of love unto ultimate self-giving in bearing witness to one's convictions and message. Unfortunately the significance of this message has been lost or distorted by the interpretation that Jesus suffered his death to pay for the sins of humanity to appease an offended God the Father.

The Sermon on the Mount

A significant omission in the encyclical in relation to the teachings and life of Jesus is the Sermon on the Mount – as in Mt. 5.1–12 and Lk. 6.20–41.

The Beatitudes present a dimension of Jesus Christ that goes beyond the charity of social service and the mere legality or correctness of loving one's friends, and the boundaries of strict obligations of justice. Jesus teaches that human happiness and the coming of the Kingdom of God are in the goodness of self-giving for others. From this disposition many conclusions can be drawn for personal and social life.

The teaching of Jesus and of the world religions is summarized in the golden rule 'do unto others as you would that they do unto you'.[19] Jesus says:

. . . the measure you use for others is the one that God will use for you.

Love your enemies, do good to those who hate you, bless those who curse you, and pray for those who ill-treat you. If anyone hits you on one cheek, let them hit the other one too, if someone takes your coat, let them have your shirt as well.[20]

Happy are those who are humble;
They will receive what God has promised.[21]

Have Christians as a community been humble? What has been the relationship of the Church towards other faiths, people of other religions and of non-Western cultures? Has it been one of humility and respect for them? Could the Church say that it has followed the teaching of Jesus?

If one of you wants to be great, they must be the servant of the rest; and if one of you wants to be first, they must be the slave of all. For even the Son of Man did not come to be served; he came to serve and to give his life to redeem many people.[22]

On the other hand has not the historical record of the Church been largely one of thinking of itself as having the unique truth concerning God and a monopoly on the path and means to salvation? For a long period before the Second Vatican Council, others faiths and religions were considered wrong, and therefore without rights. They could not only be opposed but also defeated and, if possible, exterminated as works of the devil. The interpretation of Christian revelation combined with political and military power gave the European peoples a thinking that they were superior human beings, especially loved and privileged by God.

The attitude of the Catholic clergy towards women is that men were/are considered more in the image of the Man-God Jesus Christ and hence superior to women. Women are still not considered worthy of priestly ordination and of the exercise of higher teaching and administrative functions in the Church. The exclusion of women in some places from university and seminary theological studies till Vatican II (1962–65) ensured that the point of view of women had little chance of influencing the teaching and life of the Church. This is a long history of male domination that continues even today.

The Sermon on the Mount teaches:

If you lend only to those from you hope to get it back, why should you receive a blessing? Even sinners lend to sinners, to get back the same amount. No, love your enemies and do good to them. Lend and expect nothing back. You will then have a great reward, and you will be sons of the Most High God.
For he is good to the ungrateful and the wicked.
Be merciful just as your Father is merciful.
Forgive others and God will forgive you.[23]

Jesus' prayer includes 'forgive us our sins as we forgive others'.

The world system is very far from this reign of God presented by Jesus. The norms in the dominant world system are so different from these ideals. The foreign debt of poor countries is an unbearable burden that further impoverishes poor indebted countries that have been long exploited by the former colonial rulers. The IMF and the World Bank impose Structural Adjustment Policies that compel poor indebted countries to open their economies to foreign subsidized imports that destroy local production, and to privatize their public enterprises such as their water supply, fuel and common services such as health, education, communications and transportation.

Mary's Magnificat

The encyclical ends with a reflection on and prayer to Mary the mother of Jesus. She is presented as a model of social service. Her humility and kind services as at Cana are underlined in the encyclical. But it does not connect the virtues of Mary with the active public life of Jesus. Jesus took strong positions concerning true spirituality in religion and strongly castigated religious leaders who placed unnecessary burdens on simple people. The whole of Mt. 23 is a very strong public criticism that was bound to get Jesus into grave trouble with them. 'They tie on the people's back loads that are hard and heavy to carry, yet they aren't willing to lift a finger to help them carry those loads. They do everything so that people may see them.'[24]

Mary knew that Jesus was being targeted by the high priests, scribes and Pharisees. She was with him in his mission unto the death on the Cross, and thereafter with the early Church.

The Pope comments on the Magnificat, the hymn attributed to Mary when she visited Elizabeth her cousin. The Pope praises her humble sentiments and the glory of God, but makes no mention of its important radical social message.

He does not comment on the revolutionary consequences that would follow from a serious meditation on the socially demanding pronouncements of the Magnificat:

He has stretched out his mighty arm
    and scattered the proud with all their plans.
He has brought down the mighty kings from their thrones,
    and lifted up the lowly,
He has filled the hungry with good things,
    and sent the rich away with empty hands.[25]

These radical teachings are in line with the more revolutionary messages of the prophets of the Old Testament, which are also bypassed in the encyclical.

Our Self-examination

Why do you look at the speck in your brother's eye, but pay no attention to the log in your own eye? How can you say to your brother, 'Please, brother, let me take the speck out of your eye', yet cannot even see the log in your own eye? You hypocrite! First take the log out of your own eye, and then you will be able to see clearly to take the speck out of your brother's eye.[26]

On reflecting on the history of Christianity there is much cause to regret that, as a faith community, Christians have thought of themselves as superior to others, since they claimed to be the privileged of God. Christians, when in power, were intolerant of others. Among different Christian groups there were the wars of religion that decided the fate of Catholicism and Protestantism in Europe on the basis of political power and the axiom *cujus regio ejus religio* (whose is the regime, his is the religion).

The long centuries of Christian intolerance require an examination of conscience by Christians, to see where and in what way the Church went wrong. In the past, prior to Vatican II, the Catholic Church was not accustomed to accept that it could be wrong in condemning others and even persecuting them. There was a significant change in attitude with Pope John XXIII, who convoked the Second Vatican Council to update the Church (*aggiornamento*), and Paul VI, who somewhat hesitatingly continued the conciliar process.

Pope John Paul II's Apologies

The Polish Pope, John Paul II, was quite clear in apologizing throughout his long pontificate for the wrongs and mistakes of the Catholic Church. He did so as Pope, especially during his numerous travels. He asked pardon for the wrongs of anti-Semitism, of slavery, of the Crusades, the Inquisition, of the divisions among the Churches and the wars of religions, from Islam, Hus, Luther, Calvin, Zwingli, Galileo, the native peoples of the Americas, for the compromises with dictatorships and different forms of injustice, for the mistakes in the centennial confrontation of science and faith, for the responsibility of the men of the Church in discrimination against women, for the forced conversions that accompanied the brutal conquest of the peoples of the other continents, for not resisting the temptation of 'integrism', claims of exclusive righteousness. Pope John Paul II asked pardon courageously and persistently, often alone in his position.

As the millennium was coming to a close he persistently called the Church to an examination of conscience concerning the previous millennia, to begin a new stage in the history of Christianity with the grace of the millennium 2000. He called it the 'purification of memory', as against the tendency to forget or overlook the past mistakes and wrongs of the Church, which claimed papal infallibility. Thus the ageing pilgrim Pope helped open the path to dialogue among religions, among Christians, among conflicting peoples, and generations, as in the interreligious days of prayer at Assisi, and the World Days of Youth, attended by millions. He asked the journalist Jas Gawronski, 'at the end of the second millennium: where are we? Where has Christ led us, or where have we deviated from the Gospel?' [27]

Peace and Non-violence

'Blessed are the peacemakers, God will call them his children.'[28] This has great relevance in the history of the Church and now in the twenty-first century. It includes options for peace as well as methodologies of action for peace such as active non-violence and civil disobedience.

Mahatma Gandhi was drawn towards Jesus due to the deep humanity of the Sermon on the Mount. It reveals Jesus as giving a divine message beyond the limited considerations of charity, and even of justice. From Jesus' teaching on love of enemies and forgiveness of those who offended him, Mahatma Gandhi developed the philosophy and theory and practice of non-violence in all spheres of life – including the political struggle for the liberation of India from British imperial rule, and of the black and coloured peoples from white racist domination in South Africa at the beginning of the twentieth century.

The Mahatma (Great Soul) was inspired in his theory and practice of non-violence through meditation on the Sermon on the Mount, against the background of the Indian peoples' struggle for freedom from the largest empire in the nineteenth and early twentieth century. He developed the methodology of active non-violence as a very powerful weapon of peaceful people to impact on even the most powerful regimes and ruling peoples. He promoted people power – soul force and the strategy of civil disobedience in which the leaders court imprisonment rather than take to violence. In a period in which there is much resort to violence and terrorist attacks to achieve one's objectives, Mahatma Gandhi was a pioneer in evolving the teaching and practice of civil disobedience.

He trained the poor Indian masses to be disciplined in eschewing violence. He did so by public education such as calling off a campaign of non-violence when some groups of his followers resorted to violence. His moral courage and spiritual influence on the masses was so great that it became impossible for the British to continue their rule in India with Mahatma Gandhi and the Congress leadership in British jails. He led by being in the front ranks of the resistance – being the first to go to prison on 9 August 1942 in support of the Congress resolution demanding the British to 'Quit India'.

He was followed by Martin Luther King in the struggle of the black people for their rights in the USA in the 1950s and 1960s. King was a Christian minister who mobilized the people of goodwill in the USA to protest non-violently against racial discrimination. He was a disciple of Mahatma Gandhi and a teacher of active non-violence out in the field – till his assassination.

Nelson Mandela of South Africa, influenced by Gandhi and King, also showed the world a magnificent example of forgiveness at the point of victory in calling on the people of Africa to forget past grievances and live together in peace as South Africans of all races – after having been 28 years in an apartheid prison.

Although there were Christians, including Religious, who offered themselves as ransom for prisoners, it would seem that it is Mahatma Gandhi who first brought out this dimension of spirituality as soul force in the public and political sphere. It is a hope and belief in the ultimate triumph of love that inspires peace and non-violence, because self-sacrificial love can teach a lesson to the offending parties and powers. It is not to be a position of mere passive acceptance of injustice, but a strong active resistance to evil and injustice that does not bow the knee before insolent might (as Tagore calls it) but holds the head up high, asserting justice and practising supreme love even unto death. These inspiring examples of some of the greatest personalities of the world in the twentieth century can be invoked as very meaningful lessons for humanity in the twenty-first century. They give principles, methods and sacrificial fidelity to the God of love and love of one another.

In a sense this was the message of the martyrs of the early Church during the period of persecution of Christians. It got submerged in theology and spirituality when the Christian Church joined the ruling state powers in persecuting dissenters from proclaimed orthodoxy after Nicene in 325. This omission or distortion was passed on from generation to generation up to recent decades. It is opportune that the Churches return to the teaching of

Jesus. This would be one dimension of the re-evangelization of Christians that is said to be necessary today.

Twenty-first Century – Violence and Christianity

The twenty-first century was born in violence, with the 'terrorist' air attack on New York on 11 September 2001 and the invasion of Iraq by the USA, the UK and Australia on 18 March 2003. It is now well known that the invasion of Iraq in 2003 was not motivated by fear of a nuclear attack by Saddam Hussein or due to the desire of the invading forces to install democracy in Iraq. It was a step in the efforts of the USA and its allies to exercise superpower domination, especially over the Middle East, largely due to its oil riches. This war has now gone on for over three years without an end in sight. There is even the possibility of it spreading to other countries such as Iran.

One of the greatest challenges for Christians in the twenty-first century is that it is mainly they who control world power after the end of the cold war with the fall of the Berlin Wall in 1989 and the end of the Communist empire in Eastern Europe.

In the encyclical *Deus Caritas Est* there is no significant reference to this war of the twenty-first century, and to the worldwide movement for peace. This war is causing the death of several thousands of innocent men, women and children.

The superpower world of the twenty-first century has been built up by force and invasion during the five centuries since 1492, when the Christian Churches were partners with Europe in global conquest. These crimes call for reparation. The Church has been far from being an effective witness to the God of love during the building of this unjust racist world (dis)order. Most of the saints mentioned by the Pope as icons of social charity were far from being champions of the rights of the oppressed and conquered peoples of the Americas, of Africa and Asia. Global social justice was hardly their concern during the times when the exploitative world system was being built up. They were inspired by a theology and spirituality that presented the message of Jesus in a manner that legitimized the Western colonial adventure.

How and why did this happen? How has it been possible that, despite innumerable saintly persons in the Church, and millions of periods of prayer and meditation by thousands of millions of good Catholics through-out a millennium and more, the basic message of the Beatitudes did not become the way of life of the Christians and of the Church? They did not inform the spirituality and moral theology of the teaching Church to become their guiding principles, and the core inspiration of Christian culture and civilization.

Need of Purification

It can be asked how and why did the Church go so wrong for nearly 1,500 years of its 2,000-year history concerning such significant issues as the salvation of those not of the Christian faith? Was there not a mistaken emphasis in the three major functions of the Church?

- First in preaching the Word in an exclusivist and dominant sense;
- Second, in the celebration of the Eucharist being performed alongside the grave injustices of slavery, feudalism, colonial invasions and present-day growing global injustice and inequality; and
- third, in the ministry of charity being conceived as social service and not requiring reforming social action from the church leadership.

We cannot help but see an inadequacy in this interpretation of God and of the mission of the Church as service of charity. The world injustice of 20 per cent of the population having 80 per cent of the wealth and millions going hungry each day is too well known to require repetition.

Background Thinking to the Encyclical

(1) Human redemption is explained as paying the required price to God the Father.
(2) This gives an understanding of the life of Jesus that does not emphasize the positions he took for justice in the society of his day. This dilutes his strong critical message concerning the injustices of the prevailing social order and the faults of the religious and civil leaders.
(3) This gives an explanation of his death as being due to the need to make amends to the Father for original sin, rather than as being due to his strong critical stance against the social-religious injustice and struggle for the liberation of the oppressed of his day:

> This divine activity now takes on dramatic form when, in Jesus Christ, it is God himself who goes in search of the 'stray sheep', a suffering and lost humanity. When Jesus speaks in his parables of the shepherd who goes after the lost sheep, of the woman who looks for the lost coin, of the father who goes to meet and embrace his prodigal son, these are no mere words: they constitute an explanation of his very being and activity. His death on the Cross is the culmination of that turning of God against himself in which he gives himself in order to raise man up and save him. This is love in its most radical form. By contemplating the pierced side of Christ (cf. Jn 19.37), we can understand the starting-point of this

Encyclical Letter: 'God is love' (1 Jn 4.8). It is there that this truth can be contemplated. It is from there that our definition of love must begin. In this contemplation the Christian discovers the path along which his life and love must move.[29]

The Pope speaks of a lost humanity. His definition of divine love, 'God is love', begins with the hypothesis of a lost humanity to be saved by a divine act of reconciliation.

(4) Consequently another worldly interpretation is given to the spiritual discipleship of Jesus, to the meaning of prayer and to the understanding of salvation and Christian mission. Christian holiness is understood mainly as leading to charitable activity and not so related to action for justice and peace that transforms social structures.

There is no practical application of the demands of 'God is love' for peace with justice in the world of the twenty-first century. This could give the unfortunate impression that the sacramental life goes on side by side with the killings of wars, an economy of grave exploitation and pollution of nature.

A Eucharist which does not pass over into the concrete practice of love is intrinsically fragmented.[30]

(5) The sacrament of baptism was given an effect of automatic redemption of infants. The sacraments of penance and Eucharist were not closely related to the need of justice and peace in society, as oppressors, slave drivers and colonizers could receive the sacraments without meaningful remorse for their social evils. They could be at peace with the Church with a good conscience, especially if they did charitable works.

(6) Correspondingly for a long time there was a downgrading of other faiths, and opposition to friendly interreligious relations.

(7) The Kingdom of God preached by Jesus is seen as being realized in the next world, rather than on this earth. Hence a neglect of the care for nature, God's gift for all humanity to be safeguarded for succeeding generations and shared equitably among all peoples.

If the church leadership does not undertake a critical social analysis of a given situation, it cannot and will not be able to influence the laity and church organizations to take political action to bring about justice. Without a clear option for justice, especially to the poor, the Church could not fulfil the responsibility which the Pope entrusts to it: 'the Church is duty-bound to offer, through the purification of reason and through ethical formation, her own specific contribution towards understanding the requirements of justice and achieving them politically'.[31]

A Mission for the Pope

May we humbly suggest that in a subsequent encyclical he develops the radical demands of the Christian gospel of Jesus. The Pope could propose very effective remedies to this unjust situation in a relevant meditation on the Sermon on the Mount. If the Pope listens to the present cries of humanity expressed by the global protests and peace movements, he will discern the potential that the Church has for bringing war to a halt. The Christian leadership can inspire active non-violent protests, including civil disobedience, such as by refusing to pay taxes for war and the armaments industry that supports and profits from war. This would be at least as meaningful as the encouragement to charitable social service within the grossly unjust world order of violence and international lawlessness.

The Pope could lead the Christian churches and peoples to develop methodologies of non-violent protest that are far more feasible now with the present rapid global communications. If the Pope and the Christian leadership of North America, Europe and Oceania are firmly determined to stand up courageously for a just peace in a coordinated manner, the Iraq war can be brought to an early halt. The price would be the severing of the unholy alliance between the Church and the dominant Western colonizers, an option not effectively made since the time of Constantine.

Reflecting on the wider implications of the message of Jesus, that God is love, the Christian churches in the world can rethink the core of their teaching in the present world situation of war and grave injustice. Catechesis can highlight the different dimension of the demands of love that could lead to the transformation of persons, relationships and structures. We need to develop our thinking and methodology of peace with justice to be achieved by non-violent methods. Otherwise the alternative at the world level is vast, unimaginable destruction, given the divisions in the world and the accumulated powers of self-destruction available to many.

In a subsequent encyclical or instruction the Pope could give the leadership that the world needs. The world religions have the common core message of peace and strategies to save humanity from the impending tragedy to humans and nature itself. Throughout the world there are numerous persons, groups and movements that yearn for peace with justice, beyond the limits of the dominant neo-liberal capitalism. The gospel of Jesus gives inspiration for another possible world that can give a better chance for most humans to live a full and meaningful human life. The World Social Forum meeting in Poto Allegre in Brazil and elsewhere expresses the hopes of humanity for such a peaceful transformation. This present situation is a great challenge for all of us to bear witness to the God of love revealed by Jesus. We hope Pope Benedict XVI will help us all to face this challenge wisely, courageously and peacefully.

'Blessed are the peacemakers for they will be called the children of God.'

If, as the Pope writes in the introduction, the encyclical is meant to be a guideline indicating his thinking, we need to reflect carefully on its intents and limits, 'since I wanted here – at the beginning of my Pontificate – to clarify some essential facts concerning the love which God mysteriously and gratuitously offers to man [sic], together with the intrinsic link between Love and the reality of human love'. If Part II intends only to direct and support organized church social action as 'Caritas', then the sidelining here of the mission and action for justice and peace can be understood. We will then await another encyclical on the justice and peace of God that will deal with all such issues directly and give the required leadership to the whole Church.

Notes

1. Acts 2.44–45.
2. Pope Benedict XVI, Encyclical Letter *Deus Caritas Est* (Libreria Editrice Vaticana, 2006), no. 20.
3. Acts 3.1–10.
4. Pope Benedict XVI, op. cit., no. 40.
5. Acts 6.1–6.
6. Pope Benedict XVI, op. cit., no. 28a.
7. Pope Benedict XVI, op. cit., no. 28a.
8. Cf. Mt. 23.13–27 '. . . Teachers of the Law and Pharisees! You hypocrites . . .'
9. Mt. 27.37.
10. Mk 15.10.
11. Jn 19.12.
12. Pope Benedict XVI, op. cit., no. 28a.
13. Synod of Bishops, *Justice in the World* (Vatican Press, 1971).
14. Cf. Tissa Balasuriya, *Planetary Theology* (New York: Orbis, 1984), ch. 2, 'The World System'.
15. Pope Benedict XVI, op. cit., no. 31b.
16. Col. 3.22–4.
17. Pope Benedict XVI, op. cit., no. 31b.
18. Pope Benedict XVI, op. cit., no. 25a.
19. Lk. 6.31.
20. Lk. 6.27–30.
21. Mt. 5.5.
22. Mk 10.45.
23. Lk. 6.34–37.
24. Mt. 23.4–5.
25. Lk. 1.51–53.
26. Lk. 6.41–42.

27. Luigi Accattoli, *Quand le Pape Demande Pardon* (Paris: Albin Michael, 1997), p. 18, *et al.*
28. Mt. 5.9.
29. Pope Benedict XVI, op. cit., no. 12.
30. Pope Benedict XVI, op. cit., no. 14.
31. Pope Benedict XVI, op. cit., no. 28a.

Chapter 4

Social Justice in Protestant Thought

Duncan B. Forrester

There are profound similarities between Protestant and Roman Catholic under-standings of justice, but the differences of emphasis are also important. Both see Scripture as a, or the, major authority; both have recourse to the Fathers of the Church. But Protestants tend to be more sceptical about the insights and theories of the philosophers, including Aquinas, and to have rather different understandings of the relation between the secular and the religious realms or spheres. Charac-teristically Protestant thinkers see justice as central to any Christian political or social ethics, and they wrestle with the relationship of love and justice. The cen-trality of justification in Protestant, and particularly Lutheran, thought deeply influences Protestant understandings of justice. In today's Protestant theology much attention is given to the public reliance of Christian understandings of justice, forgiveness and reconciliation, with examples such as the South African Truth and Reconciliation Commission. Justice is seen as healing and forgiving, and the Church is called to exemplify in its life the divine love/justice. Christian understanding of justice can thus play a very significant and healing relationship in public debate today.

There are, of course, profound similarities between Protestant and Roman Catholic thought on social justice. It would indeed be strange if this were not so. For these two major strands in the fabric of the Christian faith draw on a common tradition, accept the same authoritative Scriptures, have interacted down the centuries with very similar cultural contexts, were for long locked in more or less acrimonious controversy with one another, and in more recent times have become partners in ecumenical dialogue.

The cultures in which Christianity has flourished prior to the missionary expansion of recent centuries were deeply influenced by Christian notions, and in their turn shaped and perhaps sometimes distorted the expression of the Christian faith. It should not then be surprising if we discover that distinctively Christian ideas about justice which Christians, both Protestant and Roman Catholic, would wish to support and affirm have been deeply implanted in many modern cultures. The boundary between the religious and the secular in such matters is not always clear-cut or easy to discern. Themes like the human equality that the American Declaration of

Independence thought 'self-evident' were not accepted as at all obviously true in a very different cultural environment such as that of traditional India. Indeed, in the course of time ideas and values absorbed from religious sources can become the almost unquestioned assumptions of later generations, commonly believed to be axiomatic, or the conclusion of a purely rational argument.

The complicated interaction between Christian thought on social justice and its intellectual, social, ecclesial and political context continues today. It is at this point that the first, and most obvious, distinction between Protestant and Roman Catholic thought on social justice emerges. In general terms Roman Catholic thought draws on classical Aristotelian philosophy as mediated and moderated by St Thomas Aquinas, whereas Protestants tend to be suspicious of secular reason and seek to ground their thought on justice on revelation contained in Scripture. The distinction is not as clear-cut as this remark might suggest. Roman Catholics have always used Scripture, of course, and have a high doctrine of scriptural authority. Indeed it is not hard to see an increasing emphasis on Scripture in recent papal encyclicals. Nor have Protestants a uniform conviction that when addressing temporal issues such as social justice, Scripture should have the primacy it must possess within the heartlands of theology. Luther, for example, denounces Aristotle as 'this damned, conceited, rascally heathen' when considering his influence on theology.[1] And elsewhere he writes, 'Virtually the whole *Ethics* of Aristotle is the worst enemy of Grace . . . No syllogistic form is valid when applied to divine terms . . . The whole of Aristotle is to theology as darkness to light.'[2] But in relation to temporal affairs – and Luther would include social justice under this heading – the same Aristotle becomes a reputable authority:

> The heathen can speak and teach about this very well, as they have done. And, to tell the truth, they are far more skilful in such matters than the Christians . . . Whoever wants to learn and become wise in secular government, let him read the heathen books and writings.[3]

Most Protestant thinkers would not accept the sharpness of Luther's disjunction between the sacred and the secular realms, or his suggestion that the one is the sphere of divine truth and revelation, while the other is to be governed by secular reason. Theology, most Protestants would say, has something to contribute in the secular realm, while reason has a role in theology. But it is *fallen* reason that is at issue here, and most Protestant thinkers agree with Calvin in being suspicious of 'the great darkness of philosophers who have looked for a building in a ruin, and fit arrangement in disorder'.[4] It is incorrect, he continues, to 'maintain that reason dwells in the mind like a lamp, throwing light on all its counsels and, like a queen governing the will – that it is so pervaded with divine light as to be able to consult for the best, and so endued with vigour as to be able perfectly to command'.[5]

Protestants, therefore, in their thinking about social justice, have a continuing ambivalence about the role of reason, and in particular about natural law forms of thinking. They are not agreed among themselves as to where the boundary between the realms of the spiritual and the temporal comes, or about the role of a Scripture-based theology in temporal matters. Some, like Luther and many Anglicans, affirm the role of reason in temporal affairs. Others, like most Calvinists, draw a less sharp distinction between the sacred and the secular, and argue that revelation should hold sway in both spheres. And the majority of Protestants in their treatment of issues of social justice seek to root their thinking in Scripture and, particularly among liberals and charismatics, on experience of the justice of God.

Protestant accounts of social justice are diverse and tend to be episodic rather than systematic. Lacking a central authority like the papacy, Protestant thought on justice emanates from many quarters and is rarely coordinated. It is not cumulative, like official Catholic social teaching over the last century and more. Positively, this may mean that it can respond more creatively to changing challenges in the various contexts without the need to demonstrate that it is an unchanging and universally valid teaching. But this virtue of flexibility is sometimes at the expense of consistency.

What almost all Protestant theology shares with the whole of the Christian tradition is a belief in the authority of Scripture. For most Protestant social thought this stress on scriptural authority is the strongest single emphasis and the *sola scriptura* principle tends to make Protestant thinkers suspicious of using any secular language – say, that of John Rawls – as an adequate vehicle for communicating Christian insights. Theology or Christian thought must have something *distinctive* to offer to the discussion, or it might as well keep its mouth shut – such is a typically Protestant approach. Since Scripture is at its heart gospel, a scriptural theology of justice may be understood as public confession of the faith.

Social Justice in the Bible

Biblical teaching on justice comes primarily in the garb of narrative and of injunctions, denunciations and the announcement of coming judgement and the restoration or establishment of God's just ordering of things, the messianic age or the Kingdom of God. It is not a *philosophy* of justice, something that can appropriately be put alongside Aristotle or John Rawls. It cannot be detached from the faith of the people of God, of which it is an integral part. Its primarily narrative form allows it to articulate the cry of the oppressed for justice, and confidence in a God whose faithfulness is the assurance that the divine justice will be established, that God's just ordering of things will be fully expressed in the new Jerusalem, in the city of God, in the Kingdom, in the coming age.

James L. Mays speaks of 'the priority of justice for the prophets', for they believed that 'the entire history of Israel under God is subordinated to one purpose – righteousness expressed in justice'. The prophets understood justice as a theological term, inseparable from 'their knowledge of Israel's God, who is himself just and requires justice of people'. Talk of justice, accordingly, has a confessional element, for justice is an element of God's being and action. Justice is also a moral value which can be expressed in social relationships at least as much as in the courts.[6] Justice is integral to the faith of Israel and of the Church. As Father John Donahue puts it, 'The doing of justice is not the application of religious faith, but its substance; without it, God remains unknown.'[7]

The prophet Micah's famous response to the question, 'What does the Lord require of you?' – that we should do justice, and love kindness, and walk humbly with our God – is a fitting reminder of the centrality of the call for justice in the Hebrew Scriptures, where justice is regarded in a remarkably broad and specific way. Justice is here linked with *hesed*, the steadfast loving-kindness which characterizes God's covenant love, and with the humble walking with this God of justice and of love. And justice is regarded as something to be done, something that is inherently relational or social.

In the New Testament in the Matthean form of the Beatitudes, the little band of disciples hear that those who hunger and thirst after justice (*dikaiosune*) are blessed and will be satisfied.[8] Justice is something about which we should be passionate, for it is essential to a fulfilled life and social flourishing. In the Bible justice appears again and again as the vindication of the poor and the oppressed. They can turn with confidence for redress to God and to those who seek to follow in the way of God. For the prophets 'made the treatment of the poor and the weak the functional criterion of a just society'. Furthermore, 'the justice they advocated must be capable of exception, of responsiveness to the individual's needs, of an estimate of worth based on the simple existence of a person.'[9] Justice here is proactive, healing, reconciling, forgiving, setting matters right so that people can live together in peace.

Justice in the Bible is always set within an eschatological frame; it is something we hope for, something that is not fully realized here and now, for the full realization, vindication, restoration lie in the future. Any manifestations of justice here and now can only be provisional and relative when measured against the coming justice of God. Thus disciples and others are enjoined to 'seek first the Kingdom of God and his justice'.[10]

Because it is the justice of the Kingdom we can give it its distinctive content by examining the parables of the Kingdom, and the practice of

Jesus as a proleptic manifestation of the life of the Kingdom. These parables characteristically depict the conviviality of the Kingdom as something at which everyone is welcome, but at which there is a kind of preferential invitation to the poor, the marginalized and the excluded. This was also manifested in the practice of Jesus, particularly in his relationship to women and in his open table fellowship with all sorts of people. In both, Jesus breaks through the traditional rules of purity in order to establish a new form of community, anticipating the fellowship of the Kingdom founded on justice and love. He ate with Zacchaeus and with Levi, with Pharisees and with quislings, with prostitutes and with notorious sinners. And at this table people found forgiveness, acceptance and the ability to make a new start in life. Zacchaeus was moved at the table to make restitution of what he had misappropriated. The forlorn found acceptance. In Jesus' eating and drinking the message of the Kingdom was enacted, the life and justice of the Kingdom exemplified. The strange and complex relationship between the meals of Jesus and his death suggests that it is not at all fanciful to see these meals as a significant part of the work of reconciliation which is the establishment of justice by the creation of a new community through the breaking down of the dividing walls of hostility and suspicion, the bringing near of those who were far off, and the welcoming of strangers into the new Israel which prefigures the Kingdom.

We see God's justice embodied and expressed in action most clearly in the life and death of Jesus, in his action as well as his teaching, and in his suffering. Bishop Lesslie Newbigin puts it thus: 'At the centre of the Christian understanding of justice there stands the cross, not a symbol but a historic deed in which the justice of God was manifested in his covenant faithfulness right through to the point where the just died for the unjust.'[11] In Acts Jesus is declared to be 'the just One'.[12] And Paul proclaims that Jesus has become our justice.[13] In him we see the summing up of the Christian understanding of social justice.

The justice of the Kingdom has an objective reality; it is something that we seek; we do not construct it or make it. It is a gift, not a prize to be earned. But the gift carries with it a call. Those who seek God's righteousness are called to walk in the ways of justice, to anticipate in their practice the justice of the coming Kingdom. Justice is pervasively relational. It has to do with the proper structure of relationships between God and people and among people.

Justification and Justice

Justification, according to the thought of the Reformation, is 'the article by which the Church will stand or fall'. Luther's own experience of justification was definitive for his whole theological and reforming project. It gave him a radically new understanding of God's justice and indeed of the nature of God which helped him to a fresh reading of the Bible, particularly Paul's Epistles, and an altered assessment of the significance of human ethical striving. Before this experience, Luther says he:

> 'did not love a just and angry God, but rather hated and murmured against him'. When he realized that 'the justice of God is that right-eousness by which through sheer grace and sheer mercy God justifies us through faith . . . The whole of Scripture took on a new meaning, and whereas before "the justice of God" had filled me with hate, now it became to me inexpressibly sweet in greater love.'[14]

For Luther now knew God to be gracious and God's justice to be loving and forgiving.

God's justice is not blind, impersonal, mechanical or retributive. It is rather gentle, forgiving, reconciling and, above all, loving. God's justice *is* his grace and forgiveness. We cannot earn the divine justification; we put our trust in God's faithfulness and grace, in the knowledge that God cares for us and accepts us just as we are. God's justice is displayed most clearly in God's grace and love, in his acceptance as just of those who are still sinners, and his special care for the excluded, the forgotten, the poor and the marginalized. In the experience of justification we discover the true justice of God, which is justice itself. In justification we encounter the justice of God, who declares us to be just, and sets us free to act justly and lovingly to our neighbours: we serve God and our neighbours for their own sakes, not because we wish to win our own salvation.

Lutheran thinkers have tended to treat justification as a rather private transaction between the believer and God, and to draw a sharp distinction between justice and justification. A number of biblical scholars have recently argued that the Lutheran reading of the Pauline doctrine of justifi-cation is far too dominated by Luther's characteristically late medieval concern for the salvation of his soul. In fact, they argue, Paul's teaching on justification and on justice is set entirely within the context of the dispute about whether Jews and Gentiles could be reconciled to one another within the one community of faith, with the breaking down of barriers and the establishment of a community in which ancient hostilities and suspicions are overcome. 'Justification by faith', writes Professor James Dunn, 'is a banner raised by Paul against any and all such presumption of privileged status before God by virtue of race, culture or nationality, against any and all attempts to preserve such spurious distinctions by practices that exclude and divide.'[15] Justification and justice are relational terms; it is social justice which is at issue here, not a private transaction between God and the believer, or the measuring of people and actions against some impersonal ethical yardstick. God's justice is experienced as pure grace, and this justice is expressed in inclusive community in which there is a special care for the weak, the poor, the stranger, the orphan and the widow.

The Lutheran tradition has been particularly apt to draw another sharp division between the righteousness of faith which we experience in justification and in the Church, and the 'civic righteousness' which is appropriate in secular affairs. It is often suggested that the justice of God that we encounter in justification may be radically different from the 'worldly justice' which is operative in temporal affairs. During the German church struggle of the 1930s this issue was thrashed out between more conservative Lutherans, who taught that they had no mandate to challenge Hitler and the Nazis because they operated in the secular realm which was beyond theological scrutiny, and the leaders of the Confessing Church, particularly the Calvinist, Karl Barth. 'Is there an inward and vital connection', Barth enquired, 'by means of which in any sense human justice . . . as well as divine justification, becomes a concern of Christian faith and Christian responsibility, and therefore a matter which concerns the Christian Church?'[16] Barth answers his own question with a resounding 'Yes', and an increasing number of Lutheran thinkers who have learned from the experience of the past would now agree with him. The experience of the divine justification displays a model of social justice which is also of relevance to the secular sphere. And a prominent contemporary American Lutheran theologian, Ronald Thiemann, adds a crucial afterword:

> Because we know that God will remain faithful to his promises, we are liberated from the devastating fear that the accomplishment of justice in the world depends solely upon our efforts. The primacy and priority of God's grace frees us from the self-defeating effort of seeking our salvation in the quest for justice. Since our salvation has been secured by Christ's death and resurrection, we are now free to seek justice for the neighbour in need . . . We seek justice freely, because we have been freely justified.[17]

Justice, Forgiveness and Reconciliation

Mercy, forgiveness and reconciliation are at the heart of the divine justice which Christians believe they experience, and which provides a model for human justice. This theme is contained famously in Portia's speech in Shakespeare's *The Merchant of Venice*. Portia, a woman disguised as a man, brings the generous, merciful, healing and Christian understanding of justice characteristic of Belmont into the mechanical and impersonal justice of Venice. She argues that God's justice is enriched with mercy and forgiveness and that only thus can true justice be established:

The quality of mercy is not strain'd;
It droppeth as the gentle rain from heaven
Upon the place beneath: it is twice blessed;
It blesseth him that gives and him that takes:
'Tis mightiest in the mighty; it becomes
The thronèd monarch better than his crown;
His sceptre shows the force of temporal power,
The attribute to awe and majesty,
Wherein doth sit the dread and fear of kings;
But mercy is above this sceptre'd sway,
It is enthroned in the hearts of kings,
It is an attribute to God himself,
And earthly power does then show likest God's
When mercy seasons justice. Therefore, Jew,
Though justice be thy plea, consider this,
that in the course of justice none of us
Should see salvation; we do pray for mercy;
And that same prayer doth teach us all to render
The deeds of mercy.[18]

Mercy and forgiveness, Portia claims, season – that is, bring out the true flavour of – justice, reveal what justice is really about. It is not vindictive, unrelenting or mechanical, nor is it the cheap grace which disguises the gravity of offence and broken relationships. Justice is essentially the healing of relationships, the overcoming of animosities. Its *telos*, its goal, is reconciliation and the restoration of community. Justice seasoned with mercy is in the last analysis gracious. And narrower, thinner accounts of justice as fairness, or impartiality, or giving to each one what is due, are actually harmful in as far as they are lacking in generosity, mercy and forgiveness.[19]

The Church as Exemplar of Justice

The American Methodist, Stanley Hauerwas, in a key passage wrote:

The task of the church [is] to pioneer those institutions and practices that the wider society has not learned as forms of justice. (At times it is also possible that the church can learn from society more just ways of forming life.) The church, therefore, must act as a paradigmatic community in the hope of providing some indication of what the world can be but is not . . . *The church does not have, but rather is a social ethic.* That is, she is a social ethic inasmuch as she functions as a criteriological institution – that is, an institution that has learned to embody

the form of truth that is charity as revealed in the person and work of
Christ.[20]

But *how* is the Church a social ethic, how does it 'pioneer new institutions
and practices', how does it function as 'a paradigmatic community', demonstrating and exemplifying the justice of God? The Church, Hauerwas is
saying, is called to be a kind of anticipation of the Kingdom and its justice, a
preliminary and partial demonstration of the justice of God. Likewise John
Milbank argues that although Augustine is right in suggesting that the world
cannot yet live by the justice of God, the Church ought to be an asylum, a
place of refuge from the injustices of the world and a space within which
a serious effort is made to pursue just practices and exemplify the justice of
God.[21]

Hauerwas and his disciples are quite clear that the first ethical task is to
be the Church: 'Put starkly, the first ethical task of the Church is to be the
church, the servant community . . . What makes the church the church is its
faithful manifestation of the peaceable kingdom in the world '[22] The talk
here is of the calling of the Church rather than its empirical reality which is
often sadly different. A church which is serious about its faith must seek
to shape its life by that faith; before it addresses 'the world' about God's
justice' and calls for obedience, it must make serious efforts to frame its
structures and its relationships so that they show something of the truth and
worth of what it proclaims. A blatant and unacknowledged contradiction
between the teaching and the life of the Church is a scandal which makes
the message implausible.

Hauerwas and his allies have been deeply influenced by the Mennonite
tradition, and tend by 'church' to mean the small local congregation of
disciples, nurturing an absolutist ethic and existing as a kind of counter-
culture, in tension with the broader society, when they speak of the church.
But similar principles are true when different and broader ecclesiologies are
involved. Magisterial social teaching on justice, on subsidiarity, on any
social issue loses credibility if the Church concerned appears to make little
effort to apply the teaching to its own life and structures. In this sense it is
indeed necessary to be a social ethic if that ethic and the faith of which it
is an expression are to be credible in broader circles.

In worship, what Hauerwas calls 'the essential rituals of our politics',[23]
there is an enacted anticipation of the Kingdom and its justice, a proclamation and a call. Here Christians believe they have an authentic
anticipation of God's future and a real, if incomplete experience of the
justice of God, a guarantee of its coming, and an encouragement to
continue to seek the Kingdom of God and his justice with courage and
steadfastness.

The Church, Bishop Lesslie Newbigin says, is called to be 'an agency of
God's justice, and in so doing it confesses the faith:

In its liturgy it continually relives the mystery of God's action in justi-
fying the ungodly. In its corporate life and the mutual care and discipline of its members it embodies (even if very imperfectly) the justice of
God which both unmasks the sin and restores relation with the sinner.
In its action in the society of which it is part it will seek to be with Jesus
among those who are pushed to the margins. But in all this it will point
beyond itself and its own weakness and ambivalence, to the One in
whom God's justice has been made manifest by the strange victory of
the cross . . . it can continually nourish a combination of realism and
hope which finds expression in concrete actions which can be taken by
the local community and more widely, which reflect and embody the
justice of God.[24]

Christian Justice in Contemporary Debate

There appears to be an extraordinary amount of confusion today about
justice and social justice in particular. Hayek dismisses the concept as a
dangerous mirage, a 'humbug', a dishonest notion, intellectually disreput-
able, socially divisive and subversive of freedom.[25] John Rawls develops with
immense sophistication the theme that justice is fairness. Richard Nozick
disagrees fundamentally. Alasdair MacIntyre and the communitarians
declare that the Enlightenment project has come to an end, and enquire
whose justice we are speaking about, and to which community and tradition
it relates. Disputes which appear to be irresolvable about justice and goodness represent not only academic difficulties but major problems of practice,
for practitioners 'on the ground', as it were, and for ordinary folk, particularly for the victims of injustice. In such a context, politics and policy
making easily degenerate into, in MacIntyre's telling phrase, 'civil war
carried on by other means',[26] an arena in which interest groups compete
for control, using ideas as weapons rather than constraints, and as justifica-
tions for volatile policy changes which in fact are little influenced by over-
arching moral considerations. Or the ideological pendulum swings from
one extreme to another without the reasons for the change being clear or
generally acceptable.

Practitioners often feel that they are making do with fragments of moral
insight, and fragments which are frequently in unacknowledged conflict
with other fragments, or are not recognized in the way the system or institution is run. And practitioners sometimes recognize that the fragments
which are most important for them as insights into reality, as in some sense
true, and which are central to the sense of vocation which sustains them in
their practice, are derived from a tradition which was and is nurtured in a
community of shared faith to which they may or may not belong, and which
is now a minority view in society. There is a widespread awareness that

the foundations of the practice of justice have been shaken. And in such a situation it is the weak and the poor who are hurt the most. But their cry of protest is often drowned out by the theoretical argument.

Roman Catholic social teaching is articulated in such a way that it is not too difficult to see where it may fit into the contemporary debate about justice. But the debate itself is flawed, MacIntyre suggests, by the fact that there is no agreed criterion against which conflicting views might be measured. Protestant thought, as we have already seen, is far more diverse and episodic. And in as far as Protestantism suggests it can only speak with integrity if it speaks theologically, whereas Roman Catholic social thought uses for the most part a more theologically neutral language of natural law, the question arises whether Protestant thought on justice can be more than the inner discourse of religious communities. Can it contribute creatively to the confusing debate on justice which is taking place in the public arena today? I think it can.

Theological Fragments

A Protestant theologian should not, I think, be ashamed of offering initially in public debate in the conditions of postmodernity no more than 'fragments' of insight. Postmodernists (and sociologists of knowledge) are, after all, right in affirming that systematic, carefully developed theories (even theological theories!) can sometimes conceal practices which are inhumane and brutalizing; ideologies can serve as the emperor's new clothes, so that the theologian's first task, as a little child, is to cry out, 'But the emperor's got no clothes on!': a fragment of truth reveals that by which most people have allowed themselves to be blinded. Truth-telling in a fragmentary way becomes even more important when the scheme to conceal the emperor's nakedness is something that is hurting people and destroying community.[27]

Such a fragmentary theology assumes that in this life we never see save 'in a mirror dimly', and only at the end 'face to face'.[28] This might make us more generally cautious about regarding theology as some grand coherent modernist theory rather than a series of illuminating fragments which sustain the life of the community of faith which nurtures them, and claim also to be in some sense 'public truth'. After all, the Gospels and even the Epistles do not present a system. Rather they are full of parables, stories, epigrams, injunctions, songs; fragments, in short. Perhaps theologians should sympathize with the postmodernists' suspicion of systems and system building!

Kierkegaard's suspicion of systems and grand theories was well grounded. He knew that the castle of theory often serves in its magnificence to conceal what is actually going on, to disguise an often unpalatable reality, and even to legitimate awful practices. He understood thought, and above all thought about God, as something which must be *dwelt* in, which

73

must relate to experience and which must expose untruth and injustice wherever they are found. The castle of theory needs to be cut down to size, demystified as it were, so that humans can live and flourish there. Accordingly, Kierkegaard saw his role as a theologian as like that of Socrates, asking questions, exposing falsehood and, gadfly-like, stinging people into awareness of the truth. He wrote in parables and epigrams and meditations which were deliberately unsystematic. And in communicating so, Kierkegaard perhaps gives us clues as to effective theological communication in the modern, or postmodern, age at a time of moral fragmentation. The truth about justice is not something to be comprehended, controlled, used or appropriated. It is rather to be indwelt, and lived out in action.

Are there theological fragments about social justice which might be recognized as public truth and serve to give some coherence and integrity, even in 'the desolation of reality that overtakes human beings in a post-religious age that has grown too wise to swallow the shallow illusions of the Enlightenment' (John Gray)? And might these fragments perhaps be the aptest way of confessing the faith in the public realm today?

So let me conclude by suggesting some examples of how Christian theological fragments may enrich, broaden and challenge the contemporary debate about social justice, injecting or offering insights or emphases derived from the gospel, the Christian narrative. First, two examples from the interface of social and criminal justice. In a working group on punishment, after much rather unrewarding discussion of theories of punishment which tended to suggest that theories hid as much as they illumined and were as often abused as used creatively, the group turned to the theologians for *the* Christian theory of punishment. Instead of producing a grand theory, an experienced Christian woman prison governor commented simply that few people involved with criminal justice today seemed interested in guilt in any broader sense than the sentence of the court, or in forgiveness, reconciliation, restoration of community, and the healing of relationships. After an exciting discussion, the group, of whom only some were religious, agreed that any system of punishment which was not directed towards reconciliation lacked all moral credibility. A profoundly Christian insight from the heart of the gospel had been recognized as public truth.

Again, a few years ago the leading judges in England and Scotland got locked in controversy with the Home Secretary who was demanding a rigorous and mechanical sentencing tariff for repeat offenders. The judges insisted that justice demanded that they should have the ability to adjust sentences to the person and the circumstances. In doing this, they were affirming an understanding of justice as concerned with healing and restoration, with the good of the offender as well as the good of society, which was originally derived from the Christian tradition.

Again, more directly in the field of social justice, Christian theological fragments would suggest that more than fairness is necessary at the heart of a decent society. If Rawls is right that justice is 'the first virtue of social institutions', it must surely be a justice which is informed by love, by the *agape* of the Christian story, a justice which is more than fairness, a justice which is sometimes generous and sometimes is capable of eliciting sacrifice for others. Generous justice sometimes means giving people other than what is due to them, their deserts. In the Gospel parable of the labourers in the marketplace, each receives the same wage independently of how long they have worked, of their desert. Their equality as human beings is recognized. But those who have worked throughout the heat of the day complain that they have been unjustly, unfairly treated. And so, in a sense, they have. But the parable expands the notion of justice beyond the rules which protected the worker by insisting that a worker should be paid fairly to a broader, more generous justice which responds to the misfortune and need, rather than the work, of those who stood waiting to be hired all day. Such a generous understanding of justice must find its place in public policy if we are not to have welfare policies which despise and mistreat the non-achievers, the disabled and the poor.

The final example is a now familiar one from South Africa: the Truth and Reconciliation Commission, presided over by Archbishop Desmond Tutu. Here, issues of guilt and of retribution are not avoided, and requests for amnesty are not invitations to amnesia: the memories of the past must be faced and healed. The truth must be confronted and moral responsibility accepted, for reconciliation is the aim. In the Commission's work they are using, according to its research director, 'a different kind of justice' which is restorative and sees forgiveness as an essential element in justice. They believe this broader frame and fuller understanding of justice is necessary for the healing of South African society. And there is little doubt that this healing, restorative, relational understanding of justice comes as a Christian 'theological fragment' which has significant affinities within African traditional culture and is thereby recognized as public truth.

So perhaps fragmentary biblical insights into justice of the sort that Protestantism characteristically offers may still have something useful to say in the public forum and in the support of those who are striving to act justly, and to love kindness, and to walk humbly, with or without knowing that such is the way of God.

Notes

1. Luther, 'To the Christian Nobility of the German Nation', in *Philadelphia Edition of the Works of Martin Luther* (Philadelphia: Holman, 6 vols, 1915–32), II, p. 146.
2. Luther, 'Disputation against Scholastic Theology', Clauses 41, 47,

50. *American Edition of Luther's Works*, ed. J. Pelikan and H.T. Lehman (St Louis: Concordia c. 1955–86), XXXI, pp. 4ff.

3. Luther, 'Commentary on Psalm 101', *American Edition*, ibid., XXXIII, p. 198.

4. Calvin, *Institutes*, I.15.8.

5. Calvin, *Institutes*, II.ii.2.

6. James L. Mays, 'Justice: Perspectives from the Prophetic Tradition', in David L. Petersen (ed.), *Prophecy in Israel: Search for an Identity* (Philadelphia: Fortress Press, 1987), pp. 146–7.

7. John R. Donahue, 'Biblical Perspectives on Justice', in J. Haughey (ed.), *The Faith that Does Justice* (New York: Paulist Press, 1977), p. 76.

8. Mt. 5.6.

9. Mays, op. cit., p. 155.

10. Mt. 6.33.

11. L. Newbigin, 'Whose Justice?' *Ecumenical Review* 44 (1992), p. 310.

12. Acts 3.14; 7.52.

13. 1 Cor. 1.30; cf. Rom. 1.17.

14. Cited in Ronald Bainton, *Here I Stand: A Life of Martin Luther* (New York: Abingdon-Cokesbury Press, 1950), p. 65.

15. James D.G. Dunn, 'The Justice of God: A Renewed Perspective on Justification by Faith', *Journal of Theological Studies* 43.1 (1992), p. 15.

16. Karl Barth, *Church and State* [Rechtfertigung und Recht] (London: SCM Press, 1939), p. 1.

17. Ronald F. Thiemann, cited in V. Mortensen (ed.), *Justification and Justice* (Geneva: Lutheran World Federation, 1992), p. 15.

18. Shakespeare, *The Merchant of Venice*, Act IV, scene i, my italics.

19. I have argued this case in my book, *Christian Justice and Public Policy* (Cambridge: Cambridge University Press, 1997).

20. Stanley Hauerwas, *Truthfulness and Tragedy* (Notre Dame: Notre Dame University Press, 1977), pp. 142–3 (my italics).

21. John Milbank, *Theology and Social Theory: Beyond Secular Reason* (Oxford: Blackwell, 1990), p. 422.

22. Stanley Hauerwas, *The Peaceable Kingdom: A Primer in Christian Ethics* (London: SCM Press, 1983), p. 99.

23. Hauerwas, ibid., p. 108.

24. Newbigin, op. cit., p. 311.

25. See F.A. Hayek, 'The Mirage of Social Justice', in *Law: Legislation and Liberty*, 2nd edn (London: Routledge, 1982).

26. *After Virtue*, p. 236.

27. Notice that Z. Bauman characterizes 'the post-modern perspective' as 'above all the tearing off of the mask of illusions; the recognition of certain pretences as false and certain objectives as neither attainable or, for that matter, desirable' (*Post-Modern Ethics*, p. 3).

28. 1 Cor. 13.12.

Chapter 5

Searching for the Faith to Do Justice

Judith A. Merkle

Forty years ago there were efforts in the Catholic Church and other Christian communities to identity faith in its relationship to action for justice in society. At that time Christians asked how their fundamental faith commitments were related to the efforts in society at large towards reform. Did faith support involvement in better race relations, work to improve the conditions of the poor, or more concern for the earth? Theologians asserted faith was not just an intellectual assent or what identified one as a Lutheran or a Catholic; faith was related to justice. Today, however, the conditions in which this question is asked have changed. Changes within Churches and culture frame the search for faith to do justice in different terms. This chapter explores these new conditions, and the relevance of our response to this important question.

In the 1970s Avery Dulles wrote an article on the nature of Christian faith and its relationship to justice.[1] Dulles' concern was not to write an article which defined faith. Rather he sought to address faith as it exists, or should exist, in modern society. What is faith in a 'socio-technical' civilization characterized by the capacity of men and women not only to exercise control over nature, but to shape the specific institutions which make up society: economics, education, science and politics? Christians had been accused not only of failing to promote justice in the world, through centuries of collusion with colonial forces which shaped the global society, but also of counselling the poor to accept their place in the world, in hope of a better life in heaven. Dulles, in contrast, wanted to make clear the theological connection between faith and investment in the reform movements of the postwar era. How did involvement in civil rights, women's rights, action against poverty, participation in the anti-war movement and the like relate to the Christian life? Was this an abandonment of one's deepest religious commitments as a Christian, or an embracing of them?

While Dulles wrote for a primarily Catholic audience, the question was raised in Protestant circles as well.[2] For Catholics and Protestants alike, faith was commonly understood as belief in the doctrinal content of Christianity. For some, it marked denominational identity. I am a Lutheran, I am a Catholic, and I am a convert to the Anglican faith. The question, however, was how faith related to action. How was the core belief that the Christian life unfolds under the norm of neighbour-love related to the situation of modern society? By the 1970s it was difficult to avoid the paradox then clearly present in the world: some suffered from the inequalities of modern society and others were thought to possess the tools to shape society in a manner never before possessed by humankind.

Dulles' article addressed faith in three main ways: as belief or conviction, as trust which affects decision making and as a way of action. 'Faith' which comfortably ignored the social movements of the times was lacking. Today Dulles' distinctions still hold true. In Micah we hear, 'Act justly, love tenderly and walk humbly with your God.' This biblical paradigm assumes that for the Christian, faith is lacking without justice and love, action is lacking without ongoing encounter with God in Jesus Christ. Yet, in the search to find the faith to do justice in the new millennium we face new questions. New conditions in modern society set a different terrain than we faced 30 years ago for articulating just how Christian faith relates to justice.

New Horizons for Faith in Modern Society

Traditional approaches to the role of faith in human life rest on an anthropological foundation and frequently a specific theological and ontological anthropology. These invaluable insights ground the search for faith in every age. At the same time, the credibility of faith in one's life and in its witness in society still lies in its reference to the unresolved problems or limit-questions that plague the modern person. Modern technology, wealth and all the advantages of globalization as we know it still leave us facing the timeless issues of human finitude, guilt and the unavoidable reality of one's own death. In addition, we have to ask, to what degree are our modern ethical systems working to provide a moral compass for our world? After years of an active pursuit of justice on the part of the Christian Church, is the world better off? Or do the unresolved problems of our global society, and not only the timeless issues of the human life cycle, call us to a new search for the meaning of our faith in its relationship to justice?

As we encounter Kant's famous three questions – 'What can I know?'; 'What must I do?'; 'What can I hope for?' – faith is integral to our reply.[3] Christian faith provides its own response to each of these challenges. In the decades immediately following the 1960s, there appeared to be a growing consensus that these questions could no longer be answered only in one's personal life, but also had to address social life as well. Both the World Council of Churches and the Vatican Council in the Catholic Church sought to draw the link between faith and justice in their documents.[4]

Theological reflection tackled the question of faith in this world as well. After the Second World War, faith in Europe was challenged by secularization and its twin, materialism. Political theology in Europe arose in Protestant circles from Karl Barth's anti-bourgeois theology and from the experiences of the Confessing Church in its resistance to National Socialism. For Catholics, Karl Rahner linked the tradition to the search for meaning in modern times. He claimed that faith allows one to live creatively, faithfully, hopefully and honestly in face of life's ultimate questions.[5] Johann Metz added that the individual is also embedded in a social-political context. Faith has to address this social reality to be relevant to modern experience. Metz charged that a mark of faith is the courage to name the suffering in this world, and acknowledge those who are not experiencing the world as 'progress', the promise of postwar life. Rather they are left behind, in unspeakable limits and suffering. Faith challenges one to be truthful in the world, yet remain hopeful and future oriented, living in solidarity with others and working to transform the world.[6] Theology therefore must be 'political', that is, Christianity's essence had to be related to faith and action in society.

In Latin America faith was challenged by dehumanizing injustice. There, the challenge to Christian faith was no longer doubt, or a vision of life in which faith was unnecessary, since life was to proceed according to the inevitability of the myth of progress of the economic system.[7] Faith in Latin America was defined in face of the non-person, who was the refuse of the world capitalist system, and its own version of the good life.[8] Latin American theologians charged that Christian faith inspires one to work for the human development of all, and to engage in the struggle for national development in their developing nations. At this time, the divergence of quality of life between the North and the South gave rise to two languages of faith in Christianity responding to two different life questions. Why should I believe in the face of sufficiency? How can I believe in the grasp of unrelenting poverty? The concerns of Latin American theologians were echoed by African, Asian, Feminist, Hispanic and Black Christians as they took cultural marginalization, poverty, racism, sexism, colonialism and the search for cultural identity as starting points of their reflection on the meaning of Christian faith.

J. Matthew Ashley claims that today even this context for responding in faith has changed in the First World. Now the believer faces a radical pluralism in which there has been a privatization of spirituality, delinking it from social and institutional contexts.[9] The postmodern criticism not only of society but of religious institutions challenges the adequacy of religious institutions as reliable ways to God. This criticism names their patriarchal, colonizing, racially segregated and militaristic tendencies.[10] However, voices of criticism to create a better sense of religion in society and movements of indifference merged in modern culture to leave people in a quandary as to how religious belief functions in modern human identity. Faith still faces the question of human meaningfulness but it does so in light of modern assessments of what threatens this meaning. In earlier times faith was rooted in contexts of family and community, which were the only guarantees of survival in a world of indigence and insecurity.[11] Today these traditional boundaries of identity are overshadowed by a culture of radical pluralism where most institutions of late modern capitalism are being rethought, including that of the significance of the Church to one's life of faith. This new context in which we search for the faith to do justice reframes the old question, what is worth my effort?

What is Worth My Effort?

The problem of faith today is not disbelief; it is paralysis before the question of what is worth my effort. First-world culture too often limits the scope of this question to material success. We live in a consumer society, which frees us from want of the material necessities of life. It is not uncommon to feel positive about one's own life in this situation, as life as a whole remains basically without conflicts, at least in comparison to others. But we can be hopeless about the problems of the wider society. Some feel nothing of significance can be done to change the world, or even the condition of religion in our societies. The systems and power of the globe are beyond our control. Any vision for change is dismissed as unrealistic. The hope we want to feel that we can make a difference is dulled by the feeling that there are no alternatives. Some might say our hope for a better world is hijacked by this cultural pessimism. The temptation to find some niche, a fit, where we can be immune to the problems of the world and work out some private version of peace and happiness is difficult to overcome. Instead of investing in a broader vision, we focus on our own upward mobility, which we believe will insure us against having to mix with others who might put demands on us.[12]

The same hopelessness can be true regarding the Church in our societies. Thirty years ago when Dulles wrote his article, the conflict in the Church was between people who saw themselves as conservative and those who saw themselves as progressive, wanting to modernize the Church. These divisions assumed people were members of the Church, active in it, and had opinions regarding its direction. Today sex-abuse scandals, public perceptions of irrelevance, the failure of one generation to evangelize the next and the general cultural climate of spirituality divorced from its institutional framework have left some wondering if the Church is like Humpty Dumpty, broken beyond repair. This is true in the Catholic Church as well as many Protestant denominations.[13]

Even disbelieving in God or leaving the Church today is different. We do not grapple with the atheism of the 1960s and 70s when disentanglement from church ties often involved ruptures in family, friendships and social networks. Today the choice between acceptance and rejection of religious faith may not be a particularly dramatic choice. Rejection may simply take the form of evasion or postponement. If meaning comes from culture alone, from money, from upward mobility, then receiving meaning from an active relationship to God appears to some to be 'unnecessary'.

For those who are believers, formation in faith in light of one's religious tradition can also have new challenges today. Vincent Miller argues that consumer society actually shapes people to approach religious beliefs as if they were consumer commodities. The result is that when members of consumer cultures actually embrace religious traditions they encounter them in a commodified, fragmented form. Beliefs, symbols and practices appear abstracted from their connections to one another. They thus lose their capacity to convey the alternative logics and desires of the gospel which can draw believers' lives away from conformity with the status quo. The gospel therefore fails to create a community of contrast to society. Miller charges that religious belief is always in danger of being reduced to a 'decorative veneer of meaning' over the emptiness of everyday life as it is already spelled out in advanced capitalist societies.[14] These questions direct us to revisit some basic understandings of faith, and the compass they provide in searching anew for the faith to sustain the commitment to justice today.

Faith and the Modern Era

The modern context of faith reflects both shifts in the Church's theology over the past centuries and changes in modern culture. The obedience of biblical faith (Rom. 1.5; 16.26) as a radical and total opening of the self to the content and message of the gospel, Christ himself and shared by the community of believers, has been interpreted in later centuries with two main tendencies. Thomas Aquinas stressed the intellectual aspect of this surrender as an act of judgement directed to the first Truth, God himself. By means of grace through the power of God, the believer surrenders to the truth of the reality of God. Martin Luther emphasized the trust involved in the surrender of faith, where the believer who is summoned by God to a new life of grace, recognizes and accepts God as the one who is for me.[15] Tension between the head and the heart in the surrender of faith, and concern to maintain faith as a personal encounter with God, are seen in subsequent theological debates in the following centuries.

The nineteenth-century debate between fideism and rationalism in the Catholic Church reflected the challenge to maintain a balance between the head and the heart in the consideration of faith. Fideism denied that human reason, through its own unaided power, could acquire any certain knowledge about the world's transcendent creator. Faith was entirely 'a leap'. Rationalism, on the contrary, refused to concede that the knowledge of God transmitted through Christian revelation exceeded its range.

Rationalists gave little attention to the work of the Holy Spirit in the life of faith. Fideists gave too little credence to natural reason; rationalists demanded too much of it. Philosophical knowledge of God was impossible for fideism; rationalism submitted revealed knowledge of God to the criticism of philosophy.

Whereas earlier theology stressed revelation as a series of supernatural truths which God makes known to the human being, twentieth-century theology in both the Protestant and Catholic Churches saw revelation as salvation history. God who was revealed in the covenant of the Old Testament, revealed himself in Jesus Christ. Revelation is identical with the person of Christ, and to discover God's revelation one is referred precisely to Jesus Christ (*Dei Verbum* §4). The obedience of faith, as a biblical foundation, is a surrender in which a person entrusts themselves freely to God. Faith is made possible through a gift of the Holy Spirit. This surrender involves not just the head or the heart, but the entire personality.[16] In this encounter, one meets God, not just knowledge about God.[17] In the revelation of this encounter in faith the truth of God and the truth of being a human being are revealed together. *Gaudium et Spes* §22 says, Christ reveals the truth of every person to themselves.

Yet, the journey of faith for modern theologians is not an intra-psychic one of consciousness between God and the human person. It is one which happens in real time and history in light of all our interactions and relationships. God touches more than our interiority. Faith in God does not bypass this world and its challenges. Yet, religious faith is required to discover God's presence in them. Amid the darkness and light of our times to act with God in action for justice is an act of faith.

While our concern is how action for justice is related to Christian faith, Rahner acknowledges that for some a faith response is present in its effects on one's life, but not acknowledged in its fullness. Even those who expressly deny God, may also implicitly experience God in their efforts to be faithful:

> Wherever there is selfless love, wherever duties are carried out without hope of reward, wherever the incomprehensibility of death is calmly accepted, wherever people are good with no hope of reward, in all these instances the Spirit is experienced, even though a person may not dare give this interpretation to the experience.[18]

Religious faith involves the human search for meaning, not only of my life but of all life. The experience of faith in the Spirit of God is the positive and unconditional acceptance of one's own existence as meaningful and open to a final fulfilment, 'which we call God'.[19]

Cynthia Moe-Lobeda reclaims from the Lutheran tradition that a unity of faith in God and action in society is deep within Luther's sense of faith. Faith does not distract us from the tasks of building a better society, as Marx once charged. Yet faith is not just a personal relationship with God, it grows in the faith community and through its practices. Luther held that where moral power is missing, the community is not maintaining certain practices through which the living Christ is known, received, builds abode in the faithful and loves through and with them.[20] Action for justice, neighbour love, concrete behaviours in economic life which take into account the common good are not just personal moral decisions, they are empowered by Christ's indwelling presence. For Luther, two practices which sealed this essential relationship between the understanding of one's faith and its practice were the practice of the Eucharist and the practice of solidarity.

We acknowledge today that the assent of faith involves not only acceptance of meaning about sacred truths handed down in the tradition but the significance of those truths for the contingencies of daily life and the challenges of global society. Discernment of this relationship requires an ongoing practice of faith. It was important 30 years ago to link social commitment and faith and to provide a vision of faith which went beyond intellectual assent. However, a new problem in the Christian community is that today, people may feel more comfortable with social involvement than with the challenge of the commitments of religious faith practised in a community. At a recent weekend meeting, an acquaintance was worried she would not get home on a Sunday in time to keep her commitment to work in the soup kitchen. However, she was not concerned about attending communal worship. At one time, this might be viewed as 'getting one's priorities straight'. One should not be a perfectionist about religious duties and avoid the call of charity. However, when this becomes a pattern, it causes us to revisit the important question: what relevance do other commitments of faith, like worship, have to our search for justice in society?

What Can I Hope For? Faith, Church and Vision for Justice

Faith is a movement of the entire personality which affects how one thinks, acts and feels. Faith is not just an intellectual pursuit. Rather a person of faith lives by a horizon of beliefs about life and its meaning. When we work for 'a better world', 'global peace' or 'sustainable community', we reach into this horizon for direction and purpose.

Our vision of life and its meaning is decisive for the acceptance or rejection of specific values because it has to do with the possibilities for satisfaction which those values can or cannot provide. Is sacrifice worth the effort? Can our vision of human flourishing be adjusted by our reading of and praying over the gospel? These ideas about what is worth our effort, to whom we owe help, what is necessary for our happiness, influence our decisions. They account for the human experience that ratiocination seems to be able to do very little to 'convert' human beings from one meaning

83

structure to another. Because this vision is learned primarily in relationship, its formation is also related to religion and the community called the Church.

The cultural context in which we live today can be characterized by a shift in the experience of human embeddedness and the impact of radical pluralism. Structures and horizons which once told us our place in the world are not as secure as in the past. Modern times are often characterized by a loss of meaning. Yet, how we understand a problem in our world involves our comprehension of the meaning of the world and essential relationships in it. In the search for the faith to do justice, we find ourselves in a quandary. On the one hand, ethical deliberation requires we have some idea of what a problem means by comprehending what meanings of life underlie the problem and constitute it. For example, a vision of human rights is a backdrop for understanding rights violations. On the other hand, when this wider framework is lacking, technical solutions alone appear insufficient to move the human spirit to action.

When religion and church communities raise deeper questions about the meaning of life, they are not avoiding the 'hard questions' by retreating into idealism. For what and for whom am I responsible? What can we hope for from the human spirit? What can we hope for the world? These definitions of the meaning of human living are essential frameworks for addressing problems in global society.

Contemporary ethics tend to embrace functional values as absolutes, rather than these deeper questions. For example, it is not uncommon to meet in public policy debates the limits of the ethical and purely moral argument to address underlying dimensions of a problem. Questions such as to whom are we responsible often frame the extent a group even pursues a solution.[21] This type of question relies on values often formed or not formed in places like a church community. When our contemporary ethical systems leave the affectivity that moves us to act untouched, justice is not done. Technical solutions alone will not bring justice to the world without addressing the relevance of deeper dimensions of the issue. Who is God? What is the meaning of the world? Who are we to one another?

Across the globe today there are many interpretations of these questions. Yet amid this pluralism we seek a global ethic. In the search for the faith to do justice it is important to acknowledge the role which religion has to contribute to this search. Can we work towards a common vision of life's meaning that transcends the particularity of a religious tradition but upholds a truth God wills for all humanity? The faith to do justice is found as relational beings, those who are always acting, not simply as lone individuals, but as people in relationship with God, the world, with neighbour and with self.

The actions of a living Christian faith therefore are not irrelevant to this dilemma. For instance, prayer is an active ingredient of Christian faith. Prayer generates affections, towards God, self, neighbour and the world.

Intellectual beliefs alone do not suffice to generate countervailing affections to what we learn in our culture.[22] In prayer, the religious belief that God wills all human beings to prosper and reach their potential can be experienced interiorly in religious experience, exteriorly in worship and reinforced in the action of the community. Here faith confirms what we strive for in hope, and its practice in community continually opens us to its meaning in our lives. Through liturgy, community and the life of the Church we are continually drawn into knowledge of this saving reality, and the change which occurs is not simply in our heads, it occurs in our hearts as well. In this way, there can be a belief–practice circle that points to the inseparable unity between religious beliefs, values and action for justice in the Christian life. This type of belief–practice circle is implicit in the search for faith that grounds justice.

What Must I Do? Faith and Ideology

Finally, a serious challenge in searching for the faith to do justice is the determination of how to apply the insights of our faith to concrete problems in society. Because society operates by its own laws, we must calculate how to make our values effective in 'real situations'. We need to know the best and most economical way to combine the meaning of existence with the know-how to manipulate reality. We employ two types of knowledge in this discernment which is constitutive of faith: faith and ideology.[23]

Faith is more than a relational sense of confidence regarding the next life. Rather, faith is the act of risk through which one devotes the use of one's freedom to the positive task of love.[24] Thinking and acting from the stance of faith is something which produces tangible results. Faith, then, is more than a religious act. Faith is a deeply centred aspect of all human life. It is an outlook that orients the total meaning structure of life. Religious faith is related to this more fundamental and salvific human faith. Through basic human faith people form relationships, create values and respond to the problems in society. Religious faith in the Christian sense builds on this more fundamental type of faith. It is an identification of the ultimate possibilities and limits of human life and the universe with the revelation of Jesus Christ. Faith is the surrender of one's whole being to the person, community and teaching of God, who saves us not only ultimately but from evils which impinge on us, here and now in this life, and lead to the paralysis, enslavement and culture of death we encounter in modern society. Faith in this sense is essential to the struggle for justice in society today.

The spiritual depth of religious faith is marked by its concern for history and the task of love. True religious faith seeks to establish the divine will as the Kingdom of God on earth, as Jesus did in his life. The conscious God–human relationship that religious faith involves, fuels conversion, a process of growth or change in values and meaning structure. Faith is a salvific outlook that relates us to a God who is concerned about the problems of our history and who calls us to greater growth through the events of our human experience.

For faith to impact the problems in society, the Christian requires another kind of information, that is, data about politics, economics, trade and culture. He or she must turn to the social sciences, economics, anthropology and environmental studies. Action on behalf of the concerns of justice requires a combination of faith and ideology.

Ideology has many meanings. However, for our purposes, it simply refers to our perception and understanding of the concrete instruments in the world at our disposal to realize our values. Another name for ideology is worldview, or our current ideas as to how the world works.

The interaction between faith and ideology points to the significance of faith for action for justice. We always exercise the values of our faith in the concrete world of objective reality, measured by our ideology. The mix between faith and ideology is one where we perceive reality where the ultimate data over reality illumines what reality can offer us. Faith helps us over the hurdle, 'there is nothing that can be done'. People who want to do something, will find a way to do it. The difficulty is not in doing, but in seeing in the first place. Or we can 'see' a solution to a problem, but not have the political will to accomplish it. In the interplay between faith and ideology, we allow our faith to transform our view of the world, and our ideology to make concrete the demands of our faith. On the other hand, faith without ideology is ineffective. Ideology provides us with the knowledge and skills to make the values of our faith work in a concrete situation. We can have our heart in the right place, but make ineffective decisions concerning how to bring about social change. Both faith and ideology are needed.

The Christian community acts on values like the right to work, to participation, the inherent equality of all men and women, the right to food, clothing and shelter, and education and healthcare as outgrowths of the Church's belief in the dignity of the human person. The belief that love is worth our effort, that sacrifice is indigenous to life, that creation is for the good of all, and the belief in solidarity, are values and visions held by the Church.

Church membership therefore is linked to a value stance towards life. The ultimate possibilities and limits of life as revealed through the person of Jesus Christ constantly impinge on our realm of values.[25] Social action in the Church arises from a tradition of faith which provides a 'way' of being in society and reveals in the process more than a social theory or even a teaching. Rather, it is also a way of faith to God, and is connected to the deepest mystery of the Church.

The search for faith to do justice is never resolved. It always relies on a certain surrender to the truth and call of God, a reliance on God's mercy and care and an investment in service with and on behalf of our neighbour.

It requires community, commitment and the conviction that love is worth the effort. However, for Christians, this is a way which is not new, but a path which many have followed with integrity and love. In this, the search for faith to do justice is the tradition of faith and, as the tradition, it rests in the surety of the presence and accompaniment of the risen Christ and his promise of its ultimate fulfilment.

Notes

1. Avery Dulles, SJ, 'The Meaning of Faith Considered in Relationship to Justice', in *The Faith that Does Justice*, ed. John C. Haughey (New York: Paulist Press, 1977), pp. 10–46.
2. See, for example, Jürgen Moltman, *God for a Secular Society: The Public Relevance of Theology* (Minneapolis: Fortress Press, 1999); Cynthia D. Moe-Lobeda, *Public Church For the Life of the World: Lutheran Voices Series* (Minneapolis: Augsburg Fortress, 2004).
3. Gerald O'Collins, *Fundamental Theology* (New York: Paulist Press, 1981), pp. 150–2.
4. See Donal Dorr, *The Social Justice Agenda: Justice, Ecology, Power and the Church* (New York: Orbis Books, 1991), chs 2 and 3.
5. Karl Rahner, *Christian Foundations* (New York: Seabury, 1978), pp. 402ff.
6. Johann Metz, *Faith in History and Society*, trans. David Smith (New York: Crossroad, 1980).
7. Christopher Lasch, *The True and Only Heaven: Progress and its Critics* (New York: Norton, 1991).
8. For an insightful assessment of competing visions of the good life in face of the realities of globalization, see Rebecca Todd Peters, *In Search of the Good Life: The Ethics of Globalization* (New York: Continuum, 2004).
9. J. Matthew Ashley, 'New Horizons for Mysticism and Politics', in *New Horizons in Theology*, ed. Terrence W. Tilley (New York: Orbis Press, 2005), pp. 56–69.
10. See, for example, J. Denny Weaver, *The Nonviolent Atonement* (Grand Rapids, Michigan: William B. Eerdmans, 2001).
11. See Charles Taylor, *Modern Social Imaginaries* (Durham: Duke University Press, 2004), p. 17.
12. Robert Bellah, *Habits of the Heart* (Berkeley and Los Angeles, CA: University of California Press, 1985).
13. See Peter Steinfels, *A People Adrift* (New York: Simon & Schuster, 2003); Michael Jenkins, *The Church Faces Death: Ecclesiology in a Post-Modern Context* (New York: Oxford University Press, 1999).
14. Vincent J. Miller, *Consuming Religion: Christian Faith and Practice in a Consumer Culture* (New York: Continuum, 2004), p. 225.

15. See John O'Donnell, SJ, 'Faith', in *The New Dictionary of Theology*, ed. Joseph A. Komonchak, Mary Collins and Dermot A. Lane (Wilmington, DE: Michael Glazier, 1987), pp. 375–86.
16. Judith A. Merkle, *From the Heart of the Church: The Catholic Social Tradition* (Collegeville, Minnesota: The Liturgical Press, 2004), ch. 2.
17. Dulles remarks:

> Without denying the historical mediation of faith, we may continue to insist that God succeeds in making himself immediately present to the human spirit, as the transcendental theologians have so lucidly shown. If this immediacy of God were allowed to be obscured . . . faith might seem to be a reaction to the historical situation rather than a response to a personal call from God. ('Faith in Relationship to Justice', *op. cit.*, p. 39)

18. Karl Rahner, 'How is the Holy Spirit Experienced Today?', in *Karl Rahner in Dialogue: Conversations and Interview, 1965–1982*, ed. Paul Imhof and Hubert Biallowons, trans. Harvey D. Egan (New York: Crossroad, 1986), p. 142, as quoted in Declan Marmion, *A Spirituality of Everyday Faith* (Louvain: Peeters, 1998), no. 1, p. 117.
19. Karl Rahner, 'The Certainty of Faith', in *The Practice of Faith: A Handbook of Contemporary Spirituality* (London: SCM Press, 1985), p. 32.
20. Cynthia D. Moe-Lobeda, *Healing a Broken World: Globalization and God* (Minneapolis: Fortress Press, 2002), p. 123.
21. J. Brian Hehir, 'Personal Faith, The Public Church, and the Role of Theology', *Harvard Divinity Bulletin*, vol. 26, no. 1, 1996.
22. John C. Haughey, SJ, 'Affections and Business', in *On Moral Business*, ed. Max L. Stackhouse, Dennis P. McCann and Shirley J. Roels, with Preston N. Williams (Grand Rapids, MI: Eerdmans, 1995), pp. 687–90.
23. Juan Luis Segundo, *Faith and Ideologies*, trans. John Drury (New York: Orbis Books, 1984), no. 1, p. 71.
24. Juan Luis Segundo, *De la sociedad a la teologia* (Buenos Aires: Carlos Lohle, 1970), no. 1, p. 92.
25. Segundo, *Faith and Ideologies*, p. 81. It is important to note that this approach emphasizes the Church as a 'tradition' of human beings who have learned how to learn from God. In this sense, the Church as a 'tradition' is a living reality, not just a school of thought. A tradition is borne along by a chain of witnesses to certain values. A school of thought establishes continuity in the logic of preferred arguments, not in the quality of the people and their experiences. We are suggesting that the tradition of the Church to act on the behalf of justice, encompasses its official teaching. However, through the witness of its martyrs, its social action and community life, the Church also concretizes its faith in action.

Chapter 6

Working and Being: Social Justice and a Theology *for* Workers

Gerard Mannion

This chapter simply seeks to provide an overview of some of the prevalent topics in ethical discussions about the world of work and the lives of workers.[1] In particular, I wish to introduce and discuss some of the key themes that have historically and in recent years preoccupied Catholic social teaching on these subjects. Thus I explore the historical background to and recent developments in the ethics of work. Throughout, I also explore how theologically informed ethics has influenced the analysis of the world of work in order to progress towards some conclusions concerning how theology in general, and Catholic social teaching in particular, might today offer food for thought for workers, corporations, companies, employers and governments alike. Such pointers may help us appreciate that all might better prosper through attention to ensuring people are enabled and allowed to flourish through truly being rather than through spending the majority of their lives merely working in ways and conditions that are detrimental to life itself.

CATHOLIC SOCIAL TEACHING AND THE PRIORITY OF LABOUR

I. Introduction

Human work not only proceeds from the person, but it is also essentially ordered to and has its final goal in the human person. Independent of its objective content, work must be oriented to the subject who performs it, because the end of work, any work whatsoever, always remains man. Even if one cannot ignore the objective component of work with regard to its quality, this component must nonetheless be subordinated to the self-realization of the person, and therefore to the subjective dimension, thanks to which it is possible to affirm that *work is for man and not man for work*.[2]

In exploring so many wider ethical questions today we find ourselves returning to considerations of the world of work – how the nature and

89

understanding of work has changed, along with radical transformations in how work is organized, managed and regulated. In particular, the implications of these changes for our communities have been increasingly explored. For no less today than in the past, changes in the world of work do have an enormous impact upon the lives and well-being of human individuals, families and societies alike. Work is and always has been a very live issue for ethical analysis. Any company, organization, corporation or indeed government which does not recognize or would rather wish to ignore this fact, might nonetheless sit up and take notice of the fact that research would seem to indicate that those organizations who take on board the need to engage in the ethics of work, find themselves enjoying greater success and, indeed, even profit in the long term.[3]

For example, one only has to point to the many surveys that illustrate how workers in Germany and, especially, in France, who put in considerably fewer hours than their UK counterparts, are nonetheless also considerably more *productive* than their UK counterparts.[4] Gerry Robinson, serially successful entrepreneur, chief executive of a series of multinational 'blue chip' corporations and well known as a 'troubleshooter' for failing companies and other institutions alike, recently offered managers what he deemed to be one of the most important pieces of advice his decades in business had taught him: it related to the adage 'The longer you work, the more you contribute'. Robinson argued that anyone who failed to realize just how false a myth this adage is, would never succeed in business:

> This [statement] strikes me as just about the saddest thing about business life. At any level of management, if you are working all the hours God sends, you will be causing more harm than good. When I was chief executive of the leisure group Granada I got some flak from some sections of the press for stating that if I couldn't fit my job into a nine-to-five day I was either being unreasonable or I was mucking it up. But I stand by this, and in fact quite a few people thanked me for taking a stand against the unreasonable hours that are often expected.[5]

Robinson went on to chart just how dangerous for the success of any business working long hours actually is, including leading to the invention of pointless and counterproductive tasks to fill time, the establishment of an unhealthy culture throughout the business and the loss of 'big picture' thinking and creative energies, indeed of clear thinking altogether. As Robinson (who, at the most, worked a four-day, nine-to-five week in such high-profile jobs) said, '*There is no way you can approach your job with enthusiasm if you are working twelve hours a day*.'[6]

Or examine how even governments in parts of Europe and the United States of America are finally coming round to recognizing that questions of 'work–life balance' are issues that should not and indeed cannot be ignored by anyone in the world of business, the public sector, the arena of trade, or indeed by governments themselves. So one hopes this wards off the sceptics who feel that somehow only those from within the world of business and economics (and perhaps politics) should seek to determine possible future directions for the way in which we perceive, organize and manage work and workers. The professor of economic history at Oxford University, Avner Offer, has recently given rise to much debate with his study of the 'hedonic consumerism' that shapes the lives of so many in the English-speaking countries of the world.[7] Research elsewhere demonstrates that one of the main reasons behind the alarming decrease in the birth rate of countries such as Britain is the slavish dedication by young people of their lives to their workplace in an unprecedented, intense and all-consuming fashion, leaving them seeking only escapism of the more instant kind. This, as opposed to wishing to strike a happy balance through putting their lives into a more genuine and healthy perspective. One quality daily newspaper duly announced the result of one such survey with the headline 'Britons Put Work and Fun before Babies'.[8]

Now of course, many company managers and owners might delight in such a culture, some even believing that work hard and play hard is good for their profit margin. But such would be crass short-termism, for with such alarming declines in the European birth rate, they may find that their company has a very bleak future indeed as workers, particularly those with the necessary skills, become ever more short in supply.[9]

What is happening in the world of work is having a major impact on the health of individuals, indeed upon the health of communities in general. It has an impact upon relationships, upon families, upon the values and norms of our societies. It impacts upon the level of involvement in voluntary activities, including in politics. Work-related 'stress' is now seen to be one of the world's leading health issues, according to the World Health Organization (WHO).[10] As noted, it also has a major impact even upon the success of the very businesses and organizations that individuals work for. So it is a live issue indeed.

This far down the line from the monumental historical events of the early and mid-twentieth century, as well as in the 1970s, 80s and 90s, we might finally be able to edge towards realizing that the waves of unfettered capitalism which many believed were necessary conditions for the prosperity of certain powerful nations need to be reassessed. Indeed, they should now be viewed as the very specific and frequently misguided and politically and ideologically driven expediency of certain interest groups and governments, as opposed to the inevitable way that 'things must be'. Crude determinism has proved as groundless and indeed as destructive a foundation for any economic or political worldview, as it long did for various theological, philosophical and political worldviews. If we jettison such crude determinism with regard to the morality of institutions and especially with regard to the world of work and the lot of workers, then much good might come from doing so.

Here I am not going to focus, primarily, upon the many contributions we have seen, particularly in the last 60 or so years, in the theology *of* work. Instead, I wish to argue that the only reason why theology engages with the world of work at all is because it wishes to influence the social and so anthropological implications of work and how it is perceived and organized. 'Work', per se, needs no theology, at least from a moral standpoint. On the other hand, those who engage in 'work' can gain very much from theological scrutiny of the world of work. So *not* a 'theology of work' – for work seems to take care of itself! But rather a theology that seeks to do justice for workers.

What I especially hope will here become evident, is that, contrary to the increasing 'withdrawal' from the world of many Christian ethicists in recent years, the issue of work and the plight of contemporary workers will help demonstrate that, as with all the major moral challenges of our postmodern times, the Church is neither a voice crying in the wilderness *in toto*, nor does it have nothing to offer those in secular and civil society who do not share the Christian faith. Instead, as the Church has always done, partnerships can be built with all those of 'goodwill', in order collectively to confront and go on to defeat the sinful malaises, both social and personal, of our times. So, in this chapter, for example, we will see the Church learning from and in turn informing (just as it had originally informed in a more indirect fashion), philosophical, social scientific and economic theories with regard to the world of work.

II. Human Dignity in the Catholic Social Tradition[11]

1. A century of social teaching

As reflected in so many other chapters in this volume, from 1891 onwards, the Roman Catholic Church has increasingly seen the need to reflect in a sustained and authoritative fashion upon the plight of workers.[12] And, by and large, this has usually meant theological and moral reflection more upon the persons who do work themselves, and the forces which control their 'working lives', than upon the nature of work itself. In other words, such official teaching, itself, should most often be categorized as a theology 'for workers' as opposed to being any theology '*of* work'. Of course the rapid developments brought forward by the Industrial Revolution and the developments in science and technology, as well as in politics and economics throughout and since the nineteenth century, have meant that the Church could do no other than to engage with such issues. This is because the Gospels were initially the stories of Jesus' proclamation of 'good news' to those whose lives were conditioned in similar ways to those of the majority of the world's population today: mostly poor or not especially wealthy in relative terms for their day and society.

In other words, human beings whose dignity and hence whose opportunity to be fully open to grace, and hence whose capacity for closer communion with what Christians understand by the term God and with their fellow human beings, were being stifled and routinely demeaned by the forces of the society around them. The majority of their lives and of their energies were given over to the forces of the world of what today we call 'work'. In other words, these people led lives which were largely stories of oppression, the absence of fulfilment and were, in so many ways, exploited. Many of them perhaps lived and died without ever having the opportunity or inclination to realize the fact and they thus had little chance of breaking out of the vicious circle of exploitation in which the lives of themselves and their families were trapped.[13]

2. Our social nature

The Church, in much of its social teaching (with due acknowledgement to Aristotle in some aspects), proclaims that human beings are called to community. Why is this? The answer involves that which lies at the very heart of the Christian faith itself. Christianity proclaims *one* God understood in a threefold sense: God is a community of co-equal, co-eternal and co-divine persons. This communion, whereby the very being of God is understood in terms of a wondrous mutual 'indwelling' (*perichoresis*) of the divine persons is taken to be an indication of the life to which God calls each and every human person.[14] The term 'person' here being understood in the ancient sense as being linked to one's role and part in a community, as opposed to the modern sense of an isolated individual.

We humans are neither well suited to nor best served by isolated and individualistic existence (ironic, given that this is the form of existence that has increasingly become the norm, thanks to those same industrial, scientific, technological, political and economic forces in the modern and contemporary eras). Thus our 'social nature' implies a mutual dependency and, with it, mutual responsibilities. The Church could never sanction a 'dog-eat-dog', *laissez-faire* form of society whereby the prevailing ethos is each to their own, for such runs counter to the very core of the most sacred truths to which Christianity bears testimony. No, the Church teaches that, because we are called to social existence, to communion, we must understand that human dignity is also the benchmark for our ordering of our shared existence – our communities – and hence must also dictate the ways in which we live out that social existence. This presupposes cooperation, sharing, supporting, caring. Mutuality, not individuality, is the key here. And all such teaching has profound implications for the world of work and, indeed, for any situation that lends itself to furthering the erosion of human dignity and to the promotion of exploitation.

3. Society grounded on *truth*, *justice* and *love* (and *freedom*)

Much of the legacy of the rich heritage of Catholic doctrine about communal human existence (that is simply what 'Catholic social teaching' means) points towards allowing the being of God to shape our own relations and communities and day-to-day existence. It points towards establishing the values of the 'Kingdom', heralded in the gospels as the foundational principles of our societies, organizations and institutions, of our utilization of goods, including property, and of our treatment of others.

Above all else, Catholic doctrine concerning human shared existence makes a powerful case for the fact that the best societies, the most flourishing communities, the best organizations and institutions are ones which are grounded upon and – on a daily basis – are attentive to truth, to justice and to love (*caritas*, charity). Hence such are those most in touch with the vision espoused in the gospels and in subsequent theological interpretation and additional Christian insight. Of course, underlining all three is the prerequisite of human freedom. And yet in the world of work, in how we manage our workplaces, in our treatment of workers (even within church-linked institutions), we see that truth, justice, love and freedom appear to be viewed more as 'vices' that such organizations, such workplaces, such societies can ill-afford to indulge or can only pay lip-service to at best. We see this as well in the broader organization and political and economic management of our communities, of society in general.

4. The relation between labour and capital

Which brings us to a further fundamental theme common to much of the heritage of Catholic social teaching since the nineteenth century, just as it is a theme common to most discussions of work and of the lives and treatment of workers. That subject is the understanding of the relations between 'labour' and 'capital': or, to demythologize this and to repersonalize it (for its depersonalization best serves the interests only of those who would perpetuate the cycle of exploitation and the crushing of human dignity), the relationship between the human beings, the persons who give their time and energies in exchange for some (usually unfavourably disproportionate to what they give) financial return, on the one hand, and between the forces of finance, of money, property, of wealth and, we might add, of power, on the other.[15]

5. Conceptions of the state

Thus much of church teaching on these issues sought to remind the political classes who run the various nation 'states' that came to represent the most common form of organizing communities in the modern era, that they had certain duties towards working people and indeed towards the members of their societies in general (as well as their relations with members of other societies, of other 'states').

The *polis*, of course, refers to the community, to the 'city' or the 'state' or, perhaps better, to the 'social' (the 'shared existence'). Hence the Church, as with much classical and modern political philosophy and the emergent 'social' sciences, thus sought to contribute to the ongoing debates about how we understand, organize and regulate our communal existence – in other words, the Church entered into the ongoing and often divisive debates in the modern era pertaining to the conceptions of the state. With regard to the world of the workers, this was very important: for conflicting conceptions of the state went hand in hand with conflicting conceptions of the world of work and the ways in which states would order and regulate the relations between 'labour' and 'capital'.

6. Beware 'false ideologies'

Much of the official Catholic social teaching then, especially in the middle third of the twentieth century, was concerned with trying to raise awareness of the dangers of building and maintaining societies around ideologies that, ultimately, worked against truth, justice, love and human freedom. In the 1930s, in particular, the Church sought to unmask the evils of fascism on the one hand and state totalitarianism of a pseudo-communist kind on the other. Indeed, the Church has also consistently sought to steer a middle way between all forms of overt individualism and collectivism alike.

The principle of subsidiarity is a crucial concept here. It demands that autonomy (whether of groups or individuals) be respected and facilitated, the only exceptions being where a larger or broader organization or collective might bring about greater enhancement of truth, justice, love and freedom than if certain actions were left to a more localized form of control. And, of course, this again has significant implications for the understanding of the rights of workers and of how the workplace should be organized and managed, as well as with how and when the state should intervene on behalf of workers and their families.

But the battle against dehumanizing ideologies, which deify states, collectives or markets, did not end with the defeat of Nazism following the Second World War, nor with the collapse of the totalitarianism of Eastern Europe in the early 1990s. Indeed, perhaps the single most 'false ideology' that the Church has consistently had to speak out against in its social teaching since the nineteenth century, has been that which became the supreme guiding ideology across the globe towards the final decades of the twentieth century.

7. The 'sins' of liberal capitalism[16]

The rampant *laissez-faire* capitalism, whereby the forces of the 'market' (read powerful elites) dictated the lot of the majority of the human race, reared its ugly head anew in a still more dehumanizing form in the final third of the twentieth century. Just when the world, in the aftermath of the second horrific global conflict of that century, had seemed as if it was moving towards a sensible balance between collective efforts to shape better societies and respect for diversity and the rights of individuals and smaller communities, powerful and influential political theorists, economists and politicians themselves began to champion anew a minimalist version of the state (at least in terms of positive and welfare-oriented intervention in the affairs of its citizens).[17] There emerged a new form of liberal capitalism, one driven by aggressive monetarist policies which deified the market anew and which sought to strip away as much state interference in the 'market' as possible. 'Market forces' became the new determinism. As Jürgen Moltmann put it:

> The global marketing of everything and every service is much more than pure economics. It has become the all embracing law of life. We have become customers and consumers, whatever else we may be. The market has become the philosophy of life, the world religion, and for some people destroys community at all levels, because people are weighed up only according to their market value. They are judged by what they can perform or by what they can afford.[18]

Nothing was supposed to stand in the way of the 'market', this 'new religion', and if the cost was untold human misery, mass unemployment, deprivation, malnourishment and poverty, then so be it: 'market forces' dictated the situation. In the early 1990s, for example, one British Chancellor of the Exchequer said that high unemployment of record levels was 'a price well worth paying' in order for economic expediency to triumph.[19] And if workers became more and more exploited, if governments and large corporations sought to smash or nullify their hard-fought-for (over the course of two centuries) collective bargaining mechanisms and trade unions, then so be it: 'market forces'.

And if companies, industries and all manner of workplaces were closed down or pared to the bone of their 'human resources', if entire communities were devastated by the removal of industries that had employed generations of the same families, then so be it: 'market forces'. If the wealth and property of, first, certain nations and then the world in general became concentrated in the hands of fewer and fewer individuals, if multinational corporations began aggressively to foist their wares upon every corner of the world, undermining and undercutting local initiatives and thereby taking the profit from local sweat and toil away from the locality and into the hands of fewer and fewer in already very wealthy countries elsewhere, then so be it: 'market forces'.[20]

If those rights and benefits of workers, for which so many had campaigned during the 200 years or so since the dawn of the Industrial Revolution, were gradually being eroded to the point of disappearance, even to the point where companies could gamble with the 'saved' future benefits of the workers (i.e. their pension funds, and lose them without any recompense for the workers whose final years now looked very bleak), then 'market forces' were the simple conclusion. If political parties which had been founded to speak out for, stand up for and to represent the very same rights of workers, of 'labour', moved further to the right so as to be indistinguishable from their once sworn opponents, whose only substantial difference from them now was simply the fact of who at a particular time was in power, 'market forces' provided the explanation and supposed 'necessitation' of such developments. If members of parties that once saw the unfettered market as nothing less than evil, were seen now, like 'pigs with snouts in the trough', to abuse their positions of power and influence, primarily for personal gain, selling generations down the river in the process, as they helped the forces of capitalism greater concentrate the world's wealth ever more in still fewer hands, then market forces could be pointed to once again as the root cause.

Selfishness, then, was preached from political pulpits. 'There is no such thing as society', proclaimed Britain's first woman Prime Minister. Even not a few churches profited from investing in or conniving with the exploitation of workers or indeed even engineering such exploitation themselves.[21]

The world, paradoxically, considering what the first wave of postmodern theorists had predicted, was becoming, in many ways, a 'smaller' or more localized place: globalization became the new ideology, the new form of spreading the gospel of liberal capitalism into areas where even the tainted and variably functional forms of Western 'democracy', let alone capitalism, were alien to the spiritual and cultural inheritance of the people whose lives and communities were turned upside down as the world became populated by more and more drastically poor and exploited people.[22]

In the world of work, even in those wealthier countries where people were 'duped' into thinking of themselves as fundamentally free to do as they choose, the clock was also turned back to workplace practices more redolent of the days before the first modern encyclical on social teaching and the plight of workers was released – *Rerum Novarum* (1891). Increasingly, the genuine rights of workers were eroded once more. 'Work–life balance' became a fundamental issue but even much talk of this really meant trying to stack the odds in favour of those in control of workers and the profits they generate – hegemony again: how to dupe people into thinking they are not neglecting their families, their communities and themselves when they are increasingly doing so.

The world, then, at the end of the twentieth century was working harder than ever, more hours than ever and was creating more wealth than ever. And yet at no time had there been more poverty, more deprivation, more death from starvation and from easily curable or preventable illnesses and diseases. At no time had so few owned so much. The world was richer or rather, a relatively few individuals and institutions and, of course, still fewer countries, were very, very, very rich – all from the sweat and toil of the many whose percentage of the 'rewards' they were producing became ever more minuscule.[23]

The Church did not stand by and refuse to speak out. And yet, ironically, it was in the age when people began to speak of the Church's social teaching as its 'best kept secret' that the Church's social teaching became ever more ignored by many, even within the Church itself. And, perhaps for some, there is a surprising element to the Church's social teaching in recent years that is still very underplayed in certain quarters: for, as we shall seek to illustrate, Pope John Paul II did not just denounce totalitarianism in the Eastern Europe from which he hailed. He was utterly vociferous in his denunciation of the evils of liberal capitalism, too – and this even more frequently than his pontifical predecessors. The Polish Pope was one of the most ardent critics of the dehumanizing effects of globalization itself.[24]

III. Working and Living

Let us turn then to engage in some further contextualizing of our theological explorations into the world of work and into the lives and aspirations of those who do it – workers.

1. Theology and anthropology

Contra the German philosopher/theologian Ludwig Feuerbach,[25] his compatriot, Karl Rahner, famously wrote that theology and anthropology are, in essence, the same thing viewed from differing perspectives.[26] In other words, in seeking to discern the mystery and nature of God so, also, do we engage with the mystery and nature of what it is to be human and vice versa (whether one believes 'natural theology' to be possible or not – for example, John Calvin spoke of the fundamental link between knowledge of self and knowledge of God).

If we bring this down to our narrower focus upon the world of work, then it follows that our attempts to understand God's will and purpose for humans – God's call to communion with Godself, in other words our paths to salvation – obviously affect *any* theology of work or any theology for workers. For God's call to communion with Godself takes place not simply in church on Sundays but rather in the midst of our everyday existence. Therefore, how we spend the majority of that existence obviously has a profound bearing upon whether or not we are in an existential, social, psychological, emotional or physical position to be receptive to God's offer of self-communication, i.e., to grace.

Thus work – that is to say, that activity in which the majority of adult human beings (and in many societies even children) spend the vast majority of their existence – can be, on the one hand, something which moves us further away from God, through being an obstacle to our capacity to receive grace and so become closer to God (and indeed with our fellow human beings which is part of the continuum of grace and the path to salvation). Or, on the other hand, it can be something through which we develop more fully as persons, become fulfilled – more fully human – as well as contribute towards the common good and a more just community and wider society ('building the Kingdom' of love, justice and righteousness), and so partake in God's plan of salvation for the world.

We have noted that an unswerving acknowledgement of the value of each and every human person – the inherent dignity of each person, which is in the gift of no person nor any institution or organization because humans are made 'in the image and likeness of God' – is a fundamental principle of Christian social doctrine. And yet, in the sphere of work – the arena in which most humans spend the majority of their (waking) lives – human dignity is routinely ignored, undermined, deprived and often crushed. What has theology and the Church to say of such a situation?

2. To earn a 'living'

When discussing work, which usually refers to the situation whereby people offer their time, energies and particular skills in exchange for financial remuneration, we often speak of 'earning a living' – which is something most people at one stage or another perceive to be a necessity. Hence this need is seen as the means by which we will be able to enjoy the things that are necessary for human life and, for those in more fortunate positions, many things which are perhaps not necessary as such for sustaining existence, but which go a long way towards enhancing and fulfilling human existence. For the more fortunate still, the financial rewards of work can bring with them the means to purchase things which are not necessary at all but which can bring greater satisfaction, happiness and sense of contentment (i.e., luxuries).

But is this saying 'to earn a living' not, in itself, something misleading? For do not the vast majority of people engaged in work today – due to the very nature of much work – actually do something other than truly 'live' when they are engaged in working? Here we can except many forms of employment but not, I suggest the majority. And does not much, perhaps most work actually take away not simply the 'time' necessary for a fulfilled life, but also the necessary energies and motivation and so on for living? In other words, when many people are working, they are not truly 'living' and when they have finished their day's work, they frequently have little energy left *for* true living. Indeed, again perhaps for the majority of the world's workers, their arduous labour does not even buy them much beyond the bare necessities of *existence*. So it is strange to speak of *earning* a 'living', as such. It seems, at best, a category mistake. At worst it is part of that hegemonic process whereby the majority of adults (and to reiterate, in many societies, of children) are cajoled into giving up the greater part of their biological, chronological, often physical and indeed spiritual *capacity* for living.[27]

3. Labour, property and human fulfilment

Hence many of the theological, as well as philosophical and social scientific considerations of work and the plight of workers, focus upon themes such as the nature of work itself – i.e., labour, as well as upon what the rewards of such labour can and should be. Naturally this leads into a consideration of what work and its rewards can enable people to purchase and to own – hence property. It is somewhat obvious that those who own the least property already (or have the least means of purchasing such) are those who are necessitated to engage in labour in order to be able to gain what little property they can eventually own.

Paradoxically, then, in the world of work it seems that to those who have to work, more work will frequently be given. To those who do not have to work, or who enjoy the means to purchase property to a high degree already and so do not have to work as much or for as long, less work is foisted upon them and many may choose not to work at all. So, too, with property: to those who have, the means to gain more is proportionate to what they already have.

To those who have not or have little, the same applies – their lack of property (including existential necessities here), or the means to purchase such, means that most of them are unlikely ever to improve their situation significantly here. What they *do* have is their time, their energy, their skills, and so they 'mortgage' their existence by engaging in labour, i.e. they 'mortgage' their 'living' in the usually vain hope that they might one day not have to do so or might be able to do so less often. This 'mortgage' is really a fiction, for, by the time most of them cease to work, they are either at the stage of their life where they have only a limited amount of time left for 'living', and/or they have also used up the majority of the 'rewards' of their labour along the way to get to that point.

Thus we are, once more, brought back to the fundamental question of human dignity. The situation of the majority of workers, if accurately reflected in our (admittedly generalized but necessarily so in such a short essay) deliberations thus far, is one whereby their dignity is not allowed to flourish. Let us explore some aspects of what the Catholic tradition has had to say about such matters in the modern and contemporary eras. We begin by noting that, in exploring the pertinent issues for a theology for workers today, one particular issue deserves our undivided and ongoing attention.

III. One Fundamental Problem, from *Rerum novarum* (1891) to the Present Day . . .

We are still . . . in the civilization created by industrialization and democracy, still caught in the clash between contradictory forces, the domination of instrumental reason with its dehumanizing consequences and the movements of resistance based on the conviction, be it secular or religious, that humanity has an ethical vocation.[28]

It would appear that the lot of workers – for those who care or have the values as well as the energies left to do so (for one of the great triumphs of liberalism capitalism from the mid-1980s onwards was the increasing depoliticization first of youth and then of the workforce in many countries in general) – has returned centre stage. For the majority of workers in recent decades have been suffering, albeit in new and alarming ways, from a much older malaise. And, once more, this despite all the collective and enlightened efforts (many of which were inspired, sponsored or very much supported by the Churches) to improve their lot and to make work more fulfilling, rewarding and literally *dignified*. In other words, efforts towards the enhancement of human well-being and fulfilment have gradually been unravelled. Such developments gathered apace in the final decades of the twentieth century.

Despite the increasing discussion of work–life 'balance' in societies such as Britain and the USA today, I suggest this really masks the more fundamental underlying problem. For it tends towards the mentality that work and life are on an equal footing, i.e. are of equal importance, and the core challenge today is to convince people that this is simply not true and should never be seen as true. To speak of 'balance' masks a malignant evil that has grown and now grows anew within our midst.[29]

This malaise, this evil, is the fact that workers are becoming increasingly detached from that very part of their selves, that aspect of their spiritual and existential lives, to which they devote the greatest part of their waking lives. In other words, the majority of workers have once more become utterly *alienated* ('cut off', 'estranged') from the dominant working aspect of their lives and hence in their personal, familial and communitarian lives. And the social cost of such has been immense – so much so that some theorists came up with the term 'social capital' in an effort to measure the effect of dehumanizing liberal capitalism and, conversely, the positive benefits that might be forthcoming from enlightened steps to address the evils of such capitalism once again.[30]

Thus the focus has switched back to anthropological concerns once more: are workers in much of the world today actually earning a true 'living' or are they simply gifting the best part of their lives towards the ends of selfish and immoral individuals and organizations, not to mention governments? Let us – albeit briefly and in very general terms – attempt to sketch some of the theory behind this issue.

IV. The Concept of Alienation

1. Living in a state of estrangement: a brief history of the concept of alienation

In exploring the history of the concept of alienation, in the modern sense of the word, many of the key philosophical articulations of the concept can be traced back to the work of G.W.F. Hegel (1770–1831).[31] But, with regard to the world of work and the monumental historical, economic and political consequences of mass alienation, no thinker has been more influential, of course, than Karl Marx (1818–83).[32]

Marx's own definition is as instructive today as it was in the middle of the nineteenth century when the plight of the workers in places such as north-west England moved Marx and his revolutionary collaborator, Friedrich Engels, to devote so much of their own energies to the cause of raising awareness of the *literally* inhuman conditions in which most persons laboured. They sought to suggest what steps were necessary to rectify this and to stave off the worst consequences if no such action was taken. Thus, amongst Marx's voluminous literary output we find what would later become a very famous definition of the concept indeed:

> What constitutes the alienation of labour? First, that the work is *external* to the worker, that it is not a part of his nature; and that

consequently he does not fulfil himself in his work, but denies himself, has a feeling of misery, rather than of well-being, does not develop freely his mental and physical energies, but is physically exhausted and mentally debased.[33]

Indeed, Marx foresaw the inversion of values and the confusion between means and ends to the detriment of the lives of millions of workers – a development to which we shall return in our analysis of Catholic social teaching on this subject:

> We arrive at the result that man (the worker) feels himself to be freely active only in his animal functions – eating, drinking, and procreating, or at most also in his dwelling and in personal adornment – while in his human functions he is reduced to an animal. The animal becomes human and the human becomes animal.[34]

Now, of course, so much ink has been spilled on the concept since, but here let us simply keep to outlining the most significant aspects of the concept for our own debates today. I suggest the continued prevalence and worsening effects of alienation essentially focus our attention upon three fundamental aspects of the concept that have characterized it from the days of Marx onwards:

1. *Alienated from self and others.* As we shall see, below, this aspect of the concept relates to the fragmentation of existence itself and the breakdown in existential and social equilibrium.

2. *Alienation increased by technological advances.* On this point, in addition to Marx, one can find much agreement in the works of some perhaps surprising people such as Martin Heidegger and John Paul II, himself; on alienation they share much in common.

3. *Private property and individualism result.* Alienation leads towards the desire to amass material goods and private wealth. A vicious circle ensues and this drive to accumulate 'private' property leads to the greater spread and worsening effects of alienation all the more. Indeed, our postmodern age has seen it spiral out of control in some societies altogether.

2. The prevalence of alienation

Indeed, as alienation has spread and, thanks to the rapid developments in technology, taken on ever more new and diverse forms that are ever more difficult to counter, so it has come to dominate human existence in so total a way that perhaps the most apt analogy to describe its effects really is that of a global and mutating disease. In some societies, alienation has triumphed over each and every aspect of human existence to such an extent that it has reduced human existence in those places to a pale imitation of what meaningful existence might be like. It has reduced human existence, in the words of one famous theorist, to one dimension alone.

3. One-dimensional existence

That theorist was, of course, Herbert Marcuse (1898–1979), whose now famous work, *One-Dimensional Man* (1964) might be said to chart the next key 'stage' in the development of alienation after that stage addressed by Marx. There, Marcuse details the rise of what we now all familiarly refer to as the 'consumer society' – whereby alienation masks its true effects and so enlists the help of people in furthering its spread all the more, by leading us to believe that the patterns of life we follow are really good for us in a way that they were perhaps not for workers in the past:

> The people recognize themselves in their commodities; they find their soul in their automobile, hi-fi set, split-level home, kitchen equipment. The very mechanism which ties the individual to his society has changed, and social control is anchored in the new needs which it has produced. The prevailing forms of social control are technological in a new sense.[35]

Thus, if Marx and others rightly pointed the way towards a realization that alienation shattered the meaningfulness and wholeness of human existence, the explosion of mass consumerism has since dulled human consciousness of workers' true plight, through making them believe that they really do enjoy 'worthy' rewards of their labours. As such it replaces both religion as the 'Opium of the People' and gin as the preferred escape route of nineteenth-century workers. But, as Marcuse continues:

> However, the reality constitutes a more progressive stage of alienation. The latter has become entirely objective; the subject which is alienated is swallowed up by its alienated existence. There is only one dimension, and it is everywhere and in all forms. The achievements of progress defy ideological indictment as well as justification; before their tribunal, the 'false consciousness' of their rationality becomes the true consciousness.[36]

4. A *mutating* disease

In terms that are as enlightening today as they are depressing, Marcuse goes on, in that now classic study, to speak of the continuingly seductive nature of alienation itself:

It is a good way of life – much better than before – and as a good way of life, it militates against qualitative change. Thus emerges a pattern of *one-dimensional thought and behavior* in which ideas, aspirations, and objectives that, by their content, transcend the established universe of discourse and action are either repelled or reduced to terms of this universe. They are redefined by the rationality of the given system and of its quantitative extension.[37]

In other words, we become locked in the cycle of believing that, in the words of that profound political commentator Billy Bragg, 'As Long as You're Comfortable it Feels Like Freedom . . .'.[38] Indeed, things have since spiralled ever further towards the realization that we have long since ceased to be simply hunter-gatherers and nor, of course, did we ever come remotely close to approximating the ideals of 'Renaissance man' or 'Renaissance woman'. We can no longer even take some semblance of reflected dignity from the fact that we are producers – we are now simply consumers who work and exist primarily to consume more and thus most work is geared towards offering something that others will be willing to consume (or at least willingly duped into consuming).[39] The cycle perpetuates itself.

Whilst this has yet to take root in so all consuming a fashion in every society (pardon the pun) – cultural and ideological pockets of resistance do thrive in many parts of the world – it is nonetheless the case that in societies such as Britain and North America we are willingly duped into conspiring to keep ourselves chained to the forces of dehumanizing capitalism which moves us ever further away from a life with meaning, purpose, direction and fulfilment. Those who might think such is overstated should open their newspaper or switch on their television sets – which may or may not be the latest plasma screens but will communicate the reality of this analysis all the same.

V. Consumerism

Here philosophers such as the French existentialist Gabriel Marcel, and Erich Fromm, that kindred spirit of Marcuse who also branched out from the Frankfurt School, have sought to counter the spread of this disease by trying to remind us of a simple truth that is shared by many of the world's faiths. It is an insight one will find even in medieval texts such as St Thomas à Kempis' *Imitation of Christ*. It points towards the difference between a life of *being* and a life of *having* – in other words, a life of authentic existence or a life driven by consumerist escapism.

In the latter form of 'life', all become commodities – including our very *selves*. The apathy that maintains such a society in existence breeds . . . only further apathy. Thus new and increasingly seductive and even addictive forms of escapism become the only real 'goals' and 'ends' of people caught on such a treadmill. For such allows us to suppress and deny our alienation. Superficiality and short-termism become virtues in a further twist to the inversion of values that alienation causes. The emergence of the '24-hour society' drives this process on relentlessly, and hence the elusiveness of meaning and fulfilment become ever more serious.

For human life, dignity and community are literally 'priceless': they are in no person's gift – they are far too valuable. Here the works of Marcel's *Être et avoir*[40] and Fromm's *To Have and To Be*[41] continue to be most instructive – we should aspire towards true, authentic 'being' instead of allowing our lives to be ruled by 'having'. Here the Church shares such concerns: we should *always* strive to be persons in community and not be driven by the desire to amass material wealth and possessions. Fundamental to all this is the fostering and sustenance-in-being of community. The German political theologian Jürgen Moltmann offers the following suggestion with regard to our contemporary situation brought about by mass alienation and the very consumerization of human existence: 'How can the human person protect their dignity and freedom in spite of the pressure of individualization? By becoming capable of community, and prepared for community. That is the truth of the communitarian network.'[42] So property and wealth should not be weapons or the criteria of/means to authentic human existence. We need a *being* society, not a *having*, a consumer society.

THE CHURCH'S ONGOING BATTLE AGAINST THE CONTINUING DISEASE OF ALIENATION

I. Changing Methods in Catholic Social Teaching

The Church's response to the plight of workers has considerably evolved in a number of ways, just as the mutating disease of alienation itself has changed since the nineteenth century. Thus, Catholic social teaching (as with much Catholic theology in general) has witnessed a methodological shift from a 'classicist' worldview to one which pays due attention to historical consciousness: reading the 'Signs of the Times' became increasingly important from the 1960s onwards. Likewise this marked a shift (as witnessed in the major church teaching documents on social issues) from *deductive* reasoning to *inductive* reasoning. So, too, was there a shift from a singular emphasis upon natural law and the notion of a 'universal plan' for the world towards due attention being given to contextual and cultural considerations.[43] In all this, the Church was also witnessing changes in the operative understanding of human nature itself, i.e. of anthropologies, in its own teaching.

II. Changing Attitudes Towards Socialism

The Church gradually moved away from its opposition to socialism towards a recognition of a shared emphasis with many socialists on fundamental issues such as *equality*, *participation* and *freedom*. Hence, in the 1960s again, the official Church, as had many Catholics at the grassroots level before it, underwent a significant transformation in its position vis-à-vis socialism and particularly Marxist-inspired communism. This marked a move from a position of hostile opposition towards one of mutual respect and recognition of the 'common ground' the Church shares with many socialist ideals, hence a move that has been 'from anathema to dialogue'

One key player in all this was Pope John XXIII (1958–63) who initiated what became known as the 'opening to the left' and who acknowledged the common causes shared by the Church and the political Left. This was facilitated by the recognition that different *forms* of socialism existed and so not all could be either condemned or indeed collaborated with on equal terms.

Thus (and not for the first time in its long history) church teaching with regard to private property also began to change. In particular, the Church moved away from acknowledging any *absolute* value of property towards a qualified recognition of the *instrumental* value of private property. And this was further qualified still by an emphasis upon the *universal* utilization of private property.[44] Hence private property in itself was deemed to have no value – only the uses to which it is put have potential value and then only if it is put to the use of the whole community, rather than exclusively kept for the benefit of the few.

Of course, further developments in the world of theology helped transform Catholic approaches to the world of work, towards capitalism and towards socialism further still. Hence movements such as political theology, liberation theology and even the employment of Marxist social analysis all played a significant role here, as did the further renewal of the anthropological dimension to theology in the works of those such as Rahner, Bernard Lonergan and Juan Luis Segundo.

But, to bring the story more up to date, one recent pope played a major role in developing the Church's attitude towards capitalism and towards worker alienation further still. And the picture of his influence is perhaps often skewed by the emphasis that the secular media puts upon his legacy.

III. John Paul II, Alienation and Work

It is true that John Paul had much to say in condemnation of those forms of Marxism that he had personally experienced in Eastern Europe[45] – in personal, political and philosophical terms, he had much to say contra Marxism. It is also true that more broad generalizations returned to church teaching during his pontificate. And there were not-so-hidden agendas afoot in the Church as in the world at that time. Conservatism was on the rise as was centralization.

So John Paul's teachings demonstrated a further shift in methodology once again – the organic, deductive and Natural Law reasoning more reminiscent of papal teaching prior to the 1960s came back into play more.[46] John Paul II remains a paradoxical pope on this as on many other issues, but let us briefly look at the actuality of his teaching on the topics in hand to attempt to discern some possible insight into his own thinking here.

IV. 'Reading' John Paul II's Social Encyclicals

John Paul II issued a veritable litany of official statements and made numerous addresses on the issues of worker rights, capitalism, globalization and social justice.[47] But perhaps the three best-known and most significant are his three encyclicals in such areas, *Laborum Exercens* (1981) – 'On Human Work'; *Sollicitudo Rei Socialis* (1988) – 'On Social Concern'; and *Centesimus Annus* (1991) – 'The Hundredth Year' (i.e., anniversary of *Rerum novarum*).

The esteemed moral theologian, Charles E. Curran, has warned us always to beware of bias in seeking to interpret the social teaching of any pope or era of the Church: '. . . one should note the frequent tendency of Catholics to find support for their own particular approach in the official church teaching'.[48] So we must be attentive to the dangers of any 'selective' reading, just as we must appreciate the significance of differences in the audiences to which certain teachings are aimed and, accordingly, the employment of differing forms of rhetoric within. Hence any assessment must take into account both ecclesiological and theological factors alike. But it is beyond doubt, and here Peter Phan, one of the world's leading experts in Catholic social teaching, has very recently demonstrated in a synoptic and incisive fashion that this is the case,[49] that John Paul II was at least *as* vociferous a critic of global capitalism as he was of state totalitarian communism.

Indeed, during his papacy, several new themes came to preoccupy what has become known as John Paul's variety of 'postmodern theology'. These included the importance of developing a global outlook and vision on social and moral issues, given the onset of globalization itself; second, the emergence of a 'culture of death', whereby human life was increasingly cheapened and therefore the sanctity of life gave way to an emphasis upon the 'quality of life'. Thus, for example, euthanasia, abortion on demand, mass warfare and the genetic manipulation of human life all became commonplace without much resistance on the part of many societies. And, third, I would go further than other commentators and suggest that if, as we have already acknowledged, John Paul has much to teach that was contra Marxism, then it is also clear that he had even more to say that was contra capitalism.[50] In particular, he lamented and continuously attacked the 'cancer of consumerism' that we have outlined above. Fourth, he constantly addressed the needs and exploitation of the so-called 'developing' world that was becoming increasingly exploited anew in this age of globalization.

1. John Paul II on alienation, work and property

Let us illustrate the commitment of John Paul II to the enhancement of the lives of workers and, indeed, towards the development of a theology *for* workers by focusing upon typical passages from his many writings on the subject of alienation. Thus, on the one hundredth anniversary of *Rerum novarum*, he declared that the entire notion of selling oneself for material gain, i.e. of the prevalent capitalist model of work, was fundamentally flawed and self-contradictory from a Christian standpoint.[51] For John Paul, alienation deprives human beings of their capacities for those very aspects of human life that set it apart and make it extraordinary:

> . . . a man is alienated if he refuses to transcend himself and to live the experience of self-giving and of the formation of an authentic human community oriented towards his final destiny, which is God. A society is alienated if its forms of social organization, production and consumption make it more difficult to offer this gift of self and to establish this solidarity between people.[52]

And for anyone who doubts the severity of John Paul II's critique of global capitalism, let them ponder the following definition of the contemporary forms of alienation that beset the workers of the world today:

> Alienation is also found in work, when it is organized so as to ensure maximum returns and profits with no concern whether the worker, through his own labour, grows or diminishes as a person, either through increased sharing in a supportive community, or through increased isolation in a maze of relationships marked by destructive competitiveness, in which he is only a means and not an end.[53]

Much in John Paul II's teaching – despite certain methodological backtracking – contributed to the formation of a critical yet constructive Catholic social ethics and political theology for these times. John Paul wrote at length on most of the key issues that we have addressed in this chapter and offered a particularly incisive critique, perhaps most of all, against neo-liberalism and its capitalistic consequences for human life:

> A system known as 'neo-liberalism' increasingly prevails, based on a purely economic conception of the human being. This system considers profit and the law of the market as its only parameter, to the detriment of the dignity and the respect due to individuals and peoples. At times this system has become the ideological justification for certain attitudes and behaviour in the social and political spheres, leading to the neglect of the weaker members of society. Indeed the poor are becoming ever more numerous, victims of specific policies and structures.[54]

Indeed, John Paul also offered a damning indictment of that life-numbing consumerism,[55] our self-destructive propensity for desiring what *cannot* make us happy, to which we have already referred.

But, naturally, critical questions must also be acknowledged here. John Paul II's social teachings raise further questions. In particular, elsewhere I have questioned the consistency of his teachings on globalization.[56] And Gregory Baum has discussed the Church's general 'ambivalence' on several key issues pertaining to social justice and, in particular, the option for the poor, throughout history.[57] But nonetheless great hope can come from the ongoing engagement of the Church with the most pressing social problems and challenges of the day. Baum even speaks of the sadness Christians feel over the realization that the Church has, at times, been complicit in injustice as being 'moments of divine grace delivering them from blindness. They are released from their dark night when they are allowed to acknowledge God as the infinite source of liberation, justice and mercy'.[58]

Hence, in the final analysis, we have cause for much hope for there is so much *continuity* in church teaching on each and every one of the key issues pertaining to the world of work and the plight of workers, from the groundbreaking developments in the 1960s, throughout the pontificate of John Paul II and down to the present day. In particular, such continuity can be seen in how, in both John Paul's teachings and those debates in Catholic social ethics that were contemporaneous with his papacy and since, there is a demonstrable continued centrality of such crucial themes as human dignity, authentic human being, and the priority of labour.[59] Here compare these uncompromising words from John Paul's address to the Canadian Episcopate in 1984:

The needs of the poor must take priority over the desires of the rich, the rights of workers over the maximization of profits, and the preservation of the environment over uncontrolled industrial expansion, and production to meet social needs over production for military purposes.[60]

And, finally, of course, the fourth area where greater continuity has thankfully been witnessed in recent decades is in relation to the Church's (because of its historic testimony to God's own) preferential Option for the Poor.[61] On each of these issues John Paul II frequently surprised and indeed at times even shocked those Catholics who believed that theological and ecclesiological conservatism naturally goes hand in hand with political and economic conservatism. Thus Peter Phan has charted a shift in the thinking of many within the Church here, through attention to the concept of 'political holiness':

> . . . political holiness fosters a set of virtues and practices that were either neglected or even derogated by traditional spirituality. For example, whereas traditional spirituality uniformly regards anger as a vice to be controlled, political spirituality sees it as a necessary and beneficial emotional reaction to systemic and organized injustice and oppression. This anger is the opposite of indifference and lack of courage. Rather than a vice to be avoided, this moral indignation is a force impelling compassion for the victims and action to help them regain their humanity.[62]

Indeed, one might well conclude that, on social issues, John Paul II could even be labelled as what most schools of thought would term a *radical*. And in this he is in very good company throughout the history of the Christian tradition in its entirety.[63]

2. The future of Catholic social ethics?

Thus, despite the best efforts of those on the political and economic Right, or even, today, in the 'centre' as well as for any who choose expediency over principle, Catholic social ethics remains and will continue to develop further as a powerful ally for oppressed and alienated workers. Let us attempt to draw towards some constructive conclusions, then, by distilling the wisdom of Catholic social ethics in the service of shaping a contemporary (and enduring) theology for workers. In order to do so, we must first revisit the horror of the 'dark night of the working soul'.

V. Authentic and Inauthentic Existence

In the main, then, this 'old' problem and its mutating and rampant contemporary forms represent the primary 'evil' (in terms of consequence, as opposed to causality) for the workers of the contemporary world today. For if God calls us to fuller being, which means a positive response to the offer of God's self-communication (given *in the midst* of our day-to-day lives), then if workers today are alienated from their very selves, their ex-istence – their standing out – is one, not of closer union with God and with other persons, but is rather a standing out from their own souls and the souls of their community. It thus prevents them from 'seeing' God, from responding positively to that gracious offer of self-communication, that call to communion with the divine Trinity, for they are caught up in the literally dehumanizing forces of alienating work.

St Richard of Chichester prayed, daily, for three things: to see God more clearly, to love God more dearly and to follow God more nearly. Alienating work prevents today's workers from even aspiring towards a greater awareness of God's loving and communal self, the first of these prayers. It thus stands in the way of our capacity for growth in our loving God. If alienating work stands between the worker and the awareness of God, the love of God, and prevents the worker from better following God's ways, then such work is a daily occasion of dehumanizing sin. It is nothing less than an evil, a 'social sin'.

Note, the Church is called to play a significant role in discerning, confronting and defeating *social sin*, which 'is every sin committed against the justice due in relations between individuals, between the individual and the community, and also between the community and the individual', just as social sin involves all infringements of rights, against human dignity and against the common good itself.[64] What of the nature of this alienation and the Church's various responses to it?

Inauthentic existence

Those who accuse the Church of being too timid in its critique of injustice might here find much to comfort and inspire them. For here the teaching of the Church – in tandem with numerous other voices – would appear to be saying something along the following lines.

1. 'The herd'
Inauthentic existence, admittedly, can sometimes be easier, less complicated and even, at times, more alluring. But it means we simply follow the crowd, we designate our freedom and so eventually lose it. We follow the 'herd', we seek to be like others more and more, rather than be authentic selves (here

globalization appears only to ensure that difference and true choice are eradicated as much as possible). Fear drives such slavish conformity.

And in the world of work it is easier not to stand up for the rights of either oneself or others. Instead play the games, drown in the bureaucracy. Undermine colleagues as if that could ever *truly* benefit yourself. Refuse to face the startlingly obvious fact that collectivistic action is in the interests of *all* workers. Stand alone and you are alone. Align yourself with coteries and the powerful and you compromise your dignity more than their exploitation of you could ever do. Refuse to support unions, to take industrial action to secure more just terms and conditions and to oppose all forms of injustice. Connive in undermining such, and you wipe away further elements of your own subjectivity and so the possibility of authentic human being in the process.

Play the game of 'presenteeism', of only ever telling those with power and authority what you believe they wish to hear, and you are well down the road to a fully blown form of alienated existence. Neglect your health, your loved ones, your friends, even your soul, for the sake of 'the job' or 'the firm' or 'the organisation', 'party', even 'church' etc. and you insult the gift of freedom, dignity and that transcendent character that God has so lovingly bestowed upon you. You have fallen prey to the vice of alienation and you have connived in making your life a thousand times less fulfilling and less extraordinary than it might have been. You have blotted out the sense of God, you have stifled your capacity to respond to God's love and to love God in the midst of everyday existence and to love others in return. You have wandered as far from the path that God calls you to follow as is possible. You may perceive of yourself as a 'good', a 'hard', an 'efficient' or even a 'loyal' worker, but that is worthless – you are as a 'whitewashed tomb': inside your very soul is relentlessly decaying.

2. The new slaves

Far too many, perhaps even the majority of workers today, then, connive in their own enslavement. This comes about because of an 'inversion of values', whereby what is detrimental to our personal and collective well-being is deemed to be 'good' and worthy of pursuit (or at least '*necessary*' to pursue), and what is *actually* good for our personal and collective well-being is at best seen as a luxurious path we cannot pursue or at worst is seen as somehow harmful to our own best interests. Thanks to such an inversion of values, and the subsequent effect this has, *capital* gains priority over *labour*: in other words, the pursuit and accumulation of greater wealth on behalf of the privileged few overrides the well-being and best interests of those who constitute the majority of the workforce who will never amass capital at such exorbitant levels and rates.

3. Means and ends

And so a confusion comes to pass about what are truly means to ends and what are the ends themselves. What really are literally (and can only ever be) means – such as the pursuit of greater capital or, indeed, work itself, become gradually installed as the actual *ends* for the sake of which all else must be undertaken. What are truly ends – the meaningful and existentially rewarding lives of human persons – become simply *means* to the greater accumulation of wealth. Subjects become objects and objects become subjects. The result is the greater prevalence of meaninglessness and absurdity in the lives of the many so that they seek only escapism from the truth, that they literally are throwing their lives away – they are pawns in someone else's game and nothing more. Such escapism, by definition, never brings anything but the most fleeting form of satisfaction and seldom any true fulfilment. It further adds to the sense of alienation from true self, from true life.

4. Fragmentation

Hence existence itself loses the sense of meaning, purpose, direction and fulfilment that we humans are inherently given to seek. Life loses its sense of balance, of worth even. Existence loses any notion of wholeness. Instead our lives become fragmented. We fill various roles here, and perform certain duties there, and seek momentary glimpses of satisfaction elsewhere. But we seldom are able to integrate, or rather re-integrate, the various aspects of our lives. Tension and torsion, often with as many physical and psychological, spiritual and existential consequences are the result of such fragmentation.

In theological terms, we become . . .

5. Cut off from God, from others, and from our true 'self'

But Catholic theology does not allow such inauthentic existence to go unchallenged. Karl Rahner spoke of the phenomenon of sin, which is the result of disharmony 'between what is within us and what is outside, between freedom and necessity, flesh and spirit, the individual and society'.[65] Such disharmony can be 'overcome only by God's grace'.[66] Rahner here captures the essence of the disease of alienation very well. And the antidote?

> Christ delivered us not only from death, the most radical effect of our fall, but from every other outward sign of our separation from God. In this way he has delivered us also from the tiresomeness, drabness and (virtual) depersonalization of work. Through the grace of Jesus Christ, therefore, and not through any merit inherent in itself, work, when 'done in the Lord', helps to form in us the attitude and disposition which God desires in those he invites to his eternal feast: that patience by which we can bear everyday witness to our faith, that faithfulness

and detachment which spring from the Christian sense of responsibility, and that unselfishness which is the very food of love.[67]

If this be true, what then does the collective and accumulated wisdom of Catholic social teaching have to suggest as an alternative? What might constitute *authentic existence*?

Authentic existence

1. Well-being, fulfilment, fully human

The 'authentic' life that Christians believe God calls all to live is a life where we exist well – literally of human 'well-*being*'. Such an existence consists in 'fulfilment' – life, love, happiness, community, a sense of making a positive difference, a sense of wonder, awe and sublimity on occasion, the freedom and energies to be creative (here taking the Christian doctrine of creation fully seriously), to restore those energies, to re-*create* – to play. To share, to sense the collective binds of partner, of family, of community, of society, of the human family. To *be* fully human – i.e. to live out the Christian anthropology – to be able, in each and every day, to try and respond in a positive fashion to God's loving offer of self-communication and hence communion. To have the understanding and/or guidance, as well as the means and energies necessary to avoid wandering off the path to true fulfilment, to avoid 'missing the mark' of *being* truly, i.e., to avoid sin.

2. Being 'whole': human equilibrium

Thus to learn from Jesus' healing throughout his mission: he said that faith made people 'whole'. All of his healing worked towards the miraculous transformation of human lives (in the face of a society beset by the exploitative and alienating forces that made authentic human existence so difficult). In today's terms, we might speak of trying to find 'equilibrium' in our lives, in our very selves – trying to restore our souls to that sense of wholeness, rather than allowing our very selves to be torn apart in a destructive multitude of directions.

3. Relation to God – being itself

Christian anthropology, then, relates so much to Christian theology. As articulated so well by theologians such as Karl Rahner, God is that limitless horizon upon which all other horizons (i.e. the individual and collective lives of human persons) meet. God is closer to us than we are to our very selves, for God is being itself: insofar as anything exists, God is the condition for the possibility of its existing at all. And human beings are called to exist, to *be* in as full a form as possible. To do so, we need to stay in touch with, close to, that which brings us into and sustains us in our existence – to God.

4. Subject and object

Thus authentic human existence consists of being able to orient the life of oneself and make a contribution towards orienting the lives of one's multitudinous communities (from partner to family to school, community, society etc.) – being able to exercise one's freedom towards the ends of truth, justice, love and freedom itself. Towards both personal and collective fulfilment, towards fuller being. In this sense the Danish philosopher Søren Kierkegaard has so much inspiration to offer, both in his famous maxim that 'truth *is* subjectivity', and in the tragic stories within his own life where he felt that he could not fully actualize his own subjectivity.

The path towards alienation begins when we literally 'lose control' – by which I mean forces remove the possibility of our actualizing our subjectivity. Thus we become mere 'objects', things to be 'used' towards the ends of others, towards the inhuman ends of inhuman organizations, corporations, governments and, sadly, sometimes even of churches. We are deprived of autonomy and subject to heteronomous control.[68] We become object not subject, commodities to be used and abused, we become dehumanized. And thus we are not our true selves. We are alien to that self which God called into existence and calls to fuller communion.

5. Dignity and rights – our intrinsic worth

But such can be resisted if we, collectively and individually, never lose sight of that very fact that our dignity is inherent and no one has it in their gift, nor can it ultimately be taken away – it can only be crushed, suppressed, denied, but the light of this dignity never fully goes out because of the very fact that it is fundamentally linked to the belief that we have been created in the image and likeness of God. Thus, on the basis of this inherent dignity, which is the gift of no person or institution, we therefore have numerous inalienable rights that should be upheld. In the world of work, then, the Churches – in partnership with other individuals and organizations[69] – must stand up for and be proactive in defending our intrinsic worth and those rights which safeguard both this and our inherent dignity. The alternative is a very vicious circle indeed.

6. The transcendental character of human nature

The concept of alienation needs to be led back to the Christian vision of reality, by recognizing in alienation a reversal of means and ends. When man does not recognize in himself and in others the value and grandeur of the human person, he effectively deprives himself of the possibility of benefiting from his humanity and of entering into that relationship of solidarity and communion with others for which God created him. Indeed, it is through the free gift of self that man truly finds himself. This gift is made possible by the human person's essential 'capacity for transcendence'.[70]

Hence theology and anthropology interplay once more. Our inherent dignity and intrinsic worth point towards our created being and therefore our at-one-ness with that which called us into being. In the midst of our everyday lives we sense the pull towards that which brought us into being. Both Rahner and Bernard Lonergan, as with so many of the mystics in Christian history (as in so many other faiths), speak at length of the transcendental character of human nature. But the important thing to appreciate, and here we simply consolidate our earlier considerations, is that they seek to emphasize that we attend to the transcendental aspect of our existence *in the midst* of our everyday lives – it is not a question of trans-cendental/mundane balance but rather one of realizing and appreciating that every aspect of our lives can be fired with wonder.

As the Protestant theologian, Paul Tillich, might have put it then, this, literally, is authentic ex-istence. A standing out of the literally mundane to glimpse not simply eternity but to be dazzled by the blinding and unconditional love of God. Gerard Manley Hopkins said that the world is charged with God's grandeur and in doing so, I think he – like Andrew Marvell and the other metaphysical poets before him – had something similar in mind: look around you and see beyond what presently encapsu-lates your soul. Realize the glory of that soul's freedom and strive to ensure that its freedom and purity of unfettered being is seldom sacrificed for any other end. The Church's *Compendium on Social Doctrine*, itself, thus states that, 'The human person, in himself and in his vocation, transcends the limits of the created universe, of society, and of history: his ultimate end is God himself, who has revealed himself to men in order to invite them and receive them into communion with himself.'[71] Indeed, at the opening of §49 of the *Compendium*, the Church is charged with the mission of being both a sign of *and* a defender of 'the transcendence of the human person'. As Gregory Baum has argued:

> Christians believe that the infinite and incomprehensible source of all life, love, and justice, which they call God (and see revealed in Jesus Christ), is operative in human history, especially in people's struggles against injustice and oppression. To stand against the established powers in solidarity with workers and the poor is for Christians a place of new religious experience.[72]

Concluding remarks

'Workers of the world unite' is thus a call to communion. Insofar as Christianity retains empowering deontological moral pathways (i.e. the notion that something is a 'Christian duty'), workers must cease to be complicit in maintaining the forces of alienation. Hence the Church can and does enter into all forms of partnership[73] that strive to fight for justice for all workers so that true and authentic being might prosper.

Unless it is truly fulfilling and oriented towards the good, *working is antithetical to being*. Any Christian who is complicit in such is therefore in a state of sin. Any Christian who exploits workers whom they employ or manage (including within the Church) and who demeans their *God-given* dignity in any way whatsoever, is in a far more serious state of sin altogether.

No tortured separatist Church/world, grace/nature form of thinking will suffice here. The judgement of the Catholic Church's teaching on these matters is unambiguous. The alienation and exploitation of workers are sinful conditions. Those who are complicit in such are therefore sinners.

Better to repent and believe the good news: consider the lilies of the field and this may help wean oneself off the 'market forces' mantra that leads to the lie of the work ethic, which is neither truly Protestant nor Catholic and is not even simply irreligious, but is rather *counter* to everything the world's major religions stand for, including, perhaps especially, Christianity. I end by echoing some further inspiring words, in this book, by Peter Phan, who, in all his many works, helps to illustrate just how much Christianity truly is a spirituality that does justice:

> Christian social spirituality also professes faith in the triune God, but it sees the problem of faith today to consist not so much in atheism as in idolatry. The real issue for Christian social spirituality is not whether God *exists* but whether the God one worships is the *true* God, a masked idol or the God who reveals himself as the Father of Jesus and the Sender of the Spirit and whose reign is one of truth and justice and peace, especially for the poor and the marginalized. This triune God, constituted by the three divine Persons in absolute equality, perfect communion, and mutual love, is Christianity's social agenda in a nutshell. Like the all-embracing Trinity in Andrej Rublev's famous icon, Christians welcome all, especially those deprived of human dignity, to the table of life, peace, justice, and love.[74]

Notes

1. In this chapter I address, in the main, the situation in the Euro-North American world (particularly the English-speaking sectors of it). Nonetheless, many issues have a global relevance and are becoming issues of global concern all the more due to the impact of globalization itself.
2. Pontifical Council for Justice and Peace, *Compendium of the Social Doctrine of the Church* (Rome: Libreria Editrice Vaticana, 2004), §272 cf. also, John Paul II, *Laborem Exercens* (1981), §6, *Catechism of the Catholic Church*, §2428 and *Centesimus Annus* (1991), §832.

3. No less a person than the former director-general of the CBI admits this fact: http://www.globalagendamagazine.com/2005/howarddavies.asp. See also, http://www.tuc.org.uk/work_life/tuc–11782-f0.pdf, and http://www.worksmart.org.uk/workyourproperhoursday.

4. This too is admitted by the former director-general of the CBI: http://www.globalagendamagazine.com/2005/howarddavies.asp. See also, http://www.tuc.org.uk/work_life/tuc–11782-f0.pdf and http://www.worksmart.org.uk/workyourproperhoursday.

5. Gerry Robinson, *I'll Show Them Who's Boss: The Six Secrets of Successful Management* (London, BBC Books), p. 175. As the adage goes, if you continuously chop wood without ever pausing long enough to sharpen your axe, you will be always chopping with a blunt blade.

6. Ibid., p. 176 (my italics).

7. *The Challenge of Affluence: Self-control and Well-Being in Britain and the United States Since 1950* (Oxford, Oxford University Press, 2006) – as discussed by Oliver James, 'Workaholic Consumerism is Now a Treadmill and a Curse', *The Guardian* (Tuesday 2 May 2006), p. 28. See also, James' forthcoming study *Affluenza: How to be Successful and Stay Sane* (Vermilion, 2006). Cf. also, Oliver James, 'Toil and Trouble', *Observer Magazine* (7 August 2005), p. 57.

8. 'Britons Put Work and Fun before Babies: ICM Poll Reveals Changing Social Attitudes Behind UK's Low Birthrate', leading article, *The Guardian* (Tuesday 2 May 2006), p. 1. See the results of the *Guardian/ICM* survey discussed in the same edition (pp. 6–7) and further discussed in editions later that week.

9. Cf. 'How Parenthood Lost its Charm', a Special Report also in *The Guardian* (Wednesday 3 May 2006), p. 23.

10. Cf., for example, World Health Organization (WHO), *Global Burden of Disease Survey*, which predicts work-related stress will be the second most common cause of disability by 2020. Its reports are available at http://www.who.int/whr/2006/en/index.html.

11. Here cf. also a brief article by Gerard Mannion, 'Defending Human Dignity in the Catholic Workplace', *The Pastoral Review*, vol. 1, no. 2 (2005), pp. 36–9.

12. Cf. David J. O'Brien and Thomas A. Shannon (eds), *Catholic Social Thought – The Documentary Heritage* (Maryknoll: Orbis, 1995); Roger Aubert, *Catholic Social Teaching: An Historical Perspective* (Milwaukee: Marquette University Press, 2003); Mary Elsbernd, 'Social Ethics', *Theological Studies* 66 (2005), pp. 137–58; Rodger Charles, *Christian Social Witness and Teaching: The Catholic Tradition from Genesis to Centesimus Annus* (Leominster: Gracewing, 2001) and also his *An Introduction to Catholic Social Teaching* (Oxford: Family Publications, 1999) (and accompanying *Study Guide*, 2001); Charles E. Curran, *Catholic Social Teaching, 1891 to the Present: A Historical, Theological and Ethical Analysis*

(Washington, Georgetown University Press, 2002). See also, Peter Henroit, Edward DeBerri and Michael J. Schulthels, *Catholic Social Teaching: Our Best Kept Secret* (Maryknoll: Orbis, 1988); P. Misner, *Social Catholicism in Europe* (New York: Crossroad, 1991); Donal Dorr, *Option for the Poor: One Hundred Years of Catholic Social Teaching* (Maryknoll: Orbis, 1992).

13. For a sample of key sources on Catholic social teaching on work, see Peter C. Phan, *Social Thought*, vol. 20 of *Message of the Fathers of the Church* (Wilmington: Michael Glazier, 1984); Charles E. Curran, *Directions in Catholic Social Ethics* (Notre Dame, University of Notre Dame Press, 1995); *Gaudium et Spes*, §64.

14. On the implications of this for work cf., for example, *Centesimus Annus*, §273.

15. Cf., for example, Gregory Baum (ed.) *Work and Religion, Concilium* 131 (New York: Seabury Press, 1980); Gregory Baum, *The Priority of Labor: A Commentary on 'Laborem exercens', Encyclical Letter of Pope John Paul II* (New York: Paulist Press, 1982); Marie-Domique Chenu, *The Theology of Work: An Exploration* (Chicago, Henry Regnery, 1966); Edwin Kaiser, *Theology of Work* (Westminster, MD: Newman Press, 1966); W. Charlton, *The Christian Response to Industrial Capitalism* (London: Sheed and Ward, 1976). See footnotes nos 54 and 60 below.

16. Here cf., for example, *Compendium*, §§267, 335. On 'capital and labour', see, for example, §§277, 338, 361ff.

17. Cf., for example, Robert Nozick, *Anarchy, State and Utopia*.

18. 'Freedom in Community between Globalization and Individualism – Market Value and Human Dignity', in his *God for a Secular Society: The Public Relevance of Theology* (London, SCM, 1999), p. 153.

19. Norman Lamont in John Major's Conservative Government.

20. On global 'capital' cf. *Compendium*, §§361, 368, 370.

21. Examples here are most numerous, and the annals of the courts of litigation chart the story of those who found that the Church frequently finds it difficult to practise that which it preaches on social justice and workers' rights.

22. Cf., *Compendium*, §§300, 310, 312, 321, 361–70, 442, 564. See also, G. Mannion, 'What's in a Name? Hermeneutical Questions on "Globalisation", Catholicity and Ecumenism', *New Blackfriars*, 86/204–15 (March 2005), pp. 204–15; T. Howland Sanks, 'Globalization and the Church's Social Mission', *Theological Studies*, 60 (1999), pp. 625–51.

23. Statistics which illustrate the sorry truth of this statement can be viewed at the following sites: www.globalissues.org/TradeRelated/Facts.asp (accessed 24 August 2006); www.bread.org/hungerbasics/international. html (accessed 24 August 2006); www.undp.org/teams/english/ facts.htm (accessed 24 August 2006), www.thirdworld traveler.com/ Globalization/Globalization_FactsFigures.html (accessed 24 August

2006); www.makepovertyhistory.org; and the CIA World Factbook, www.cia.gov/cia/publications/factbook (accessed 24 August 2006).

24. Cf. Peter C. Phan, 'Human Freedom and the Free Market Economy: Pope John Paul II's Critique of Capitalism', in *The World and I: Innovative Approaches to Peace* (May–June 2005), 46–55.

25. And Karl Barth in his preface to the latter's *Essence of Christianity* (New York: Harper Torch, 1957).

26. Karl Rahner, 'Theology and Anthropology', vol. IX of *Theological Investigations* (London: Darton, Longman and Todd, 1972), pp. 28–45.

27. Here, cf., *Centesimus Annus* (1991).

28. Gregory Baum, *Amazing Church: A Catholic Theologian Remembers a Half Century of Change* (Maryknoll: Orbis, 2005), p. 9. See also Gregory Baum, 'Modernity: A Sociological Perspective', in *The Debate on Modernity*, ed. Claude Geffré and Jean-Pierre Jossua, *Concilium* (London: SCM, 1992–96), pp. 4–9, esp. 7–8.

29. Such language is neither emotive nor exaggerated but, as witnessed through much of the literature, is simply a most apt analogy for this serious challenge to the realm of workers.

30. An interesting study here is John E. Tropman, *The Catholic Ethic and the Spirit of Community* (Washington: Georgetown University Press, 2002).

31. And his notion of the 'unhappy consciousness' that is separated from its own essence and hence literally suffers from a division in its own nature. See Hegel's *Phenomenology of Spirit*, 1807. The concept of 'alienation' relates to the German *Entfremdung* (estrangement) and *Entäußerung* (externalization). Hegel's own solution was, famously, the resolution of such division via dialectical processes towards a synthesis which would improve upon the initial situation. Nonetheless, despite the philosophical absolute idealism towards the ends of which Hegel employed his theory, his own personal history, with his hatred of certain jobs that he was forced – through financial necessity – to undertake, with the resulting and frequent bouts of severe depression that ensued, suggests that the notion of the 'unhappy consciousness' certainly found much inspiration in the struggles of his own life. Søren Kierkegaard appears to have realized the personal existential implications of Hegel's concept in a most vivid fashion.

32. The literature on Marx is obviously innumerable. For our purposes in this chapter: for two now-classic theological appreciations, see Denys Turner's *Marxism and Christianity* (Oxford: Blackwell, 1983) and his later 'Liberation Theology, Marxism and the Vatican' in Christopher Rowland (ed.), *The Cambridge Companion to John Paul II* (Cambridge, Cambridge University Press, 1998) and also Nicholas Lash, *A Matter of Hope* (London: Darton, Longman and Todd, 1981). A popular and readable recent study of Marx is Francis Wheen, *Karl Marx* (London: Fourth Estate, 1999).

33. Karl Marx, 'Estranged Labour', from his *Economic and Philosophical Manuscripts*, 1844 (written between April and August that year), *Marx–Engels Gesamtausgabe*, I/3, pp. 85–6. These were, however, not published until some time after Marx's death. Translation here by T.B. Bottomore and taken from Karl Marx, 'Alienated Labour', in Kenneth Thompson and Jeremy Turnstall (eds), *Sociological Perspectives* (Harmondsworth: Penguin, for the Open University, 1971), p. 55. Full text available in Karl Marx, *Economic and Philosophic Manuscripts*, trans. Martin Mulligan (Moscow: Progress Publishers, 1959), vol. 3. Available online at http://www.marxists.org/archive/marx/works/1844/ manuscripts/labour.htm (accessed 14 September 2006). Also available in vol. 3 of the 49 volumes of *Marx–Engels Collected Works* (Lawrence & Wishart, 1975–2002). Also abridged selections available in *Karl Marx: Selected Writings in Sociology and in Social Philosophy*, ed. T.B. Bottomore and Maximilien Rubel (Harmondsworth: Penguin, 1961), p. 177.
34. Marx, 'Alienated Labour', in Thompson and Turnstall (eds), *Sociological Perspectives*, p. 55.
35. Herbert Marcuse, *One-Dimensional Man: Studies in the Ideology of Advanced Industrial Society* (London, Ark edn, 1986, first published in 1964), p. 9.
36. Ibid., p. 11.
37. Ibid., p. 12.
38. Billy Bragg, 'North Sea Bubble', from the Album *Don't Try This at Home*, 1991.
39. cf. Nicholas Boyle, *Who are We Now?* (London: Darton, Longman and Todd, 1998).
40. English translation: *Being and Having* (London: Collins, 1965).
41. London: Abacus, 1979.
42. J. Moltmann, 'Freedom in Community between Globalization and Individualism', p. 157.
43. Here and in much of what follows, I am indebted to the painstaking analytical and historical work of Charles E. Curran. One essay, in particular, which offers a brief summary of many of these significant changes is his 'The Changing Anthropological Bases of Catholic Social Ethics', in *Directions in Catholic Social Ethics* (Notre Dame, University of Notre Dame Press, 1985).
44. See the works by the Benedictine, Tom Cullinan.
45. Though not, recent research would suggest, against Marxism per se.
46. For example, one question that needs to be discussed here is whether the emphasis should be upon 'social doctrine' or social *teachings*: in other words, should the Church issue official pronouncements, almost akin to a social ideology of her own, or should she seek to contribute to the ongoing debates and campaigns for justice at different times and in different places, albeit in the light of her fundamental principles in this

area? i.e., should she proceed in open acknowledgment that her own social thought and activism is also part of an evolving tradition?

47. For an at-once very insightful and readable account of John Paul II's social teaching, cf., ch. 10 of Judith A. Merkle, *From the Heart of the Church: The Catholic Social Tradition* (Collegeville: Michael Glazier, 2004), pp. 209–38.

48. 'The Changing Anthropological Bases of Catholic Social Ethics' *op. cit.*

49. Peter C. Phan, 'Human Freedom and the Free Market Economy: Pope John Paul II's Critique of Capitalism', see note 24.

50. Richard T. DeGeorge offers an assessment from a political philosopher. Yet, although he is correct in his assessment that John Paul II sought to seize the moral 'high ground' from Marxism, DeGeorge is perhaps a touch blind to the indictment of the United States in that *all* of John Paul II's teachings on these issues challenge the USA. See his 'Decoding the Pope's Social Encyclicals', ch. 18 of Charles E. Curran and Richard A. McCormick (eds), *John Paul II and Moral Theology* (New York: Paulist, 1998), pp. 255–75.

51. e.g., 'Man cannot give himself to a purely human plan for reality, to an abstract ideal or to a false utopia. As a person, he can give himself to another person or to other persons, and ultimately to God, who is the author of his being and who alone can fully accept his gift', *Centesimus Annus*, §41.

52. *Centesimus Annus*, §41, see also *Compendium*, §47.

53. *Centesimus Annus*, §42. For the various discussions of alienation in the *Compendium*, see §§47, 116, 272, 280, 348, 350, 374, 462.

54. John Paul II, *Ecclesia in America*, §56 (22 January 1999), discussed by Baum, *Amazing Church*, p. 67; cf., also, *Centesimus Annus*, §40. Here, see also, Gregory Baum, 'An Ethical Critique of Capitalism: Contributions of Modern Catholic Social Teaching', and David L. Schindler, 'Neoconservative Economics and the Church's "Authentic Theology of Human Liberation" ', chs 17 and 25, respectively, of Charles Curran and Richard A. McCormick (eds), *John Paul II and Moral Theology* (New York: Paulist, 1998), pp. 237–54 and 340–9; Phan, 'Human Freedom and the Free Market Economy: Pope John Paul II's Critique of Capitalism'; Merkle, *From the Heart of the Church*, pp. 209–14 and, on John Paul II's critique of globalization in general, Mannion, 'What's in a Name?'.

55. *Solicitudo Rei Socialis*, §28, *Centesimus Annus*, §36, 41.

56. Mannion, 'What's in a Name?'; see also, Baum, *Amazing Church*, pp. 66–8.

57. Baum, *Amazing Church*, pp. 78–82, esp., p. 80:

> Over the last half-century, Catholics have come to recognize that in the Church's long history, an ideological distortion of the

Gospel has at times legitimated oppressive structures, blessed the practice of violence, fostered the subjugation of women, promoted contempt for Protestants, produced hostility towards the Jews, and blinded Catholics to the truth and holiness found in the world's religions. These ideological distortions may have been consciously introduced by certain powerful individuals, but once they were integrated into Catholic discourses and practice, they acted like structures shaping the consciousness of believers and thus causing damage and suffering of innocent people.

58. Ibid., p. 81. He goes on to speak of the 'Option for the Poor' as leading to 'a deeper understanding of the eucharistic celebration of Christ's death and resurrection', p. 82. Along similar lines, see Phan, and Merkle, *From the Heart of the Church*, pp. 221–2 and 222 n. 12.
59. Cf. *Laborem Exercens*, §6, 12 and *Centesimus Annus*, §31, 32.
60. As discussed in Gregory Baum, *Amazing Church*, p. 59. On John Paul II on the priority of labour over capital in general, see pp. 60–8. See, also, Peter C. Phan, 'Human Freedom':

> This priority is confirmed by the very fact that 'capital,' that is, 'not only the natural resources placed at man's disposal but also the whole collection of means by which man appropriates natural resources and transforms them in accordance with his needs,' are themselves, the pope points out, '*the result of the historical heritage of human labor*' (*LE* §12.4). For John Paul, whenever there is a reversal of this order, placing capital above labor, there is 'capitalism.' This is precisely 'the error of early capitalism' when 'man is in a way treated on the same level as the whole complex of the material means of production, as an instrument and not in accordance with the true dignity of work – that is to say, where he is not treated as subject and maker, and for this reason as the true purpose of the whole process of production' (*LE* §7.3). In this respect, liberal capitalism is identical with Marxist collectivism, the pope points out, since both operate from the same errors which he calls 'economism' and 'materialism' (*LE* §13) or 'materialistic economism' (*LE* §7.3), treating human labor merely as 'merchandise' and commodities to be bought and sold, and as mere instrument to produce things and not as the way in which humans realize themselves. In other words, both capitalism and socialism maintain the priority of capital over labor.

61. Cf. *Laborem Exercens*, §8.
62. Peter C. Phan, 'Christian Social Spirituality: A Global Perspective', see

above. See also Gregory Baum on the Church's past 'ambivalence' on social issues.

63. See the collection of texts by Chris Rowland and Andrew Bradstock who introduce it thus:

> The Gospel of Jesus Christ, announcing the arrival of the kingdom or reign of God, offered a radical and subversive challenge to the world, its powers and authorities . . . Throughout Christian history – and particularly at times of crisis and social upheaval – there have emerged writings which, reflecting the values of the Kingdom, have engaged in searching critiques of the political order and promoted equality of wealth, power, gender or status. (*Radical Christian Writings* (Oxford: Blackwell, 2002), p. xvi).

64. *Compendium*, §118. Despite apparent opinions to the contrary in some quarters of the Church on the existence of such a concept.

65. Karl Rahner, 'On Work', in his volume, *Belief Today* (1964) (London: Sheed and Ward, 1973), p. 18.

66. Ibid.

67. Ibid., p. 19.

68. Here cf. Immanuel Kant on the need always to see human beings as ends-in-themselves and never as a means to another end. More theologically explicit, John Oman saw heteronomy as the fundamental root cause of all sin. Here cf. Adam Hood, 'John Oman: Personalism and Ethics', in John Elford and D. Gareth Jones (eds), *A Tangled Web* (forthcoming).

69. Cf. *Compendium*, §§12, 151.

70. *Centesimus Annus*, §41.

71. *Compendium*, §47, cf. *Dei Verbum*, §2, *Centesimus Annus*, §41.

72. Baum, 'An Ethical Critique of Capitalism', p. 252.

73. Here cf. *Laborem Exercens*, §8.

> To achieve social justice in the various parts of the world . . . there is need for ever new movements of the workers and with the workers. The solidarity must be present whenever it is called for by the social degrading of the subject of work, by exploitation of the workers and by the growing area of poverty and even hunger. The Church is firmly committed to this cause, for it considers it to be its mission, its service, its proof of its fidelity to Christ, so that it can truly be 'the Church of the poor'.

The significance of this passage is discussed by Gregory Baum, *Amazing Church*, p. 59. See also, Antonio Moser and Bernadino Leers, *Moral*

Theology: Dead Ends and Ways Forward (London: Burns & Oates, 1987), pp. 106–7. Cf. Ambassador Juan Somavía, 'The Church's Social Teaching and International Labour Organisations' "Decent Work" Strategy', in Pontifical Council for Justice and Peace, *Justice and Peace: An Ever Present Challenge* (Rome: Liberia Editrice Vaticana, 2004), pp. 84–109; Stefano Zamagini, 'Humanising the Economy: On the Relationship between Catholic Social Thinking and Economic Discourse', in J.S. Boswell, F.P. McHugh and J. Verstraeten (eds), *Catholic Social Thought: Twilight or Renaissance?* (Leuven: Leuven University Press, 2002), pp. 149–69. Baum states: 'The social struggle against the unjust order calls for the building of a solidarity network, possibly around a political party, that brings together labour unions and representative organizations of other disadvantaged groups. Such a network could receive the active support of all citizens who love justice, including church and synagogue groups' (Baum, 'An Ethical Critique of Capitalism', p. 251) – to which today we might add the support of other faith groups. Baum believes that '[w]hat emerges here is a more pluralistic concept of the left', ibid.

74. Peter C. Phan, 'Christian Social Spirituality', above, ch. 2.

Chapter 7

Embracing Leisure

Jayne Hoose

This chapter aims to explore the leisure phenomenon and lifestyle balance, moving towards a theology of leisure which might free us from some of those long-held bonds of productivity and status gained through work. The practical aim is to provide pointers which guide us to an appropriate valuing of leisure and lifestyle balance.

Being a resident in the UK, where we now have some of the longest working hours in Europe, and my past experience of working for church based employers, have both served to enhance a long-held feeling of a serious malaise within Western society and, in particular, within Christianity towards leisure. Leisure professionals and academics have fought hard to have their area of expertise taken seriously amongst both academic colleagues and professionals from other disciplines. This struggle for credibility continues despite increasing reports of work-related stress, rises in employee sick leave, employees increasingly expressing frustration about inadequate lifestyle balance and an increasing unease with the emphasis on the value of individuals being measured by their productivity and work-related status.

Whilst society at large struggles to confront and seriously address the emerging social problem of work–life balance,[1] anyone turning to the Church and theology will face equal difficulty in finding guidance and support. Indeed, it could be argued that church-based organizations are amongst the more difficult places in which to attempt an exploration of the work–life balance that encompasses *all* that encourages a healthy flourishing of *all* that makes us truly human.

Contemporary Leisure Definitions

An academic discussion of what we mean by leisure may seem superfluous to most of us. After all, we all know what leisure is, even if we feel we have a lifestyle where it is sadly lacking. It is, nevertheless, only through a more structured and in-depth examination of our understanding of the leisure phenomenon that we can identify the attitudes and beliefs which affect both societal and individual approaches to leisure. It is these attitudes and beliefs that form the basis of our difficulty in placing a value on leisure which facilitates a healthier lifestyle balance.

There are four major approaches to leisure which highlight a number of key issues that need to be addressed. These approaches involve exploring: (1) leisure as a concept of time, (2) leisure as an activity, (3) the concept of leisure as an attitude or state of mind and (4) the quality aspects of leisure.

Time

When we explore the approach to leisure which is time-based, a recurrent theme is to start from the point where leisure is presented as time left over from work. This immediately highlights core issues which are problematic for a positive and empowering approach to leisure. It sets up a leisure–work opposition. Such an approach can be clearly linked to the emergence of an industrial society and is heavily centred on the Protestant work ethic.[2] This concept of leisure prevents the freedom of discovery and expression that can be facilitated by an innate value to leisure. Leisure is benchmarked relative to other external expectations and roles. When this benchmark is specifically work it often leads to a perception of the need to earn leisure. This presents immediate problems for those who are unemployed, ill or primarily engaged in running the home and family. Not earning in the workplace can, and often is, translated into not having earned the right to leisure.

The leisure–work opposition which arises from the defining of leisure in relation to time can lead to very simplistic and constrained views and experiences of leisure. There are many more demands upon our time than simply work and leisure. There are many activities which relate to work but fall outside of the normal definition of the working day. A large group of the population, for example, spends significant amounts of time commuting. In addition, work–time boundaries are becoming difficult to define with the increasing expectations of social and so-called 'leisure' activities which relate to work, for example, evenings spent networking or entertaining visitors or clients – social and 'leisure' activities of necessity rather than choice. These activities may fall within the time definition of leisure but may not be experienced as 'leisurely' by the individuals concerned. This is a particular difficulty where a job makes the individual an ambassador for their employer – an experience that is frequently part of working for a church-based organization. Some posts can render the individual open to 24-hour, seven-day-a-week scrutiny by beneficiaries, partners and observers: for example, the aid worker who lives in the same building as colleagues or even local partners and is sharing meals, worship and leisure time with them, or the teacher living in close proximity to children, colleagues and parents. Vocational choices tend to be regarded as lifestyle choices in themselves, leading to work, life and leisure boundaries being especially blurred. This can lead to a 'feeling of never being off duty'.[3] This concept of time free from work is also extremely problematic for others whose primary occupation does not fall within defined hours or boundaries. Private domestic labour, traditionally undertaken by women, is notoriously ill-defined. Work and leisure are very difficult to separate. A family visit to the local leisure centre may equally be seen in the context of fulfilling a parental role or as joint family leisure.

Quantifying and identifying specific blocks of leisure time can actually be quite difficult. This does not, however, entirely negate the time-based approach when addressing lifestyle balance issues. The ability and/or willingness of an individual to identify any specific time slot which they would regard as their leisure time is often highly indicative of their lifestyle balance and their attitude towards it. An inability to indicate specific leisure time and space may mean the individual feels they cannot justify – have not earned – the right to leisure. A reticence to make such statements may equally arise from a feeling that others would not regard them as having earned such leisure and they therefore feel it is inappropriate to admit to the leisure they have.

Activities

Interestingly, when discussing leisure with individuals and to some extent with providers, we are most often presented with the identification of specific activities as leisure as opposed to blocks of time. This has led to the collation of numerous lists and directories of what are regarded as leisure activities. In turn, this has led to organizations and employers facilitating involvement in such activities in a bid to encourage healthier lifestyle balances. Again, this is problematic as participation in such activities can, hence, lead to an automatic assumption that the individual is therefore at leisure. This ignores the context of the activity and the individual's perception of it. For some individuals, attending the gym at work or participation in church social activities may be leisure. For others this may simply be a way of fulfilling what they perceive to be the expectations of the organization, colleagues or community. Such activities will therefore be based around fulfilling role expectations and obligations and may not be experienced as leisure at all. Accordingly, whilst an activity approach can provide a valuable tool which informs the provision for leisure and the individual's pursuit of leisure, we must avoid the pitfalls of approaching leisure purely from this perspective.

Attitude

To be truly at leisure involves much more than an allocation of time or a choice of activity. It is much richer and much more personal then either of these will allow. Much of this richness lies with the individuals themselves and their perception of what constitutes a leisure experience. Leisure is in essence highly individualistic and highly subjective. Different individuals will give value to different time, space and activities as leisure. This renders the list of leisure forms, environments and times limited only by individual perceptions. Leisure can hence take place at any time, in any place and in any form. It will also change as the individual changes. Whilst nightclubbing from dusk till dawn may be a highly prized leisure form during teenage years, such an experience may well later have none of the qualities sought from leisure by the same individual.

An attitude-based approach to leisure also means that it may well take place in time which other approaches would regard as work. A youth worker taking a group of young people rock climbing may well experience such an event as leisure. It is also possible that the same youth worker may experience one climbing trip as leisure whilst another trip is experienced very much as work. When leisure is defined using this approach, it is intrinsic to the individual and relies much more upon their attitude and perceptions. It is a phenomenon which is much more spiritual and much less about an experience which relies upon external factors like time slots, activity descriptions or social constructs and assumptions. It is much more about the meeting of individual, group and community needs which facilitate human development and flourishing.

Qualities

When exploring leisure time, leisure activities and attitudes towards leisure there are constant references made to specific qualities associated with the leisure experience. The quality most often directly or indirectly claimed for leisure is that of leisure as re-creative.[4] This re-creative quality has been strongly linked with leisure as supportive of work performance. In part, this arises from the development of leisure as a concept within industrial society and the notion of leisure being used as restorative or as a means of renewal from and in preparation for the working day. This supports the perception of leisure being earned as a reward for work and has led to leisure–work opposition becoming an essential defining quality and leisure being valued from a utilitarian perspective. Without work as the reference point, as in the case of someone who is unemployed, 'leisure' activities are often provided as and experienced as mere time-fillers.[5] As identified earlier, work–leisure opposition can be and often is socially promoted as an acceptable requirement for an individual to make a legitimate claim to leisure. Leisure's acceptance as an appropriate alternative to work for the promotion of human flourishing is rare.

Leisure activities can provide real opportunities for a sense of autonomy, a sense of achievement, a sense of belonging and outlets for creativity and self-expression. To limit these qualities to being an antidote to the work experience or mere time-filler is to define the individual from a starting point of productivity. To experience leisure qualities as intrinsic to the leisure experience requires a very different starting point which values leisure for leisure's sake and regards the individual more holistically.

Leisure for leisure's sake can incorporate a large element of personal pleasure. The strong ties of society to the work ethic have, however, limited the freedom individuals have felt in pursuing leisure for personal pleasure. Where work and productivity are highly prized and have strong societal approval and centrality, many find it very difficult to justify personal pleasure and even relaxation as motives for leisure. In such a context, leisure as personal pleasure can be viewed as unnecessarily self-indulgent. It is certainly often seen as a less admirable motive for the pursuit of leisure. It seems that there is a hierarchy of acceptability which sees recuperation from or for work closely followed by more socially accepted motives which involve commitment to family, community or society at large as clearly superior to personal development and pleasure. This perspective has also led to play being devalued as a quality of adult leisure – a quality which can incorporate the non-serious, non-productive, unpredictable, entertaining, fun, creative and escapist elements of leisure.

Personal pleasure, relaxation and play, however, do not necessitate a self-seeking, individualistic approach to leisure. An experience of community, for example, and the development of relationship skills which contribute to human/community flourishing can indeed be important by-products of the leisure experience which is sought for its own sake. This is especially the case where the leisure experience allows all masks to be dropped and a real connection to be made with others. It is after all only in such a context of honestly exposing the self to others that we can be truly open and receptive.

Leisure time is also often linked to the quality of freedom, that is, time free from other obligations. Freedom is seen as an important defining quality of leisure by most scholars. This is evident in the use of phrases like 'free time' and 'freedom from obligation' when defining leisure as a concept. Freedom can, however, be used and understood in many different ways. Freedom in a leisure context is usually viewed as involving freedom of choice, the pursuit of something from personal choice rather than because of external pressures or expectations. It is about an absence of imposition or obligation. Whilst a degree of freedom is valued as part of leisure, there is, however, much debate about the extent to which an individual can and does exercise that freedom of choice. It is indeed often argued that we never truly exercise complete freedom of choice but are merely given permission by society to exercise decision making within defined boundaries chosen by that society. How, why and by whom such boundaries are influenced and enforced then becomes an important question. There is no doubt that the exercising of freedom of choice is affected by individual relationships and by society at large. Key institutions, like the Church, can therefore exercise an important role in either the facilitation or constraining of the exercise of personal freedom.

Freedom which can occur as an integral part of the leisure experience is less explored: that sense of total abandonment of self and hence total receptivity. This opens the individual to a unique experience which allows growth, particularly spiritual growth, as opposed to simply seeking and earning a period of restorative activity. Such an experience of leisure, however, requires the development of key attitudes and skills in leisure which themselves are rarely addressed or explored.

The Church and Leisure

For anyone turning to the Church for enlightenment, support or education on a healthy attitude towards leisure, its qualities and values, they are left facing something of a void. There is little to be found in church documents specifically on leisure. As above, however, we find much that is or is not said in relation to work has inevitable consequences for leisure.

An obvious area of attention is that of observing the Sabbath, setting it apart from the rest of the week. This is often spoken of as having its origins as the day of rest following God's work on creation. The obvious trap becomes apparent when a direct link is made in setting aside the Sabbath from the 'working week'. Even where discussion centres on a day of observance as opposed to a day of rest, there is much written and much pressure brought to bear that relates this to the laws of the Sabbath and duty. There is often little recognition of the tension between the application of the law in order to facilitate human flourishing and the adaptation of human behaviour to suit the law. There is a need to be constantly vigilant to ensure that we recognize that 'The Sabbath was made for man, not man for the Sabbath'.[6] The tension between respecting such laws and laws being made for humanity and not humanity for the laws is often little recognized. Worship and prayer could, however, be seen as the ultimate leisure experience given the skills and spiritual development which allow us to abandon ourselves to God completely, especially where prayer and worship are not confined to a prescribed ritualistic pursuit and are freely chosen.

Given the close relationship we have established between work and leisure, another area where we might turn to the Church for guidance and role modelling is as an employer. In church-based organizations we often find, however, that, with the best of motives, because the work can often more readily be seen as vocational or 'forwarding the work of the gospel', there is a tendency to encourage each other to 'walk the extra mile', and to achieve more than resources would normally allow. It is easy to become task focused, as well as focused on being seen to fulfil those extra requirements, rather than taking the time to be, and to reflect on the way forward. It is easy to become focused on the individual as worker in such circumstances. Even prayer before the start of a meeting, with the best of intentions in contextualizing the meeting, can become focused on simply equipping us to be effective at the task.

It can be difficult to foster an atmosphere of promoting individual flourishing when tasks seem so urgent, but no one is equipped to walk that extra mile continually day after day after day. It is important that the Church is seen to set an example in respecting the individual much more holistically. This means not just allowing effective recuperation from the working day but also respecting the need for life space outside of work – time for genuine leisure, time to be.

This approach can no doubt at times seem counter to our commitments if we all rightly regard our work as not simply the way we earn a living but as part of the way we witness, an integral part of the way we live the gospel and are called to love. Nevertheless, there is clearly a need to confront religious values which compel any individual to work as hard as they possibly can. This culture is not Christian and should not be encouraged to be valued as Christian. It does not promote the well-being of individuals, relationships or communities. Individuals should be actively discouraged from striving to be seen to 'walk the extra mile' to feel valued. Such a work-centred culture not only leads to ill-health, poor performance, demotivation and the breakdown of healthy work and personal relationships, it denies our calling to 'love our neighbour as ourselves'.[7] Scripture calls us not just to love our neighbour but to love ourselves. It clearly implies we must first learn to love ourselves in order to be able truly to love others. Those who overwork and limit their development through a lack of lifestyle balance will inevitably require the same of others. Even if not directly expected, this will be implied through example and reflected values.

Sadly, alongside society more broadly, the Church seems to have struggled with embracing the positives of the post-industrial society from which a broader-based self-development and 'freedom' can arise – a move away from the limiting idolization of productivity and value through work.[8] We have not been equipped as Christians positively to embrace the leisure revolution and have fallen back into a work-centred lifestyle. Even outside work, we so often chase status through competitive, productive leisure and consumerism to the extent of pursuing leisure shopping as a recognized activity and hence promoting consumerism as leisure. We chase material ways of flaunting 'freedom' through affluence rather than exercising and enjoying the freedom we have. There is even a sense of the need to be seen to work hard at being non-productive and seeking status through this approach. This, however, still uses productivity as its reference point and falls back into the work-centred trap.

It is easy to criticize such lifestyles and approaches as morally and developmentally inferior, but, as a Church, we need to educate and support each other to take more fulfilling and healthier approaches which allow more effective witness and physical, mental and spiritual development.

The Way Forward

When surrounded by a society that gives value and priority to productivity and utility the Christian community needs to challenge the lack of focus on the inner life and spiritual development. It may suit church communities that individuals fill their 'leisure' time working for the Church. It may, however, be better for those individuals that they be encouraged to develop a sense of worth and security that allows greater freedom of expression and encourages a more outward-looking attitude towards leisure and fulfilment of the gospel.

The Christian Church needs to create a community where individuals feel valued for who they are, not what they do. We need to strive to fill the void that leaves individuals inwardly starved and pressurized to be more and more productive and to prove themselves more and more through their 'external' achievements. We need to promote a culture which allows individuals to value themselves and others enough to feel justified in seeking a more balanced lifestyle – a lifestyle which avoids overwork as a way of feeling valued and earning respect or a need to invent pressures to prove their value. We need to challenge the sense of guilt that some feel in pursuing leisure in a work-driven world, and free individuals to enjoy much-needed leisure. We need to support and promote a change of attitude. We need to support individuals who fear what they will find if they take the time to stand back, those who fear that if they stand back they will be faced with the reality of not feeling important or indispensable.

We must strive to find a way to promote the inner calm and silence of leisure – a silence that is not necessarily about stillness but about a place or activity where we can relax and listen – listen to ourselves and to others. This should not be about 'uneasy bursts of activity and unrewarding leisure, with which we seek compensation'.[9] As identified by Pieper, leisure:

> is not the attitude of mind to actively intervene, but of those who are open to everything; not of those who grab and, having grabbed, hold on to; but of those who leave the reins loose and who are free and easy

themselves, almost like a man falling asleep, for one can only fall asleep by letting oneself go.[10]

This letting go is achieved in different ways by different individuals and we need to encourage individuals to explore and be creative in the activities they seek as leisure whether these be meditative practices or rugby union. Recognizing the importance of leisure should not lead us into being so prescriptive and zealous with others that it becomes another area in which they need to be seen to be fulfilling expectations. We must not inadvertently force others into activities we may perceive as leisure. We need to respect and support individual choices which promote flourishing.

In fact, we need to go much further than avoiding being prescriptive. The Church needs to encourage and build the confidence of individuals in exercising freedom and being fulfilled in doing so:

> The most serious limitation . . . on the freedom of the individual in leisure arises in practice from the unwillingness of many human beings to exercise freedom, indeed from the unwillingness of all human beings, to some degree, to exercise freedom . . . For freedom which brings a feeling of strength, also brings the awareness of isolation; and that can engender doubt and even anxiety.[11]

The Church should play a vital role in supporting the positive exercising of the freedom we have. This means providing help and support in challenging the boundaries and expectations of work and a productive and consumer-driven society, as well as supporting effective education which allows healthy leisure choices and the inner security to exercise freedom. This calls us to provide appropriate role models as both employees and employers and to help address any unnecessary restrictions created by inappropriate cultural, religious and social baggage.

Most of us are already aware that to flourish we need to address the leisure issue. We instinctively know that we need leisure. Many of us, however, need to be given permission to pursue the fulfilment of that need as a legitimate human need. Here the Church can play an important role in freeing individuals to pursue the lifestyle changes they need in order to move forward and flourish. The Church has had a tendency towards the opposite, however, leisure often being seen as ineffective stewardship of time and resources or indeed simply as laziness. Many rely on the Church to tell them what to do rather than educate them into a healthy exercise of freedom. This does not encourage flourishing and spiritual development but suspends the individual in childlike dependence.

Our freedom to choose and to act is restricted by social processes, relationships and our psyche. The 'superego'[12] is a particularly potent factor and, in order to allow us to commit our freedom rather than submit it, we need to be encouraged to develop in a way which allows us to act in response to an educated conscience rather than the superego. We need to move to a place where we can choose and act in a way that we see as right and that supports our individual flourishing – physically, mentally and spiritually. We need to be encouraged into a maturity where, rather than submit to what are or are perceived to be external expectations, we make an educated decision and commit our freedom. This does not necessitate a hedonistic, freewheeling approach but means an embracing of social or authority standards. Committing one's freedom through the act of an educated conscience is about responding through love of self and others to a call to commit to value as opposed to submitting a response which is about chasing a need for acceptance, love and approval.[13]

Conclusion

The complex, interconnected nature of modern lives inevitably leads to the complexity of what individuals gain from and define as leisure. Only reflection by oneself can truly answer the question of what is the nature of leisure. This does not, however, mean that as a Church we can abdicate responsibility. There is an important role in facilitating healthy reflection. There is a need to free individuals to value leisure for leisure's sake, to indulge in an experience which helps them to flourish as physical, spiritual and intellectual beings and moves them away from the values of status and productivity.

Leisure at times will continue to be important as a way of re-energizing and recuperating from work or seeking activities which have compensation qualities in relation to work or social roles, allowing an expression of different aspects of self and an exploration of other talents. Leisure can also provide the self-esteem, sense of belonging and autonomy that are absent elsewhere.

To achieve leisure for leisure's sake however presupposes and involves a certain level of personal development which is not readily achievable. Work–life balance is a good starting point but, when the intrinsic value of leisure is recognized and accepted, work–life balance becomes less of an issue and lifestyle balance becomes more central. Effective valuing and pursuit of leisure should lead to greater respect for self and others. It should lead to the pursuit of humanitarian values which prevent an unhealthy attachment to work and work practices, that is, a more consistent and holistic approach to self and others – a development in the learning process of loving self and others. In practical terms, we should, for example, no longer be faced with the irony of those campaigning for workers' rights including reasonable hours who work themselves into ill-health in the pursuit of such ideals.

For the Church as both a body and an institution (including as an employer) the cost of not promoting and supporting leisure awareness and value will be higher than ignoring it. The promoting of lifestyle balance and hence the recognition of the innate value of leisure is essential to a healthy respect for self and others, and for physical, mental and spiritual health. It is not only essential for effective, productive employees but more importantly it is essential if we are truly to 'love our neighbour as ourselves'.[14]

This approach is not about vilifying work or ignoring obligations and duty in favour of a 'hedonistic' leisure lifestyle. It is about the need for balance and about promoting human flourishing as individuals and as community. People do gain meaning in their life through work, both paid and voluntary. A healthy lifestyle does not discourage this. It is the misuse of this and excessive work-centredness which is to be avoided. Achieving a balance helps us move from a utilitarian, pressured view of work and the worker to one which is about work being a means of cooperating in God's creativity and God delighting in all that God makes. This balance helps us to see all aspects of life as delighting in God's creation. Leisure is an essential part of that process and of the process of re-creation in Christ.[15]

The effective coming together of creative energy and relaxation in leisure ultimately leads to a contemplative, prayerful pursuit which forms an important part of our response to God – a response which allows us:

> to use what time is (or is made[16]) available for leisure positively and freely with the discernment of what is good and profitable, a discernment which is part of the Spirit's gift; and to recognize that prayer is not conditioned by 'clock time' but is a total relationship with God that enables us to move easily from the day to day demands of life into a loving familiarity with God.[17]

Leisure is ultimately an essential part of a complete and healthy prayer life and response to God. 'Knowledge of God is in passivity not in effort, because effort presupposes a predetermined objective and one can have no preconceived ideas about God. When one is still (the object of true leisure) one doesn't believe in God, one knows God.'[18] This is a very real response to the call to 'Be still and know that I am God'[19] or indeed to 'Have leisure and know that I am God'.[20]

Notes

1. Work–life balance is the commonly used reference term. This in itself shows the work-centred approach to individual lifestyles and their use of time. The author's preference is to use the term lifestyle balance to avoid using work as the key reference point. That is, work–life balance

starts from the reference point of work whereas lifestyle balance starts with the individual as the reference point, including personal and work relationships. The term lifestyle balance will be adopted for the remainder of the chapter.

2. C. Bull, J. Hoose and M. Weed, *An Introduction to Leisure Studies* (London: FT Prentice Hall, 2003), p. 8.
3. T. Lankaster, *Work–Life Balance – Guidelines for the Aid Sector* (London: People in Aid/Interhealth, 2003), p. 4.
4. It is this that has indeed led to the word recreation often being used synonymously with leisure. The word recreation arises from the Latin *recreare* meaning to re-create, to restore or to renew.
5. T. Kay, 'Active Unemployment – Leisure Pattern for the Future?', *Loisir et Société/Society and Leisure*, vol. 12, no. 2 (1989).
6. Mk 2.27.
7. Mt. 19.19, 22.39; Mk 12.31.
8. Graham Neville, *Free Time: Towards a Theology of Leisure* (Birmingham: University of Birmingham Press, 2004), p. 6.
9. Mother Mary Clare, SLG, *Leisure* (Oxford: Fairacres Publication 37, SLG Press, 1974), pp. 4–5.
10. Josef Pieper, *Leisure the Basis of Culture*, Fontana Library (London: Collins, 1965), p. 44.
11. Neville, op. cit., p. 5.
12. 'Superego is the ego of another superimposed on our own to serve as an internal censor to regulate our conduct using guilt as its powerful weapon' (Richard Gula, *Reason Informed by Faith* (New York: Paulist Press, 1989), p. 124).
13. Jayne Hoose (ed.), *Conscience in World Religions* (Leominster: Gracewing, 1999), pp. 86–7.
14. Mt. 19.19, 22.39; Mk 12.31.
15. Mother Mary Clare, op. cit., p. 7.
16. Author's insert.
17. Mother Mary Clare, op. cit., p. 7.
18. Ibid., p. 7.
19. Ps. 45.11.
20. Mother Mary Clare, op. cit., p. 7.

Part II:

The Practice of
Social Spirituality

Chapter 8

The Nature of the Catholic Advocate

Stephen Wall

In the world in which the author grew up, the place of the Catholic Church in Britain was unambiguous and many Catholics thought they were correct, if not always comfortable, in proclaiming their faith. For many Catholics, the author included, some of the moral choices no longer seem so straightforward. The author argues that carrying our faith into public life requires us to choose whether to rest on the absolute truth of the Church's teaching or to use the tools of a democratic society, including compromise, to reach our goals.

'Faith of our fathers living still . . . we will be true to thee till death.' So we sang, with heart and soul, in my youth. Even more heartfelt was the climax of this most English of Catholic hymns: 'Faith of our fathers, Mary's prayers shall win our country back to thee; and through the truth that comes from God we all shall then indeed be free.'[1]

If today, we are too politically correct to sing that hymn, we felt no such reservations in the 1950s and 60s. Our school history books (and we read only history written by Catholic authors) told the heroic story of the Catholic martyrs. My own family was related to one of them, John Wall, though it was on my mother's side that we were now a Catholic family. Her own father had converted to Catholicism after hearing Cardinal Newman preach.

It would be fatuous to suggest that we felt a persecuted minority in the Britain of the 1950s. But we did feel a conspicuous, if highly self-confident, minority. And there was a whiff of anti-Catholic feeling and discrimination there in the background. It was said that no child from the Epsom convent school my sister and I attended in the early 1950s ever won a scholarship to one of Surrey's grammar schools. Yet we were well taught by formidable French nuns who were not above some skulduggery to redress the balance: my sister was placed top in a school exam because, as one nun explained to my mother, 'we could not allow a Protestant child to come top'.

My mother used to say that her Methodist in-laws never held it against her that she was a Catholic, as if this was surprising as well as commendable. Certainly, one of my father's Methodist aunts, in his native Derbyshire, wrote to him on his engagement in 1931 urging him not to sign away the liberty of his children. Derbyshire's yeoman stock was, she wrote, 'the back-bone and breath of England' and he should not agree to bring up the children of the marriage as Catholics. I and my sisters are living proof of the fact that our father ignored his aunt's injunction, signed on the dotted line and, agnostic though he was, faithfully ensured that we were brought up as Catholics, educated in Catholic schools.

For us, as children of the 1950s, Catholic advocacy meant something more than going to Mass on Sunday and agonized debate about whether we had committed mortal sin by eating Bovril sandwiches on Friday. We Catholics were a breed apart and, though a minority in our own country, a distinctly superior one. Or so we thought. The size, extent and rigour of the Catholic Church made it the General Motors of Christian churches. The Pope could trump the Archbishop of Canterbury any day. We were told that even to go into an Anglican church would be the occasion of scandal.

When we made a family visit (I was seven at the time) to the building site of the new Anglican cathedral at Guildford, I self-righteously refused my father's request to put half-a-crown in a box which would buy a brick for the new building. It was, after all, 'Protestant'. My older sister rebuked me sharply. But not because I lacked Christian charity. It was, rather, that I lacked tactical sense: 'Do you think he will ever become a Catholic if you behave like that?' she said. He never did become a Catholic and I shall never know whether he would have done had I not dropped that particular brick.

So, the very fact of being a Catholic was a kind of advocacy. As citizens, we had nothing to prove. We waved our Union Jacks with fervour when the young Queen Elizabeth drove through Epsom. We trooped to the cinema to watch the film, in colour no less, of her post-Coronation world tour. We burned Guy Fawkes each November without the least compunction and, it has to be admitted, were pretty unmoved also by the burning of the Pope's effigy each year in the Sussex town of Lewes.

Pius XII's reputation was not then a matter of controversy. I wished he would smile more as he stared out of the front page of *The Universe*. Even his photo in full colour, almost a first for a national paper, could not soften the austere Roman features. But he still knocked spots off any other Christian leader. We were proud of the Church's courage in the face of persecution; proud that a prominent communist zealot, Douglas Hyde, had had a Pauline conversion and was one of England's most powerful witnesses against Soviet Russia; proud that, in Hungary, Cardinal Mindszenty had endured a kind of living martyrdom for his faith. We felt hugely validated when Alec Guinness, who had played Mindszenty in a successful film, *The Prisoner*, was received into the Church. It was big news in the British press.

Catholic advocacy certainly required Catholic example. The duties of devotion – Sunday Mass, fasting and abstinence and regular Confession – were the principal good activities through which most of us set that example. Catholic social action certainly existed, but it was more focused on the conversion of the heathen overseas than the welfare of the less well-off in our midst. Or perhaps that is just my perception as the child of a fairly comfortable middle-class family, living in prosperous Surrey.

The doubts that I and others carried through our teenage years were less about the faith as such, than about our ability to live up to it. A Catholic Truth Society pamphlet about the sins of the flesh was given to me when I was about 14. Far from acting as a moral cold shower, its descriptions of all the sinful pleasures to be eschewed was about the most arousing thing I had read thus far in my young life. Such was the secrecy surrounding these matters that, I am sure, thousands of young Catholics like me went through our teenage years thinking we were alone in committing what was then deemed to be mortal sin, and suffering agonies of guilt as a result.

Insofar as we did have doubts about our faith, we were encouraged at school to dismiss them as temptations and certainly not allowed to indulge them by intellectual enquiry. A school friend who suggested in a Religious Instruction class that we should study comparative religion was told that that was not what his parents had sent him to a Catholic school to learn about. So it was only at Cambridge University that I had my first exposure to intelligent, good, tolerant and persuasive Anglicans. Even then, the debate was not about Christianity compared with Islam, or about the existence of God.

John Robinson's book, *Honest to God*,[2] appeared while I was at Cambridge. It caused national shockwaves by questioning the literal truth of some of the Christian story and by its emphasis on a God who could be adapted to personal belief. But what I spent my time arguing about with my Anglican friends were the finer points of the doctrine of transubstantiation and similar issues. And, if I did begin to feel that what God did for us humans at the moment of Consecration was more significant than our ability to define it accurately, I was brought back to earth by a reminder, both challenging and comforting, of the separateness of Catholic witness. A small group of Catholic undergraduates met each week to hear Mass in a room at Newnham College, still then a women's college. 'Why not have Mass one week in my college, Selwyn?' I suggested. I duly wrote to the Master of the college, Owen Chadwick, to ask for his permission. Owen Chadwick was, and still is, a great church historian. He was mentioned in those days as a possible future Archbishop of Canterbury. Selwyn College was an Anglican foundation and had admitted, I believe, few Catholic undergraduates before me. Owen Chadwick wrote back politely but firmly: no Catholic Mass would be said in Selwyn.

I apologize for this autobiography. But there must today be as many views of Catholic advocacy as there are Catholics. It was not so 40 years ago. The drift away from the Church started with my generation and probably the biggest difference between then and now is the diversity of Catholic views and Catholic action. Fifty years ago, there was no debate. The duties of faith were clear. The division between right and wrong was absolute. What was right was what the Church thought and taught.

The reaction to the papal encyclical *Humanae Vitae* (1968) was perhaps the symptom, as much as the cause, of a sea change. The encyclical sought to determine the action of Catholic couples in an area where, for the first time, what the Church taught to be wrong conflicted with what many of those same couples themselves believed to be right. The Church was no longer exempt from the changes sweeping society. More and more Catholics started to interpret the Church's teaching in the light of their own reasoning and experience.

The history of the last 40 years has been the Church's struggle to come to terms with that uncomfortable fact. At times, the Church has seemed unsure whether to show Old Testament wrath or New Testament love. Should the Church be the city on a hill or the leaven in the mass? Many Catholic leaders try heroically to make the Church both. My subjective sense is that more Catholics witness to their faith as Christ enjoined us to do in the twenty-fifth chapter of Matthew's Gospel than ever before. In the year (2004/2005) that I worked as public affairs adviser to the Archbishop of Westminster, Cardinal Cormac Murphy-O'Connor, I was struck by the contrast between the sometimes stern official voice of the Church as heard from Rome and the dedication, fidelity and love of the Archbishop and his fellow bishops who sought to be both faithful to the Church's teaching and to reach out to a Catholic community, for whom the life of faith is not straightforward or easy, and to a wider society which searches for spiritual values but does not readily look to organized religion to provide them.

One of the paradoxes of our time is that, as organized Christian religion has occupied less and less of our public space, so the expectation that Catholics will give orthodox public witness to their beliefs has grown. There are at least two issues here. Am I obliged to adhere absolutely to every iota of Catholic teaching in order to call myself a Catholic? And am I obliged to work to translate the Church's teaching into public policy and law? A Catholic may both privately doubt the teaching of the Church on a particular issue and question the wisdom of translating that teaching into public policy. But, assuming that a Catholic accepts the teaching of the Church, is he or she obliged to translate that belief into public advocacy? Expectations have changed radically over a few decades.

The *locus classicus* of the prevalent view up to the 1980s was John F. Kennedy's handling of the religious issue in the 1960 presidential election campaign in the United States. Kennedy's Catholicism was undoubtedly a factor in the campaign, and one that appeared to count against him. 'There's only one problem,' a heckler shouted at a rally, 'he's a Catholic. That's our God-damned problem.'

Kennedy's initial response was limited but effective:

I'm able to serve in Congress, and my brother was able to give his life, but we can't be President? Nobody asked me if I was a Catholic when I joined the United States Navy. Nobody asked my brother if he was a Catholic or Protestant before he climbed into an American bomber to fly his last mission.[3]

But once he became the chosen Democratic candidate for President, Kennedy had to go further. His speech to a group of Protestant ministers in September 1960 remained, for years, the accepted definition of the duties of a Catholic politician. He declared his belief in:

> an America where the separation of Church and State is absolute . . . I believe in a President whose views on religion are his own private affair, neither imposed on him by the nation or imposed by the nation upon him as a condition to holding office . . . I am not the Catholic candidate for President. I am the Democratic Party's candidate for President who happens to be a Catholic. I do not speak for my Church on public matters and my Church does not speak for me . . . If the time should ever come . . . when my office would require me to either violate my conscience, or violate the national interest, then I would resign the office.[4]

If we fast forward nearly 25 years to 1984, the argument had already become less clear-cut. In that year, Mario M. Cuomo, the Democratic Governor of the state of New York, gave a lecture at the University of Notre Dame, South Bend, Indiana on 13 September 1984 entitled *Religious Belief and Public Morality: A Catholic Governor's Perspective*. In it, he asserted that:

> . . . the Catholic who holds political office in a pluralistic democracy – who is elected to serve Jews and Muslims, atheists and Protestants, as well as Catholics – bears special responsibility. He or she undertakes to help create conditions under which all can live with a maximum of dignity and with a reasonable degree of freedom; where everyone who chooses may hold beliefs different from specifically Catholic ones, sometimes contradictory to them; where the laws protect people's right to divorce, to use birth control and even to choose abortion . . . The Catholic public official lives the political truth most Catholics through most of American history have accepted and insisted on: the truth that to assure our freedom we must allow others the same freedom, even if occasionally it produces conduct by them which, for us, would be sinful. I protect my right to be a Catholic by preserving your right to be a Jew, a Protestant or non-believer, or anything else you choose. We know that the price of seeking to force our beliefs on others is that they might some day force theirs on us.[5]

145

Cuomo went on to argue that the question whether to engage the political system in a struggle to have it adopt certain articles of Catholic belief as part of public morality was not a matter of doctrine but of prudential political judgement: 'my Church and my conscience require me to believe certain things about divorce, birth control and abortion. My Church does not order me, under pain of sin or expulsion, to pursue my salvific mission according to a precisely defined political plan.'[6] In support of his argument, Cuomo cited the example of the decision by Catholic bishops not to speak out against slavery in the years before the American Civil War, despite the fact that the slave trade had been condemned by Pope Gregory XVI. They did so because Catholics in America were a small, mostly immigrant population, often vilified and the object of sporadic violence. In other words, the Catholic bishops made a judgement about translating Catholic teaching into action. They did not question the moral validity of the Church's teaching. They did question the wisdom of turning that teaching into public policy.

Translating that example to the contemporary instance of abortion, Cuomo argued that the American bishops had had to weigh Catholic moral teaching against the fact of a pluralistic country where the Catholic view was in the minority, acknowledging that what was ideally desirable was not always feasible and that there could be 'different political approaches to abortion besides unyielding adherence to absolute prohibition'.[7]

Cuomo's own philosophy was enshrined in his view that Catholics must educate themselves better to the values that defined their lives, following the teachings of the Church better than in the past:

> Unless we set an example that is clear and compelling, then we will never convince this Society to change the civil laws to protect what we preach is precious human life. Better than any law or rule or threat of punishment would be the moving strength of our own good example, demonstrating our lack of hypocrisy, proving the beauty and worth of our instruction.[8]

I find Mario Cuomo's argument compelling. But it was not the argument widely heard during the American presidential campaign 20 years later, in 2004, when Senator Kerry was threatened with excommunication by some American bishops because of his voting record on abortion. And Cuomo's dilemma was about how to translate belief into policy. He did not, to judge by his lecture, have to wrestle with his conscience about the basis of his belief.

Many Catholic advocates today share Cuomo's dilemma. Is a social worker unfaithful to Catholic teaching because she advises a prostitute in Soweto to insist that her customers use a condom to protect her, and other customers, from mortal disease? Is her Catholic advocacy more, or less, powerful because she leads, not from the bully pulpit of moral certainty but from the daily exercise of loving care and Christian example? Is it permissible for a Catholic law maker to argue for improvement in the law on abortion, rather than accept nothing less than a total ban, knowing that the total ban is unlikely to happen? Is it possible for a Catholic policy-maker to support a law allowing civil partnerships between gay people on the grounds that the law redresses an injustice while also upholding the sanctity of marriage, which remains a sacrament between men and women made before God?

There may be as many views as readers of this chapter. I have to say that I am with the Soweto social worker; with the Catholic law maker who argues for abortion law reform; with the advocate of civil rights for homosexuals. And I regard myself as a Catholic advocate, though not on a par with any of the people who have to wrestle with these issues in real life and not just in the pages of a book.

Perhaps, as its army of followers, in the European-North American world at least, has dwindled, so the Church has again come to demand more absolute obedience from its advocates. Today both Kennedy and Cuomo could conceivably be denied Holy Communion because of their views. There are many in the Church who would say 'and quite right too', many who do say that the Church must stand for absolute, revealed truth and that the integrity of the witness brought by Catholic advocates is more important than the numbers of the Church's adherents. I agree that the Church must be a rock in a sea of change and doubt. Yet there has been sufficient change in my lifetime in the Church's own view of what does or does not constitute serious wrongdoing to allow room for reasoned debate.

Faith as a private space which guides, but does not dictate, public positions on moral issues is less tolerated now than some years ago. And yet the same dilemmas continue to pose themselves in acute form for Catholic social workers, doctors, policy-makers and legislators – and, to a lesser extent, for all of us. How far does the individual refract the light of the Church's teaching through the prism of his or her own conscience and judgement? It is easier to be absolute if you are not confronted with having to make a decision involving both a moral and an operational choice. It is easier to be certain of the immorality of condom use when you are not confronted by the immorality of wanton death through the spread of HIV infection. Were I a legislator, the fact that I believe abortion to be wrong would not absolve me from making my own judgement about what constitutes the lesser of two evils. The sanctity of marriage does not absolve me from taking a view about whether the imposition of that view undermines the rights of others who do not share my viewpoint.

I spent the whole of my 35-year career in the British Diplomatic Service and was foreign policy adviser at Number 10 Downing Street to John Major from 1991–93 and senior adviser on the European Union to Prime Minister

Tony Blair from 2000–2004. Civil servants have the right, and freedom, to express their views on policy to ministers in private. If a civil servant feels there is an irreconcilable conflict between his or her convictions and government policy then it is open to that person to resign and express those reservations in public, or to suppress them and work within the system to change or moderate the policy he or she disagrees with. The Suez crisis of 1956 provoked several such resignations. The Iraq war provoked the resignation of one of the Foreign Office's legal advisers, who believed that the invasion was illegal in international law.

Since I left the civil service in 2004 I have said publicly that I think the invasion of Iraq was contrary to international law. I have been asked whether I made that view known to Tony Blair at the time. I did not do so. I felt in the early spring of 2003 that it would be wrong to invade Iraq without the explicit authorization of the UN Security Council. I was not involved in any of the discussions about the preparations for war. I was Mr Blair's adviser on Europe and my views were not sought on other matters. But I could have told Tony Blair my view and he would certainly have given me a polite hearing, though I do not kid myself that *my* opinion would have changed his. I rationalized not doing so on the grounds that Iraq was not my area of responsibility, that I was not privy to the information that was guiding the Government's decisions and that Iraq would almost certainly be a better place without Saddam Hussein. So I kept quiet. And I was wrong to have done so. It would have required a little courage to speak up; but nothing like the courage shown by the Foreign Office legal adviser who sacrificed a career for the sake of conscience.

I had often asked myself what were the issues which would represent, for me, a moral line I was not prepared to cross. I had thought almost exclusively in terms of European policy, since I spent most of the last 20 years of my career advising successive British governments on policy towards the European Union. I could not, for example, have worked for a government that was committed to take Britain out of the European Union since I believe that, for all its faults, the EU is essential for Europe's peace, stability and prosperity. For me, that is a moral, and not just a policy, question. In the end, that issue did not arise because the Labour Party, which was committed to leaving the European Community, did not win the 1983 election and changed its policy shortly thereafter.

The closest I came to confronting a moral dilemma over Europe was when I was Britain's Ambassador to the European Union from 1995–2000 and had to deal with the policy of non-cooperation with our EU partners introduced by the Major Government in the wake of the BSE (mad cow) crisis. I thought the policy was misguided, but not immoral. However, a rumour reached me in Brussels that government ministers were thinking of withholding our financial contributions to the EU budget in protest at the closure of EU markets to British beef. I told the Permanent Under-secretary at the Foreign Office (my diplomatic service boss) that I would be unwilling to execute such a policy since it would be contrary to Britain's international legal obligations. I argued that I should not be asked to implement a policy which would flout those obligations and that, if asked, I would not be prepared to do so. In the end, the idea came to nothing, probably because ministers were no more prepared to behave illegally than I was.

Christ chose sinners for his disciples. He chose men who were not the sharpest intellectual tools in the box. Peter comes across in the Gospels as moderately obtuse. At the moment when Jesus needed him to stand up and be counted, he denied his friend and mentor three times. Yet he was the rock on which Christ chose to build his Church. Even then, along with the rest of the disciples, he cowered in the upper room until the Holy Spirit filled him with divine fire. I take comfort from that.

In his play *A Man for All Seasons*, Robert Bolt has the Duke of Norfolk plead with Thomas More to go along with the king's wishes for fellowship's sake. More replies: 'And when we stand before God, and you are sent to Paradise for doing according to your conscience, and I am damned for not doing according to mine, will you come with me, for fellowship!'[9] Conscience has to be the ultimate test for all of us who strive to be Catholic advocates. And 'Faith of our fathers', which invites us to be ready to lay down our lives for our faith, concludes, perhaps surprisingly, that the watchwords of faith should be example, tolerance and love:

> Faith of our fathers, we will love
> both friend and foe in all our strife,
> and preach thee too, as love knows how,
> by kindly words and virtuous life.[10]

Notes

1. Frederick William Faber (1814–63), 'Faith of our fathers', in Patrick Geary (ed.) *The Celebration Hymnal for Everyone* (Great Britain: McCrimmon Publishing Company Ltd, 1995), p. 156.
2. John A.T. Robinson, *Honest to God* (London: SCM Press, 1963).
3. John F. Kennedy's answer to a question at a rally in West Virginia in April 1960, in Robert Dallek, *John F. Kennedy, an Unfinished Life* (New York: Back Bay Books/Little Brown and Company, 2003), pp. 252–3.
4. From a speech by John F. Kennedy to Protestant ministers in Houston, Texas on 12 September 1960, ibid., pp. 283–4.
5. Mario M. Cuomo, *Religious Belief and Public Morality: A Catholic Governor's Perspective*, http://pewforum.org/docs/index.php?DocID=14 (accessed 31 August 2006).
6. Ibid.

7. Ibid.
8. Ibid.
9. Robert Bolt, *A Man for All Seasons* (Oxford: Heinemann Educational Books Ltd, 1963), p. 78.
10. Faber, op cit., p. 156.

Chapter 9

Hearing the Cry of the Poor

John Battle MP

Catholic social teaching rejects the rigid dichotomy of 'Church' and 'State', leading us to look at politics positively, as the means of acting out the 'preferential option' for the poor. This chapter argues that listening to the voices of the poor should act as an imperative to push for change, countering the 'politics of despair' and the ingrained cultural pessimism that pervades modern society. The Church has a vital role to play in pushing for the transformation of institutions rather than their abandonment, with the tradition of the Church recognizing the value of mediating bodies and democratic governance. Returning to the concept of 'persons in community' can provide the means of reacting confidently to globalization and the rapidly changing economic environment we now find ourselves in.

I only want two things; I want you to set your eyes and your hearts on these people who are suffering so much, some from poverty and hunger, others from oppression and repression, then standing before this people thus crucified, ask yourselves what have I done to crucify them? What do I do to uncrucify them? What must I do for these people to rise again?[1]

Redeeming Politics

The Salvadoran, Fr Ellacuria, martyred for campaigning for justice for the poor, challenges us to set our eyes and hearts on people suffering from poverty, hunger, oppression and repression. He invites us to seek them out, get to know who they are, ensure that they are not invisible, and then to embrace them in love – set our hearts on them. We have therefore to identify the suffering, the poor and oppressed in our world, wherever they are, and take their part. Then, 'standing before' them, we are asked to examine our relationship to them publicly. Asking 'What have I done to crucify them?' means examining and confessing how I am part of the problem, nailing the suffering poor up on the cross, using the hammer or passing over the nails, holding the wood steady, or further back, providing the tree for the wood.

Accepting a sense of responsibility implies that we examine whether we are part of the political, economic or social arrangements by which the poor are kept poor so that the rich can remain and become even richer. Imagine examining one's conscience and confessing 'my bank card interest rate is low because some of the lenders to the poorest in our society charge them the highest rates of interests. My low rate is at the expense of overcharging the poor for money to provide basic necessities.' In other words, we have an interest in and responsibility for the connections that exist to deny the poor their basic human needs. As Enrique Dussel puts it in *Ethics and Community*, 'the life of the poor is accumulated by the rich. The latter live the life of the rich in virtue of the death of the poor.'[2]

Fr Ellacuria goes further, stressing that recognizing the existence of the poor, taking their part, at home and abroad, even confessing our role in their crucifixion, is not enough. 'Standing before' the crucified people, we are publicly asked 'What am I doing to uncrucify them?' – what am I doing to get them down from the cross? Rather than contributing to nailing more people up, what practical actions are we taking to get people down, and to ensure no more are nailed up? Then comes his deeper theological challenge: 'What must I do for these people to rise again?'

Hearing the cry of the crucified people has therefore to be at the heart of the role of the Church in challenging political authority. Identifying, recognizing and acknowledging the poor and suffering is itself more than half the task in the context of a dominant politics and economics that at worst crucifies and at best overlooks the poor. Insisting on the presence of the poor in the world is itself a challenge to political powers and economic arrangements. It is a particularly difficult job in the context of a present belief that actually, in 'the real world', there is no serious alternative to the current economic framework. In other words, challenging political authority is now generally regarded as futile; some suggest that the Church should retreat from engaging with the world. The gospel message, however, directs us in the opposite direction, right into the maelstrom of the world. Moreover, the Catholic Church's social teachings – including the latest encyclical of Pope Benedict XVI – exhort and encourage us to regard politics positively as a vital means of tackling laws and budgets, and building institutions that can liberate the suffering, the poor and the oppressed by widening our political imaginations in the search for an international 'community of persons', living together in justice, mercy and peace. Politics, according to the Church, should be regarded as a practical means of getting the crucified down from the cross.

Therefore, starting from a focus on the 'crucified people' locally and globally, identifying the poor and oppressed in our own decaying inner-city neighbourhoods, as well as on the scrub plains of sub-Saharan Africa, it is crucial to get beyond the present debilitating culture of pessimistic fear to a belief in the possibilities of politics as a means of change. The Church, by encouraging engagement in politics at every level, carefully refuses to regard 'Church' and 'State' as confined to separate sealed containers. The purpose of this political engagement is to ensure that a critical prophetic voice challenges political authority and economic systems with and on behalf of the suffering poor. Moreover, the deep political theology of the Church insists that this is not a superficial matter of the Church trying to 'influence' the political establishment, or being confined to a 'public Christian presence' among the powers that be. The State cannot be allowed to contain the Church or reduce its contribution to its own terms. To invert William Cavanaugh's phrase, 'citizenship' should not replace 'discipleship' as the Church's 'public key'.[3] Nor should the Church be regarded as a spiritual asocial entity that provides only back-up 'motivations' and 'values' for public action. Rather, as Church, we are responsible for 'standing before' the crucified people, getting them down from the cross by ensuring that there are institutions in place to prevent more being nailed up, and offering a new vision and practice of 'persons in community' that is truly international and 'Catholic' in character. We are thus called to be engaged in politics at every level, 'redeeming' the world of politics by our personal involvement.

The Agnostic Globe

At the 1993 Parliament of the World's Religions, 200 religious leaders signed up to a document entitled *A Global Ethic*, drafted by Professor Hans Küng. It opens:

> The world is in agony. The agony is so pervasive and urgent that we are compelled to name its manifestations so that the depth of this pain may be made clear. Peace eludes, the planet is being destroyed – neighbours live in fear, women and men are estranged from each other children die.[4]

It is a bleak testament to the close of the most violent century in human history – a century not only of two world wars but of now forgotten conflicts in Rwanda, Congo and Sudan, in which over four million have died since 1945 from conflict and famine. This is a far cry from the triumphant declarations of the successful 'end of history' accompanying the fall of the Berlin Wall in 1989 and the announced victory of the neo-liberal 'market economy'. In the 17 years since then, the ambivalence of 'globalization' has been further exposed as our world continues dividing into the rich and the poor, with most African countries remaining locked out of the trading world, and violent conflicts (including internal ethnic cleansing and a generic 'war on terror') persisting.

Of the six billion people on earth, over one billion poor are still locked out of the consumer economy entirely, forced into subsistence on less than a dollar a day. Despite recent efforts of debt relief and aid assistance, the Millennium Development Goals to ensure clean water, sanitation, health-care and education by 2015 will not be met until well into the next century. In the rich countries, in the USA and Britain, the gap between rich and poor widens daily as a substantial 'poor core' get left increasingly behind. In Britain, the targets of reducing by half by 2011 the number of children living in poverty are not being met. Despite some real progress, 1.9 million children remain in absolute poverty. As a member of parliament in a typical northern inner-city constituency, I hold fortnightly advice surgeries that involve dozens of conversations with poor people, usually focused on the need for better and more appropriate homes, struggles to sustain or sort out failed relationships and their impact on families (and the resulting financial knock-ons with bodies such as the Child Support Agency or tax offices), problems with mental and physical health, immigrants unprotected in low-paid work, others desperately seeking asylum. All present in their individual circumstances challenges from the poor and suffering to the Government's structures of laws and budgets.

The real blasphemy in the face of the plight of the suffering poor is the claim that there is 'no alternative' – a mantra that subscribes to the doctrine that things can only get worse. Sadly, as Tom Bentley put it in his article 'The Self-creating Society', 'By accepting the premise that "getting on" in today's consumer society is the main criteria (*sic*) by which citizens will assess how well government is helping them, politics has reduced its own capacity to question and to influence the ways in which aspirations themselves are formed and shaped.'[5] The depoliticized 'consumer society' disempowers, and attempts to turn everyone into 'consumers' and 'consumables'. We now live in an economy in which 'disposability' – not just of goods, but of people, relationships (and particular attachments of any kind) – is the hallmark of consumption. People are rubbished and disposed of, suffer violence and death; many disappear, more are unknown, unseen and unheard. Yet they should be the basis for any radical challenge to current political and economic systems and social arrangements. What is difficult, in the present cultural context, is presenting any vision of political hope in an age of loss of faith in politics as a process, and consumerist depoliticization.

From a Politics of Despair

In Europe, Ullrich Bech declared in 1992: 'Basically one is no longer concerned with attaining something "good" but rather with "preventing the worst".'[6] Avoiding the *summum malum* in a pervasive culture of fear is now seriously displacing working together towards the *summum bonum*. 'The

End is Nigh' is no longer a poster-board slogan hung over a religious fanatic's shoulders in the shopping centre, it is a regular headline of our broadsheet newspapers. There is no hope here, but only a counsel of despair afforded to the suffering poor. Faced with this counsel of despair, what serious hope could be developed by engaging with politics?

Over 20 years ago the cultural critic Raymond Williams warned that:

> The settled pessimism of so much of the culture [. . .] is in effect an absolute loss of the future: of any significant belief that it can be both different and better. The projection of dates is now more often an anxious calculation of the possibilities of mere survival.[7]

The demand for 24/7 news which drives the modern media, the Internet and the mobile phone, collapses any sense of time and space and creates an atmosphere of permanent, inescapable crisis. Nor can we easily turn to 'politics' to tackle it. The widespread belief that politics cannot influence events or change things for the good is now deeply ingrained. Political differences in the age of image and celebrity status are seen as confined to disputes about technical, administrative and managed matters, not related to ideological differences and real choices of worldviews. There is a feeling that there really is no alternative now to an economic framework that is totally dominant and unchallengeable. This is not an age of political ideas and alternatives but a time of anti-politics, in which 'politics' itself is regarded as part of the problem; it is a time of disillusion and disengagement. A kind of techno-managerialism seems to have 'removed the memory of the human' from the systems. Moreover, as the political philosopher Žižek points out, the paradox is that in the face of all our interconnecting technologies human beings are now more alone and isolated than ever before.[8] What has taken place therefore is a profound downgrading of human capacity and potential – we no longer believe we can make any difference through politics. It now seems easier, as Terry Eagleton suggests, to alter a person's genetic structure and make-up than it is to change governing institutions, market economies or the redistribution of wealth and power.[9] Nor is this loss of faith in politics unique, or confined to the Western world; it infects the Church.

The Brazilian Bishop Pedro Casaldaliga suggests 'immediatist disillusion' results from:

> the pretension to create immediate and tangible outcomes and victories. As a result of this pretension, politics is in crisis, civilization is in crisis and Christianity is in crisis. Christian faith itself is being turned into a recipe book of miracles and favours received, a spiritualist refuge from evil and suffering and a substitute for personal and community co-responsibility for the transformation of society.[10]

There is a hint here of that traditional monastic *fuga mundi* that marked the Church's struggle to separate itself from the contamination of the world, after ages of a dominant fusion of Empire and Church. The retreat of the Church from a hostile and fearful world not only emerges as a comfortable option, but is also reinforced by those who believe faith communities in general should be confined to the private sphere and not interfere in the public realm.

Moving Within the World

Who then puts the case for the transformation of the world through politics? Encouragingly the writer Jean Vanier, founder of the L'Arche communities, in his latest book *Drawn into the Mystery of Jesus through the Gospel of John*, demonstrates that the whole point of St John's Gospel is that 'this life is not a flight from the world of pain and of matter but a mission into it, to love people as Jesus loves them'.[11] Jean Vanier and the L'Arche communities are contemporary 'witnesses to this approach'. But even outside the Church, the philosopher Hannah Arendt (reacting to the Nazi regime and the Holocaust) boldly proclaimed that the crucial decision for all who devote their lives to politics is whether one is capable of loving the world more than one's own self.[12] The role of the Church then is engagement in the suffering world and the challenge to politics comes from our capacity to 'love the world' more than one's own self. That challenge of 'public service' thus takes us into the midst of the political, not away from it.

In the inner-city constituency of Leeds West are two monumental structures: the substantial ruins of Kirkstall Abbey and Armley Prison – a castellated structure built in Victorian times. The abbey, a Cistercian daughter foundation of Fountains Abbey, was built in 1152 and for 400 years was the home of Trappist monks who devoted their lives to silent contemplative prayer, regularly reciting the Office of the Church, studying the Scriptures and the Fathers, keeping the community going with agricultural work and offering hospitality to the neighbourhood. Today from the grounds of the abbey, Armley Prison can be seen on the skyline. Armley is a remand prison, home every night to 1,275 male prisoners over 18 years old, mostly on remand awaiting trial; others having been sentenced waiting to be moved to their sentence prison. Each working day, approximately 50 new inmates are taken in while 50 come out. It's a high turnover place and 80 per cent of the inmates at any one time have serious problems with drugs, alcohol or mental health. In Armley Prison is the evidence of the conflicts, violence, strains and stresses of the maelstrom of modern urban life. Some are accused of violence, robbery or fraud, others are illegal immigrants or failed asylum seekers; more than 70 per cent will have low levels of basic literacy and numeracy. The prison, therefore, provides a clear snapshot of the tensions and challenges facing our society. Recently, both the prison and the abbey have been renovated, and religious 'services' have returned to Kirkstall. Could there be any intrinsic relationship between the 'contemplation' represented by the abbey and the world 'action' represented in the prison? Has the prayer of the Church anything to do with economic justice, the liberty of the person, the right distribution of resources, and the nature of government? In a context in which, in Professor Raymond Plant's words, there is a focus on 'the needs of human beings whose essence is understood in terms of agency and autonomy, as centres of choice, rather than a more substantial sense of common identity and common purpose',[13] has our faith tradition got anything to offer? Can it reconnect the contemplative tradition with action in the world on behalf of the poor and the suffering, including 'those in prison' – so often tagged on to the list in the gospels and sometimes accepted in our hearts as 'prisoners of conscience' but spurned as 'common criminals' to be locked up for a long time? How are those in our prisons to be reintegrated as persons in community, contributing to a vision of the common good?

The Church's Positive Politics

The Catholic Church's social teaching is strikingly positive about the nature and role of politics as the 'prudent concern for the common good'. Working for the interests of the community at large, not least the poor, the suffering and the most marginalized in society, was spelt out by Pope John Paul II in his encyclical letter *Laborem Excercens*.[14] In an age when politics is usually regarded as the concern of a specialized, albeit elected elite, of 'a political class', and viewed as a rather sordid business, the Church's tradition – reaching back to Aristotle's positive 'political ethics' and engaging 'the full development of the human personality' through participation as a citizen opens up the possibility of renewing faith in the process of politics itself. Indeed the Church's teaching presents politics as a positive vocation, and part of everyone's vocation is the call to serve others. *Gaudium et Spes* states:

> There is no better way to establish political life on a truly human basis than by fostering an inward justice and kindliness, and of service to the common good, and by strengthening basic convictions as to the true nature of political community and the aim, right exercise, and sphere of action of public authority.[15]

In 2003, the Congregation for the Doctrine of the Faith stressed the need for involvement in democratic politics:

157

It is commendable that in today's democratic societies, in a climate of true freedom, everyone is made a participant in the body politic. Such societies call for new and fuller forms of participation in public life by Christian and non-Christian citizens alike. Indeed, all can contribute, by voting in elections for lawmakers and government officials, and in other ways as well, to the development of political solutions and legislative choices which, in their opinion, will benefit the common good. The life of a democracy could not be productive without the active, responsible and generous involvement of everyone, 'albeit in a diversity and complementarity of forms, levels, tasks, and responsibilities'.[16]

In other words, the Church tells us to become really engaged in politics at every level, working to reconcile conflicts in complex societies, but always insisting on including every person – especially the poor, those usually over-looked and left out. More recently, the *Compendium of Social Doctrine of the Church*, put together by the Pontifical Council for Justice and Peace, summed up service in politics in the following words:

For the lay faithful, political involvement is a worthy and demanding expression of the Christian commitment of service to others. The pursuit of the common good in a spirit of service, the development of justice with particular attention to the situations of poverty and suffering, respect for the autonomy of earthly realities, the principle of subsidiarity, the promotion of dialogue and peace in the context of solidarity; these are the criteria that must inspire the Christian laity in their political activity.[17]

To Transform Institutions

Getting involved in politics therefore is not a bad thing to do; it is a positive vocation to tackle laws and budgets, develop institutions which deliver justice to the poor, and help take the suffering people down from the cross. In recent commentaries (not least from campaigners for change), politics and political institutions, councillors, MPs, councils, governments, the UN and WTO are sometimes publicly dismissed as 'part of the problem', as if a kind of withering away of the state and all institutions is simply to be wished for, and replaced by a kind of anarchic local communitarianism. 'Civil society' is often set against 'the state' and the murky world of politics and seen as the positive alternative. Occasionally major NGOs argue that, though not elected, they are accountable to their large numbers of members or subscribers, and are therefore entitled to replace elected bodies and institutions as the source of moral and political authority. The Church's tradition, however, rejects this approach, challenging us not merely to reform political institutions but to 'transform' them – and to do so from the perspective of the crucified people. Rather than a crude dismissal or rejection of politics, the Church refocuses the challenge around the positive need for mediating institutions that can bind societies and the whole world into one fair, just and peaceful community. We have a duty, therefore, to dedicate ourselves to transforming political institutions, political parties, councils, governments and international organizations such as the UN (as *Populorum Progressio*[18] spelt out) rather than reject them or vainly hope they will go away. In his BBC Memorial Lecture, a former Archbishop of York, John Hapgood, challenged a crude anti-Establishment approach, arguing that:

> What we are witnessing is more than a justifiable reaction against the concept of authority itself. It therefore cuts at the roots of beliefs and attitudes and institutions which have traditionally held society together. It discounts the accumulated wisdom of past generations. It sees history as no more than a record of human folly and corruption.[19]

Abandoning struggles for the development of accepted, proper and legitimate 'authority', including political institutions at every level, is too easily adopted as a 'radical option'. It is not an option for the Church.

As the 1971 Synod of Bishops put it in *Justice in the World*, 'Action on behalf of justice and participation in the transformation of the world'[20] is constitutive (in other words, essential, central, necessary and indispensable) of the preaching of the Good News, that primary Christian obligation. We should not abandon the struggle to transform the institutions of the world, not least in the face of philosophers such as John Rawls and Richard Rorty, who argue vociferously that the Church's influence on democratic politics must be severely circumscribed.

Love of Preference for the Poor

To bring about this transformation of the political institutions, the Catholic Church's social teaching gives us a clearly developed starting point: the preferential love of the Church for the poor, as Pope John Paul II put it in his address in Puebla in 1979. The *Compendium of Social Doctrine* spells out, 'the fight against poverty finds a strong motive in the option or preferential love of the Church for the poor'.[21] Published by the Pontifical Council for Justice and Peace in Rome in 2004, it draws together the teaching of all the social encyclicals, acknowledging that 'the free market, an economic progress with positive aspects, is nonetheless showing its limits', and insisting that 'on the other hand the preferential love of the poor represents a fundamental choice for the Church'.[22] It stresses that it is the Church's role 'to invite all people to do all they can to bring about an authentic civilization, oriented ever more towards integral human development in solidarity'.[23] There is still an underlining here that the preferential option for the poor should be reaffirmed in all its force:

> Today, furthermore given the worldwide dimension which the social question has assumed, this love of preference for the poor, and the decisions which it inspires in us, cannot but embrace the immense multitudes of the hungry, the needy, the homeless, those without healthcare, and above all those without hope of a 'better future'.[24]

Moreover, in the section on 'service in politics', the Pontifical Council for Justice and Peace reminds us to build a functioning democratic system that takes account of the poor:

> . . . a context for the exercise of discernment can be found in the functioning of the democratic system, understood by many today in agnostic and relativistic terms that lead to the belief that truth is something determined by the majority and conditioned by political considerations. In such circumstances, discernment is particularly demanding when it is exercised with regard to the objectivity and accuracy of information, scientific research and economic discussions that affect the life of the poorest people.[25]

Standing before the crucified people, therefore, how do we set about transforming institutions, challenging politics and economics, to get people down from the cross and stop more being nailed up? We can start by paying close attention to the functions of the democratic system.

Pro-democracy

St Thomas Aquinas, who worked on 'political theology', following Aristotle, suggested that over-concern with dividing the world into public and private realms is a chimera, and that the real political issues are to do with how we can connect proper and legitimate authority to methods of participation of the people. He grew up in Italy during the development of local city-states and conflicts between neighbouring jurisdictions and the central authority. His family was of the nobility and active in the military and political struggles of the age. One of his brothers became a soldier and was executed for plotting to kill Frederick II. As a theologian in Paris he was working out Aristotle's political ideas at the time of the emergence of new ideas of 'democracy', popular participation in decision making, and in the sharing out of land, resources and wealth. He identified the need for 'mediating institutions' to connect methods of popular democratic participation with proper authority. In other words, St Thomas saw a positive role for the intervening 'state' and its institutions long before the emergence of the modern nation-state and twentieth-century forms of democracy. For St Thomas Aquinas, compared with other forms of governance ranging from tyranny and monarchy to anarchy, democracy was the 'least bad form' of arranging political affairs. Indeed as a Dominican, Thomas Aquinas belonged to a religious order whose every office is filled by election. As Jean-Pierre Torrell spells out, 'He knew quite well that the sense of personal responsibility is heightened through real engagement in the choice of those responsible for government.'[26]

Derived from the Greek, 'democracy' ambivalently meant rule by the people or the many, and because the many were also poor it was often interpreted as rule by the poor, the common rabble, or mob, as opposed to an oligarchy of a few of the rich and well born. Notably in his *Politics* Aristotle had insisted that he did not think that a state in which a rich majority governed could be properly called a democracy. He wrote, 'suppose a total of one thousand of these are rich, they give no share in government to the three hundred poor, who are also free men and in other respects like them; no one would say that these thirteen hundred lived under a democracy.'[27] Now, as then, 'democracy' remains an unfinished project, in which numbers alone are not the key, but perhaps as Aristotle proposes, and Aquinas underlines, the inclusion of the poor is a real test of any attempts at genuine democracy. As Professor A. Halsey put it, referring to poverty in the UK context, 'Society means a shared life. If some and not others are poor, then the principles on which life is a shared one are at issue: society itself is in question.'[28]

Democracy, therefore, is a contested concept. The relationship between proper authority and popular participation is not yet settled. There is no clear template to be imposed on societies. Even background concepts such as 'human rights' cannot be taken for granted, particularly when individual political and civic rights are extended into 'economic' and 'social rights'. Human rights, despite efforts in the last half-century at the United Nations and elsewhere, have not yet been developed into such a universal concept that intervention into individual nation-states to defend them can easily be undertaken. Even the basic notion of the 'common good' (again taken from St Thomas Aquinas, with its roots in Aristotle), so central in the Catholic Church's social teaching along with human rights, is not without its problems and challenges. Some contemporary philosophers (such as Rawls) argue that there is no such thing as 'the common good'. Increasingly the idea of the 'common good' is regarded as confined to the 'nation-state', which itself is challenged by developing globalization and the emergence of porous national borders in a world of increasing numbers of migrants, asylum seekers and refugees. If we have to rethink basic concepts dear to the Church such as 'democracy', 'human rights' and 'the common good' in order to transform our political institutions, where then do we look to establish a basis for a solid political ethics? Is the Church's tradition able to regenerate interest in democracy as a means of liberating the poor?

Politics as Love of Persons

In his first encyclical letter *Deus Caritas Est*, Pope Benedict XVI takes us back to the primary statement 'God is love and he who abides in love abides in God, and God abides in him'[29] as the heart of the Christian faith, the Christian image of God and the resulting image of humankind and its destiny. But what can the practical world of politics draw from this focus on 'love'? Pope Benedict is helpfully specific: 'As a community the Church must practice Love. Love thus needs to be organized if it is to be an ordered service to the community.'[30] He reinforces the Church's social teaching that charity understood as 'generous giving' is not sufficient to eliminate hunger or reduce poverty if it is not (as Pope Paul VI spelt out in his 1967 *Populorum Progressio*) linked to efforts at 'building a world where all people, no matter what their race, religion or nationality can live fully human lives, freed from servitude imposed on them by others or by natural forces over which they have no sufficient control; a world where freedom is not an empty word'. Pope Benedict's text centres on the early Church in the Acts of the Apostles: 'with the community of believers there can never be room for a poverty that denies anyone what is needed for a dignified life' (Acts 2.44–45). His focus remains on charity defined as the political search for justice, and echoes the 1971 Synod of Bishops: 'Christian love of neighbour and justice cannot be separated. For love implies an absolute demand for justice, namely a recognition of the dignity and rights of one's neighbour. Justice attains its inner fullness only in love.'[31] If working for justice is the political expression of charity, its 'absolute demand' is based on that long emphasis in the Church's social teaching on the dignity of the human person.

The dignity of each individual human person is a core concept within the Church's social teaching. That each individual person is unique and invaluable is embedded in the Church's ethical tradition. At a hustings as a parliamentary candidate in a general election, I recall being quizzed in a packed hall on details of policy, on education, on health, on tackling Third World poverty, on racism, on drug dealing and crime. But then one young man put his hand up and simply said: 'My question is "I am a human being" – what are you as my elected representative going to do about it?' That intervention was a real insistence that we put 'the memory of the human' back into politics. I recall a conversation with diplomatic officials who advised not to raise individual cases of disappeared persons with the

Chinese authorities. A poet had been arrested and had disappeared into the prison system. Since China was a huge country of 1.2 billion people then it therefore would be unfair to expect the Chinese ambassador to be able to trace and track down one lost person. But given that this is the age of supercomputers, which are easily capable of holding together the faces of every single one of the six billion persons on the planet, accountability for the whereabouts of each person born ought to be *more* insisted upon rather than less. There is now no excuse for 'losing' any single person. The Chinese were pressed to account for individual 'lost persons' – a few were mercifully released. Significantly the international insistence on human rights is based on this understanding of the basic dignity of the human person. But that each human person is essentially a social being is also insisted upon by the Church. The 'social nature of human beings' section in the *Compendium of the Social Doctrine* of the Church spells out:

> This is based on a relational subjectivity that is in the manner of a free and responsible being who recognizes the necessity of integrating himself in cooperation with his fellow human beings and who is capable of communion with them on the level of knowledge and love.[32]

Each individual human person is also part of a wider society.

One of the drafters of the UN Declaration of Human Rights was the French Catholic philosopher-theologian Jacques Maritain, whose life's work was an insistence on the concept of 'persons in community'. His work in turn had a profound influence on Pope John Paul II, whose key work as a young theologian at the University of Lublin was entitled *The Acting Person*.[33] Based on St Thomas Aquinas (but with its roots in Aristotle's maxim 'man is a social animal'), the individual person cannot be regarded as disconnected from society, with 'rights' (for example) in isolation from duties, obligations and responsibilities. Aquinas expands Aristotle's concept of the 'political animal' as a citizen of the *polis* to the 'political animal' as a citizen of the whole world. Pope Benedict goes further, suggesting that we only find our identity in our relationships with others. We are born into communities. This presupposition of 'community' participation as the fundamental context of personal individual action undermines recent philosophical insistence on the autonomous isolated individual. The philosophical tensions between the 'individual' and the 'community' have been mirrored in economics and in politics, in the ebb and flow between emphases on individual responsibility and collective 'state' action. In a contemporary political world dominated by a model of market managerialism which seems to have undermined all practical alternatives, and in which equality tends to be reduced to equality before the offer of the market, rendering every individual equal to any other on the sole basis of virtually being like anyone else – a 'consumer' – reassertion of the concept of 'persons in community' provides a helpful challenge. Richard Roberts suggested in *Religion, Theology and the Human Sciences*[34] that in fact managerialism has 'become the new religion', especially in the sense of control, as performance, targets, benchmarking, mission statements and middle managers (whose task is to secure the conformity of front-line operatives to the organization's goals, as the organization seeks to gain control over an 'other', namely, the consumer) now dominate. This 'technomanagerialism', centred around global consumerism, in practice reduces the individual person to an economic cipher, incapable of participating in politics as a shaping of the future. It profoundly depoliticizes, takes the politics out of politics, and leaves untouchable the dominant single economic model. In other words, these economic structures are presumed to be out of practical political reach. In these terms, politics at best is therefore regarded as a form of corrupting interference in the perfect workings of the mechanisms of economic markets. The Church's traditional insistence on 'persons in community' challenges this view.

Nor is it only Aquinas, Jacques Maritain and John Paul II who turned to 'persons in community' as a liberating political concept. The British philosopher John Macmurray insisted that 'we need one another to be ourselves'.[35] His work *Persons in Relation* led him to conclude that 'complete and unlimited dependence is the central and crucial fact of personal existence – the basic fact of our human condition'. Moreover he insisted that:

> Economic relations, however direct, do not themselves suffice to establish human community between human beings. To these there must be added a mutual recognition of one another as fellows in the sharing of common life. All human community is a structure of direct relations between human beings. Community cannot be constituted by indirect relations or defined by them.[36]

What is needed therefore is the fostering of an alternative and less competitive individualistic environment, to encourage an internal growth of shared and respected norms and values, to enable 'persons in community' to develop and grow.

Including the Poor

But even the philosophical concept of 'persons in community' is insufficient without the Church's insistence on the preferential love for the poor. An emphasis on the social constitution of persons needs to be integrated with an insistence on the presence and challenge of the suffering poor. Indeed, as the theologian J.B. Metz spells out in his seminal *A Passion for God*,[37] the true source of 'authority' comes from and is based on taking the suffering poor into account and responding to their needs as a priority. Authority in politics therefore is to be understood as founded on the suffering poor. This inclusion of the poor is vital to the Church's challenge to economic structures and political institutions. Nor is it sufficient to enter into 'democratic' or 'participatory' dialogue, as if on equal terms in a neutral economic or political debate. The explicit political mandate is to take up the cause of the suffering poor and insist on the transformation of structures and institutions until they are included, and the suffering are taken down from the cross and no more are nailed up.

Similarly, insistence on discovering and supporting 'a community of persons' is a contemporary imperative in a world in which increasing economic and communicative globalization paradoxically proves to be the antithesis of local community development. Globalization, with its homogenizing imperative, undermines and destroys local communities and their languages and traditions. Increasingly, however, with the migration of people for work, the emergence of growing mega-cities leads to environments in which people are thrown together. The global is therefore in reality increasingly local' in character, as the tensions and conflicts elsewhere in the world are replicated cheek by jowl in our terraces and tower blocks. Trade matters and migration increasingly break down national borders. In crowded urban environments the poor are least likely to be able to choose to move out. Their neighbours are 'given', those with whom they are invited to build community even in areas of the highest mobility and turnover of people. Building community is increasingly about our capacity actually to 'live where we are'. Dare we believe that 'anyone who lives and works here belongs here'[38] and work with them to make sense of a 'community of persons' locally?

Building Local Community

Notably the Church, and most other faith communities, retain a presence in poor inner-city neighbourhoods, understanding the need to 'abide with' rather than move out, or go away, when faced with those tensions, conflicts and crises of people jostling together for space and resources in urban centres. Many positively contribute to the shaping of the local public realm in terms of social service provision as well as challenges to economic and political structures. The role of the Church locally in challenging political authority often combines with the practical action of supporting the building of communities of persons, communities of shared hope, confident enough to challenge 'the powers that be' from the perspective of the authority of the suffering poor. Increasingly the Church can be and is working with other faith communities who share not only the preferential love of the poor, but also a mission to develop hope in a culture of fear, a hope strong enough to work for real transformation of economic structures and political institutions at every level, building from the local upwards.

'Trickle down' market economics still fails to improve the lives of the poor, whether in the inner cities of Britain, the slums of Manila or the scrub lands of sub-Saharan Africa. A new economic vision and practice is needed. The need to develop genuinely participatory models of democracy at every level, and institutions of respected and legitimated authority, within a common framework of law, which can eliminate poverty by tackling trading injustice and fostering peaceful relations, remains the twenty-first-century challenge. We need to be thinking and acting globally and locally simultaneously in our fragile, complex world. It is the Church that has developed this prophetic capacity. Rather than cynically write off political institutions as corrupt and powerless and retreat into a privatized ideal of 'spirituality', the real need is to engage, to move into the world of pain, suffering and poverty, and from that perspective work in detail at transforming our political institutions, insisting that real 'authority' comes from the suffering poor who must be heeded, and counted in.

Just as Kirkstall Abbey, that place of contemplative prayer, was the place of local community stability and hospitality, in Armley Prison it is the interfaith team of chaplains who are working to integrate ex-prisoners into 'the outside' inner-city communities on their release. They work with them and support them as a means of transforming lives, building up the local inclusive community, supportive of the poor and those who are suffering. If a local prison can be interpreted as a challenging place of liberation, how much more so should the Church, locally, nationally and internationally, be the source of hopeful transformation of political institutions? We are then asking with Ellacuria: 'What must I do for these people to rise again?'

Notes

1. Ignacio Ellacuria, 'Las Igesias Latinoamericanas interpelan a la Iglesia de España', in *Sal Terrae* 82 (6) (1982), p. 230, cited in Jon Sobrino, *Jesus the Liberator: A Historical-Theological Reading of Jesus of Nazareth* (Maryknoll, NY: Orbis, 1993), p. 262.
2. Enrique Dussel, *Ethics and Community* (New York: Orbis, 1988), p. 24.
3. William Cavanaugh, *Theopolitical Imagination* (London: Continuum, 2003).
4. 1993 Parliament of the World's Religions, 'Towards a Global Ethic', in *Testing the Global Ethic: Voices from the Religions on Moral Values*, ed. Peggy Morgan and Marcus Braybrooke (Grand Rapids, MI: Conexus Press, 1998), p. 5.

5. Tom Bentley, 'The Self-creating Society', *Renewal* 12 (1), 2004, accessed online at http://www.renewal.org.uk/issues/2004%20Volume%2012/Bentley.htm#top.
6. Ullrich Beck, *The Risk Society: Towards a New Modernity* (London: Sage, 1992), p. 49.
7. Raymond Williams, *Towards 2000* (London: Penguin, 1983), p. 4.
8. Slavoj Žižek, *On Belief* (London: Routledge, 2001), p. 26.
9. Terry Eagleton, *Sweet Violence: The Idea of the Tragic* (Oxford: Blackwell, 2002), p. xiii.
10. Bishop Pedro Casaldaliga, 'From Immediatist Disillusion to Hope-filled Utopia', *Concilium*, vol. 3 (2003), p. 132.
11. Jean Vanier, *Drawn into the Mystery of Jesus Through the Gospel of John* (London: Darton, Longman and Todd, 2004), p. 13.
12. Hannah Arendt, *On Revolution* (London: Faber and Faber, 1963), p. 253.
13. Raymond Plant, *Politics, Theology and History* (Cambridge: Cambridge University Press, 2001), p. 5.
14. John Paul II, encyclical letter *Laborem Exercens* (1981).
15. 'Pastoral Constitution on the Church in the Modern World', in *The Documents of Vatican II*, ed. Walter Abbott, SJ (London: Geoffrey Chapman, 1966), p. 283.
16. Congregation for the Doctrine of the Faith, *Doctrinal Note on some Questions Regarding the Participation of Catholics in Political Life* (16 January 2003), Section 1, §1.
17. *Compendium of Social Doctrine of the Church* (Pontifical Council for Justice and Peace, Libreria Vaticana, 2004), §565.
18. Pope Paul VI, encyclical letter *Populorum Progressio* (1967).
19. Archbishop John Hapgood, BBC lecture.
20. Synod of Bishops, *Justice in the World* (Vatican City: Vatican Press, 1971), p. 6.
21. *Compendium of Social Doctrine of the Church* (Pontifical Council for Justice and Peace, Libreria Vaticana, 2004), §449.
22. Op. cit., Cardinal Angelo Sodano, introductory letter, p. xxii.
23. Ibid., p. xxii.
24. *Compendium of Social Doctrine of the Church* (Pontifical Council for Justice and Peace, Libreria Vaticana, 2004), §182.
25. Ibid., §569.
26. Jean-Pierre Torrell, *St Thomas Aquinas* (Vol. II, Spiritual Masters), (CUA Press, Catholic University of America, 2003), p. 305.
27. Aristotle, *Politics* (London: Penguin, 1992), Book III, ch. 8, 1290b.
28. A.H. Halsey, Foreword to Joanna Mack and Stewart Lansley, *Poor Britain* (George Allen & Unwin, 1985), p. xxiii.
29. Pope Benedict XVI, encyclical letter *Deus Caritas Est* (Libreria Editrice Vaticana, 2006), §1, p. 3.

30. Ibid., §20, p. 47.
31. Synod of Bishops, *Justice in the World* (Vatican City: Vatican Press, 1971), p. 14.
32. *Compendium of Social Doctrine of the Church*, §149.
33. John Paul II, *The Acting Person* (The Netherlands: Kluwer Academic Publishers, 1979).
34. Richard Roberts, *Religion, Theology and the Human Sciences* (Cambridge: Cambridge University Press, 2002).
35. John Macmurray, *Persons in Relation (The Form of the Personal: Gifford Lectures, Vol. 2)*, (London: Faber, 1961), p. 211.
36. Cited in John Costello, *John Macmurray: A Biography* (Edinburgh: Floris Books, 2002), p. 229.
37. J.B. Metz, *A Passion for God* (New York: Paulist Press International, 1998).
38. Alan Badiou, *Metapolitics* (London: Verso, 2005), p. 17.

Chapter 10

Ethic, Business and Managers

Hans Küng

In this chapter, the author seeks to take the business global ethic project further by building a realistic vision which points towards the future in a global perspective, which makes clearer the outlines of a more peaceful, just and humane world. He argues that both in the sphere of politics and in that of economics we need a new sense of responsibility: firstly by constructing a responsible politics which seeks to achieve the precarious balance between ideals and realities which has to be rediscovered over and over again; and secondly by constructing a responsible eco-nomics which can combine economic thinking with ethical convictions. It is this change of inner humanness that is depicted as the task for the new millennium.

In 1971 Klaus Schwab, a professor of economic policy who had just returned from the USA at the age of 33, arranged the first annual meeting of business leaders in Davos, later to become the World Economic Forum, and at the same time formulated as a 'model for business' what was to become even more topical in the 1990s in the face of globalization: that 'all the groups mentioned in alphabetical order here have a direct interest in the success of a business' (here I quote him word for word):[1]

- The *shareholders and lenders* expect not only a safe investment but also appropriate interest on the capital invested.
- The *customers* expect a good product at a favourable price. For machinery, service is also particularly important. It does not just begin with the delivery of the machine, but at the first planning of the product, because here already the producer must already be concerned with the problems of the purchaser.
- The *suppliers* expect the business to be capable of paying them. Further-more, they have an interest that the competitiveness of the purchaser should be maintained in the long term, and grow further.
- The *employees* expect not only appropriate financial remuneration for their contribution, but also recognition and encouragement. The best results can only be achieved when employees are convinced of the sig-nificance of their work and individuals are given possibilities of develop-ing it.

- The *national economy, the state and society* expect the business to contribute in a variety of ways to the improvement of the common good (jobs, taxes, etc.).

The model must take these expectations, needs and interests into account. Thus Klaus Schwab.

1. Principles of a Business Ethic

Already at the third Davos management forum in 1973, a 'code of good ethical behaviour for executives' was presented. This saw it as its task 'to serve customers, workers, backers and society' and 'to balance their conflicting interests'. It culminates in the concluding remark that profit is 'a necessary means but not the end' of any business enterprise.[2] Now it is certainly not a coincidence that a vehement attack on this approach followed, with an explicit reference to Milton Friedman. It came from a professor of business theory, Horst Steinmann, who read out of the text a rejection of 'institutional measures to control power', an 'ideological justification and capitulation to environmental interests' and a 'repudiation of demands for reform'. However, none of this is to be found in the Davos Manifesto; nor can it even be attributed to the Corporate Social Responsibility movement which may have influenced this manifesto as a principal factor, but certainly not as the sole one. Would Horst Steinmann, who in the meantime has done very good work in business ethics, still construe 'a break-up of bourgeois liberal ideas of order' from the idea of the 'social responsibility of businesses' and discover a 'contradiction to the idea of democracy'[3] in it? Or was this perhaps a sin of his youth? Be this as it may, 20 years later one can read in the same author that 'ethical considerations' must 'systematically be put before the profit principle, not only at the level of order but also at that of business'.[4]

In the time of Reaganomics some economists thought that morality had lost its 'controlling power'. That is certainly not completely wrong, in that businesses and national economies have come to depend very closely on one another, and the economic interactions have become complicated and anonymous. But on the other hand, particularly in the 1990s, economists find themselves confronted with an unexpected return of morality in public discussion, in particular in the national economy and the business world. I shall now go on to mention two indications of the new significance of ethics in business.

(a) Not just for shareholders but for all involved

Two statements provide evidence for the 'global ethic project' that co-operation is quite possible both between different religions and between believers and non-believers, in questions of business ethics:

- The Interfaith Declaration. *A Code of Ethics on International Business for Christians, Muslims and Jews.* It was worked out under the patronage of Prince Philip, Duke of Edinburgh; Hassan bin Talal, Crown Prince of Jordan; and Sir Evelyn de Rothschild in 1988 (at Windsor) and 1993 (in Amman).[5]
- Principles For Business. *The Caux Round Table.* The Caux Round Table was founded by Frederik Philips (former president of Philips Electronics) and Olivier Giscard d'Estaing (vice-president of INSEAD) in 1986. It was taken further by Ryuzaburo Kaku (chairman of Canon Inc.), and concluded with the considerable involvement of leading business representatives from Europe, Japan and the USA.[6]

The Caux Declaration begins from the fact of globalization: 'The mobility of employment, capital, products and technology is making business increasingly global in its transactions and its effects.'[7] Yet at the same time it states that companies have responsibilities over and above earning profits, and that they cannot just rely on the 'magic' of the market for solving problems: 'Laws and market forces are necessary but insufficient guides for conduct. Responsibility for the policies and actions of business and respect for the dignity and interests of its stakeholders are fundamental. Shared values including a commitment to shared prosperity, are as important for a global community as for communities of smaller scale.' Therefore the declaration speaks of the 'necessity for moral values in business decision making. Without them, stable business relationships and a sustainable world community are impossible.'

It is significant that both declarations in no way see the task of the business only as earning profits for the shareholders, but in responsibility for all *stakeholders* who have a stake in the business. The Caux Declaration finds this point so fundamental that it makes it the first general principle: 'The Responsibilities of Businesses: Beyond Shareholders towards Stakeholders'.[8] The profit motive is seen as fully justified but not sufficient: 'Businesses have a role to play in improving the lives of all their customers, employees and shareholders by sharing with them the wealth they have created.'[9]

It is therefore consistent that both declarations should have more or less detailed sections on the responsibilities of business to all six parties: towards employees, customers, suppliers and financiers, the community (local and national governments), and finally also the owners/shareholders/investors (in the Interfaith Declaration put in last place, in the Caux Declaration in third place).

Both declarations agree on the responsibilities of businesses towards their employees. The Caux Declaration states: 'We believe in the dignity of every employee and in taking employee interests seriously. We therefore have a responsibility to:

- provide jobs and compensation that improve workers' living conditions . . .
- engage in good faith negotiations when conflict arises . . .
- promote in the business itself the employment of differently abled people in places of work where they can be genuinely useful';
- and finally, in addition to all the obligations of employers to provide information and communication, healthcare and further training, in particular to 'be sensitive to the serious unemployment problems frequently associated with business decisions, and work with governments, employee groups, other agencies and each other in addressing these disclocations'.[10]

The Interfaith Declaration emphasizes: 'Employees make a unique contribution to an organization; it follows that in their policies businesses shall, where appropriate, take notice of trade union positions'; businesses should show:

> a respect for the individual (whether male or female) in their beliefs, their family responsibility and their need to grow as human beings. It will provide equal opportunities in training and promotion for all members of the organization. It will not discriminate in its policies on grounds of race, skin colour, creed or gender.[11]

But it would take us too far were I to go on to report on the ethical responsibilities of businesses to the other five groups involved. Rather, what is important for a global ethic at a time of globalization is *what underlies the individual ethical requirements*. Both declarations are quite clear about this.

(b) Basic values and basic attitudes

It is highly illuminating that in the preface to the Caux Declaration both a 'Western' and an 'Eastern' basic value are to be found which happily supplement each other:

- not only *human dignity* and the sacredness of the value of each individual, who must always remain an end, and not simply be a means for other purposes;

- but also the Japanese concept of 'kyosei', which means living and working together for the common good, enabling cooperation and mutual prosperity to coexist with healthy and fair competition.[12]

The Interfaith Declaration makes the necessary distinction between various levels in an ethical approach to business: the intrinsic morality of the economic system in itself, then the policy and strategy of the organizations concerned, and finally the behaviour of individual employees in the context of their work. At the same time reference is made to the different legal frameworks, depending on the country in which business is conducted. However, mention may be made of some of the key concepts or *basic values* which have great significance in *Judaism, Christianity and Islam*, and for which numerous texts from the sacred Scriptures of these three Abrahamic religions can be cited:

> *justice*: fairness, exercising authority in maintenance of right;
> *mutual respect*: love and consideration for others;
> *stewardship*: human beings are only 'stewards', 'trustees' of natural resources;
> *honesty*: truthfulness and reliability in all human relationships, in short integrity.

The Caux Declaration, in which respect for the law and for national and international rules is inculcated, also stresses that one 'must get beyond the letter of the law to a spirit of trust':[13] honesty, boldness, truth, keeping promises and transparency, all of which contribute not only to the credibility and stability of a business but also to the smooth efficiency of business transactions.

It should also be mentioned that the Caux Declaration openly addresses the particularly tricky point of the 'avoidance of illicit operations'. 'A business should not participate in or condone bribery, money laundering, or other corrupt practices: indeed, it should seek co-operation with others to eliminate them. It should not trade in arms or other materials used for terrorist activities, drug traffic or other organized crime.'[14]

A question which must be raised is: are only Western values and criteria appealed to here? The strong Japanese involvement in the Caux paper already makes this seem doubtful. But the question plays a role which extends to official statements by Chinese and Indonesian statesmen.

(c) Asian versus Western values

It is easy to understand why today Asians, who are open to the West, while affirming modernization, are sceptical about the Western system of values. There was an outcry from half the American press (the other half was wisely self-critical) when a young American vandal who had maliciously damaged automobiles and other objects was subjected in Singapore to the caning customary there (though not always enforced). Singapore took its revenge with concrete figures: in the United States, where the population has increased by 41 per cent since 1960, crimes of violence have increased by 560 per cent, divorces by 300 per cent, single mothers by 419 per cent and children who grow up with one parent by 300 per cent.[15] Singapore really has no intention of being infected by this Western 'morality'. We have heard similar tones from Japan, and in America the former President's drug representative W.J. Bennett, attacking the decline in values, wrote a *Book of Virtues* which presents a 'reasonable mean between *carte blanche* for vandals and torture'.[16] Moreover it promptly became a bestseller, a sign that responsibility, honesty, loyalty, courage, sympathy, friendship, tenacity and self-discipline are being more sought after in the West as well.

However, we are not concerned here with individual virtues, but with the basic question whether the peoples of Asia will adopted *limitless individualism* (which pays no heed to the community) and *unbridled freedom* (with the associated phenomena of Western decadence), or whether, as the wise diplomat and director of the Institute of Policy Studies in Singapore, Tommy Koh, remarks, they should not maintain and encourage 'the 10 values which support the strength and success of East Asia', by attaching importance to strong families, intensive education, hard work, savings, moderation and national teamwork.[17] Already in my dialogue with Julia Ching, an expert on Chinese religion from the University of Toronto,[18] I drew attention to the researches of the French sinologist Leon Vandermersch. In his study of the 'new sinified world',[19] Vandermersch investigates the economic, political and cultural dimensions of the peoples who are bound together by the Chinese writing system or ideograms. These are the same everywhere (though they are read differently), and express meanings and reflect common basic attitudes and values that reproduce the more than 2,000-year-old Confucian tradition. We need not decide here whether this is also a reason why the cultures of East Asia have been able to advance so amazingly in recent decades by comparison, say, with the Islamic countries. Singapore, at any rate, adopted Confucian ethics in school teaching material in 1984, and similar efforts are also being made in other countries of the Far East. At all events, it is certain that the West has every reason to treat specifically Asian values with modesty and respect, despite all its reservations about a Confucian patriarchalism.[20]

Now does this mean on the other hand that Asian values may be cited *against human rights*, as was done by the Chinese Communists (and other autocratic Asian governments) at the Second World Conference on Human Rights in Vienna in 1993? Human rights emerged in the Enlightenment Christian philosophical tradition of the West and also in Asia (one can ask why). Because religion is the 'missing dimension of statesmanship', none of the Western diplomats and politicians at that Vienna conference was evidently knowledgeable enough to point out to the Chinese delegation that, for example, the concept of '*jen*', the '*humanu*', is very much a central concept of the Chinese tradition. In the present situation a great many human rights can be grounded in it which have considerable resonance all over Asia and Africa. In the long run these cannot be suppressed by force. How effective it would have been had a Western speaker pointed out that Confucius had already stated that a government could most easily dispense with the military, if need be also with food, but least of all with that trust which the people puts in it.[21]

Of course the rulers in Asia and elsewhere are often less interested in human rights than are those whom they rule. But in today's age of mass communication the fact can no longer be overlooked that from China, Tibet, Myanmar and Thailand through East Timor, West Iran in Indonesia and the Philippines to Kenya and the Congo, human rights express a deep longing of the ruled in the face of the rulers. And the 'dissidents' are no tiny minority, as one can sometimes read even in Western newspapers, but for many dictators a terrifying if oppressed power. There is no question that, given freedom of speech, those millions whom the bold Nobel Peace Prize-winner Aung San Suu Kyi was able to mobilize through free elections in Burma could also be activated in China by a man like Wei Jingsheng.[22]

However, the 'global ethic project' differs from the Western human rights movement insofar as it does not attempt simply to disseminate human rights deriving from Western natural law thinking all over the world, but rather the values, criteria and attitudes of the ethnic and religious traditions peculiar to each people, in order to make fruitful use of them for human responsibilities and human rights. As I have described, the Chicago Declaration of the Parliament of the World's Religions also came into being in an attempt to extract from the traditions of the various great religions what is common to the religions today and can also be supported by non-religious people. The opposition of Asian values to Western values is relativized by the common foundation of human responsibilities and human rights in each particular tradition. However, we are now moving from *these* questions of principle to the more practical questions of today's industrial societies.

(d) Inconvenient questions, practical suggestions

Are economics, politics and society at all prepared for this epoch-making, postmodern paradigm shift of globalization now taking place, which in its way is as far-reaching as the change from a medieval agricultural economy to modern industrial society? It is important above all to *find a new status for the state, labour and capital*. 'The globalized economy must not become synonymous with a freewheeling market economy, a train without brakes, which wreaks havoc,' remarks Professor Klaus Schwab, the president of the

Davos World Economic Forum. The 'human costs of globalization' have reached 'a level at which the whole social structure of the democracies will be put to the test in an unprecedented way'. 'The social responsibilities of businesses (and governments) remain as important as ever. What is on the agenda is the need to redefine them and to weight them.'[23]

All sides have to make their contribution to a new social consensus. Nowadays many statesmen, too, see that there must be a fair *balance of burdens*. As the German Federal President Roman Herzog remarks, with an eye to the often blind and selfish functionaries of the different interest groups:

> My experience shows that when people see that a real problem is being addressed and there are not just mischievous cuts, they contribute much that their representatives in the association hierarchies, the parties and even in the media do not understand. People may say that I have illusions, but I still believe that the population is ready to accept cuts as long as it feels that they are needed and the cards are put on the table.[24]

Thus here first of all some inconvenient but also unavoidable questions arise on all sides. I shall not offer any recipes, but present questions for discussion which are prompted by the problems above all of the Swedish and the American economic models (BI) and the discussion of neocapitalism and the social market economy (BII). To discuss them in the spirit of an ethical, responsible way of doing business (BIII) might perhaps open up ways out of the present crisis.

BI

Experiences with the American model raise the question: do we not need a new responsibility for businesses? 'Globalization is an irreversible process. One of its greatest challenges has not yet been resolved: unemployment. It would be out of the question for companies to be concerned only with their own surplus value and to leave the negative consequences of their restructurings to the world at large.'

Thus the Swiss Federal President Pascal Delamuraz.[25] The following thoughts seem to me to be worth considering:

- In principle 'lean production and management' (USA) and social responsibility (EC) must be achieved together.
- Specifically, we must get out of the vicious circle in which only the slimming down of companies and the mass redundancies connected with this lead to improved profits and thus to higher share values, so that now redundancies are often identified with gains on the stock market. The efforts of business must be concentrated on creating new jobs with new tasks instead of just saving 'superfluous' jobs.

- More success might be achieved if, rather than making workers redundant for short-term gain and in order to consolidate a company, the level of training among the workforce were improved ('upgrading') with a view to a longer-term increase in productivity and possible recruitment for an expanded market.
- Just as the share of income from dependent work must not drop arbitrarily, so too the share of income from business activity must not rise arbitrarily.
- More precise rules relating to *the responsibility of the chairmen and directors of companies* need to be aimed at, in order to protect the shareholders and the employees. Bad business decisions and mismanagement, which in individual cases result in the loss of millions or billions and threaten the very existence of a company, must also have tangible consequences for the chairmen and boards responsible.
- Not only the top executives but all employees should share in the return, the success and the resources of a company. Participation and profit sharing can increase identification with work and the company and can also strengthen motivation to personal responsibility, an awareness of costs and better performance.
- A good atmosphere at the workplace and social peace are also 'productive factors'.

Against the advocates of a pure capitalism who are miles away from a social market economy, it must be pointed out clearly that a form of economic doctrine and praxis which aims only at profit and does not take the slightest notice of either the workforce or the citizens who are also affected, and which rather *a priori* accepts monstrous differences in income and unimaginable suffering and poverty must be said clearly to be not only unrealistic and antisocial, but also downright immoral. Truly, 'What is the use of globalization if it is no more than a vehicle for cynics who want to avoid the norms of the law and morality?' That is a remark by no less a person than the director-general of the International Monetary Fund, Michel Camedessus.[26] And since some advocates of this pure capitalism still claim to be believing Christians, Jews or adherents of other religions, they should be referred to the powerful thousand-year-old tradition which, beginning with the prophets of Israel, the philosophers of Greece, the Jesus of the New Testament and the Qur'an, down the centuries to the present, has sharply required a morality of social justice from the greedy, the ambitious and the exploiters: justice and fairness to the poor, the helpless and the exploited.[27]

BII

Experiences with the Swedish model in particular make us ask: do we not also need a *new responsibility on the part of employees*? As we have seen, the global structural change has led to mass unemployment, which represents a tremendous existential burden for hundreds of millions of people. But cannot this central problem of our time be solved not just by creating new jobs but by *obliging those unwilling to work* to look seriously for jobs, or helping them to create their own independent jobs? The unemployed must not earn as much as the employed (or even more, through the black economy); the net income from work must clearly be higher than the income provided by the state for those out of work; and badly paid work is better than no work at all and therefore can be asked of people.

But can such *new flexibility and differentiation of wages* be achieved? This would mean quite a significant change both for individuals and for trade union policy. It would mean 'the willingness of large groups in our societies to take jobs which pay less well than today', and thus to accept 'larger inequalities'. That at any rate is the comment by the Social Democrat economic policy expert Kjell Olof Feldt on the Swedish model, contrary to his own party ideology.[28] A discussion is going on here. Some people are suggesting that there could be more extensive and intensive work, if labour in the industrial nations as a whole were to be made cheaper, so that it regained its competitiveness, and consumers were not required to pay high prices, so that their purchasing power diminished again, to the detriment of the economic boom. Specifically this could mean less absenteeism and more flexibility in the working week (in Japan the working year is 2,200 hours and in Germany 1,250).

BIII

Experiences with both the Swedish and the American models raise the question whether we do not need a *slimmed-down state*. The state must certainly not be made into merely a night-watchman state again, as the ultraliberals may want, but perhaps it will have to concentrate more on the core areas of defence, internal security, law and order and also education. However, a basic provision must be made for all citizens in the areas of healthcare, education with equal opportunities and social and old age welfare, so that real poverty continues to be excluded.

But wouldn't this result in a *diminution of claims on the state*? Mustn't claim and achievement stand in a reasonable relationship? Many people say that those who achieve less should also receive less; and those who have a special wish (in respect of healthcare, social security) should pay for it themselves. In this connection the following proposals are being discussed:

- The *state contribution* (in the German federation, the states and local communities) must be *reduced* and space made for the private sector.
- In times of financial need *large-scale projects costing billions*, the need for which is doubted even by many professionals (Eurofighter, Transrapid, Expo etc.), should be abandoned.

- *Subsidies running into billions* should be *reduced* and the burden on the state budget should be substantially lightened.
- *Taxes*, which are often far too high, should *be lowered*; tax legislation which only experts can understand must be simplified, and tax allowances and possibilities of writing off tax which are often misused must be abolished.
- Businesses which pay less and less tax at home should not still be rewarded with high state subsidies, but should be 'obliged' to make a relevant social contribution at home.
- Once again, more responsibility and independence should be required of the individual.

However, all these are not patent recipes, but basic reflections over which there is much argument. They have been put forward by members of very different political and social interest groups. All this aims on the one hand to relieve the state of a burden and on the other to increase not only the responsibility but also the economic scope of the individual. So these proposals are aimed at a consolidation of the budget, not through piecemeal financial measures (which are also common outside Germany) and unplanned cuts, but by a fair middle-term concept of consolidation which affects not only the large low- and middle-income group, but also the employers, their expenditure and their privileges; then tax allowances for the rich; and not least subsidies of all kinds.

If the morass of state subsidies is drained and both taxes and payments are tangibly lowered, will not *individuals* once again be able to, indeed have to, decide how to utilize their financial resources? I can decide for myself what I buy and what I do not buy, *whether I* save or spend. This brings us from the meso-level of businesses to the micro-level of persons, and here especially executives.

3. Ethics – a Challenge for Managers

There are more managers than is generally assumed who are the opposite of hardliners, thinking only of profit and shareholder value. There are managers who attempt, rather, to live out a high ethic, even in the harsh reality of business. One of them always carries around an already yellowed slip of paper with the admonition of Mahatma Gandhi on it, '*The Seven Deadly Sins in Today's World*':

> Wealth without work,
> Enjoyment without conscience,
> Knowledge without character,
> Business without morality,

Science without humanity,
Religion without sacrifice and
Politics without principles.

(a) Where does strong management come from?

Here are three cases to reflect on:

Why in a particular branch have two great multinational concerns not merged, whereas two others have? Because the man behind the decision had the conviction, which was ultimately grounded in ethics and religion, that expansion and concentration of the power of the companies were not in themselves sufficient justification for a merger: it was not necessary economically and would be at the expense of people in their various positions.

Why in a world-famous German company was a financial director quietly dismissed from the board for irregularities? Because one individual against all the rest did not agree to a cover-up on account of his ethical convictions. Long afterwards, he was thanked by his colleagues for his unyielding attitude – and subsequently recognized as an extremely wise policy-maker.

A concern known all over the world was entangled in several bribery scandals, and a number of its employees had to accept responsibility for paying bribes, while the chairman, directors and managers distanced themselves from such manipulations. A rival firm has so far remained free of all such accusations. Why? Because in the second international concern it was part of the business philosophy that any employee with a management function had to sign a paper entitled 'legality'. This stated that the company applied the principle of strict legality 'to all actions, measures, contracts, etc. of this group and its workers', regardless of any opportunistic considerations. Specifically it stated: 'Every employee is personally responsible for observing the laws in his sphere of work.' So this was a legality grounded in morality.

It is quite clear that today much is expected of executives in business, administration and politics. They must show that they are not only capable of analysis but can also take decisions and implement them. Thorough training and long experience are needed to achieve this. Executives have to set clear goals for themselves and others, employ workers and resources effectively, be able to grasp complex situations in a very short time and make the right decisions in them. In a word, strong management is required.

By contrast, weak management ('nobodies in pinstripe suits'), whether in private business or public administration, in a firm or a ministry, has a depressing, demoralizing and destabilizing effect down to the last employee, whereas strong management provides motivation and inspiration. Think of all the far-sightedness, steadfastness and dynamism that is called for. Can management be learned? In principle, yes. Think of all the books that are written and journals published, all the seminars that are held and courses taken to train first-class management and keep retraining it. Modern management consultants rightly require executives to communicate rather than to inform, to cooperate rather to delegate, to lead rather than to control. A holistic training and perspective is called for which incorporates a person's own feelings, intuition and creativity; humanity has to be learned, along with communication, cooperative partnership and social competence.

However, there should be a consensus that all this, that strong and effective management, has to do not only with actions and strategies but also with *attitude, character and personality*: leadership through personality, with the head and the heart. Hence the question: don't attitude, character and personality at the same time have to do with integrity, morality and ethos? Not just with ethics = teaching, but with ethos = attitude, inner moral attitude? And doesn't this have to do with values, patterns of interpretation and criteria for action, and thus quite often, directly or indirectly, also with religious convictions, religious upbringing, positive or negative religious experiences?

(b) No business culture without personality culture

Business culture, always important but nowadays of strategic relevance, ultimately consists in the totality of the decisive attitudes, values, criteria, norms and behavioural patterns of management and employees in a business.

A business consists primarily of people, and therefore business culture presupposes a *personality culture*. Hence my very direct questions:

- Is it not necessary, first, for *executives themselves* to be aware of their own moral and religious attitudes, and thus to understand the moral and religious aspects of leadership more clearly? So the question is: who, what, how are you – as a human being, a person, a character?
- Secondly, is it not important for *employees*, too, not only to see management from the outside as directors, executives, managers, supervisors and so on, but also to learn something of what moves their heads and hearts, what determines their invisible and yet very influential 'ethos'? The question here is, 'Where do you stand in your attitude?'
- Thirdly, in a time when the credibility of public institutions and representatives has suffered a great deal (at a time of satiation with politics, politicians and parties), must it not once again be made clearer to the *public* what the supreme values, generally binding moral criteria, norms, normative authorities are, to which our leading figures feel bound in

business, administration, politics and in education and science? So the question is a personal one: what are your fundamental convictions? What is unconditional, categorical for you, without any ifs and buts?

Since all professionals, including politicians and business executives, want to present a good image to themselves and to the public, it is worth knowing that in *America* a questionnaire[29] about the ethical standards or honesty of particular professional groups circulated among business students in the middle of the 1980s produced the following results: clergy 67 per cent, chemists 65 per cent, doctors 58 per cent, dentists 56 per cent, college professors 54 per cent, engineers 54 per cent, police 47 per cent, bank staff 37 per cent, television reporters/commentators 33 per cent, journalists 31 per cent, newspaper reporters 29 per cent, lawyers 27 per cent, leading businessmen 23 per cent.

Does this perhaps apply only to America? In Germany, in 1993 the Allensbach Public Opinion Research Institute,[30] which enjoys a very high reputation, obtained the following answers to a question as to which profession enjoys the highest respect: doctors 81 per cent, clergy 40 per cent, lawyers 36 per cent, college professors 33 per cent, diplomats 32 per cent, writers 28 per cent, chemists 27 per cent, businessmen 26 per cent, engineers 26 per cent, nuclear physicists 25 per cent, schoolteachers 24 per cent, directors of large firms 22 per cent, journalists 17 per cent, student chaplains 15 per cent, officers 9 per cent, politicians 9 per cent, booksellers 9 per cent, trade union leaders 8 per cent.

But aren't the questions raised above perhaps all superfluous? Are executives solely and exclusively concerned with the statistics of success? Is their own career more important even than the well-being of the firm? As a well-known business consultant announced: in order to remain in the 'fast lane of life', certainly one must 'always believe in something, but it doesn't much matter what', 'everything is right, everything is wrong' . . .[31]

(c) Business consultancy: Machiavelli for managers?

Back in 1967 a book appeared in Britain with the title *Management and Machiavelli*; the German publisher gave it the provocative subtitle *The Art of Keeping on Top in Our Organized World*.[32] If we look more closely at this bestseller, it is easy to see that the author does not want to argue for Machiavellianism in management, but only for Machiavelli's method 'of grasping a contemporary problem and then investigating it in a practical way with reference to the experience of others who faced a similar problem in the past'.[33]

Be this as it may, the link between management and Machiavelli was made, and in some circles *Machiavellianism in management* became respectable. I shall merely illustrate briefly here what the St Gallen specialist on Machiavelli, Alois Riklin, documents at length:[34]

- According to a test game at an elite American university (one is reminded of the diplomacy games which were so popular among Kissinger's students) a good Machiavellian is someone who rejects statements like 'One should only act if one is certain that one's action is morally unobjectionable' and accepts statements like 'The essential difference between criminals and other people is that the criminals are stupid enough to get found out.'
- There is a Machiavelli course for rising managers at a well-known American Graduate School of Business and Public Administration with the aim of recognizing Machiavellianism among others, and also being able to practise it oneself.
- The advertisement for a course in a German managers' magazine runs: 'Managers' Machiavelli, seminar on success for managers, the theory and practice of power in business life.' The slogan is: 'Guaranteed effective. Almost moral-free. Use at your own danger. No refunds.' And there are rules like: Lies are occasionally necessary, sometimes practicable. But lie only when it is worth it.
- Then at Cornell University, as a counter-movement, there has been an interdisciplinary investigation into selfishness and solidarity in student attitudes. It found that economists did much worse in tests on fairness and social behaviour than the students of any other discipline.
- Riklin's comment: 'What a tremendous difference between the patriotic common sense of Machiavelli and the egotistical career mania of the Machiavelli courses for managers!'[35]

However, more important than these Machiavelli courses which, while symptomatic, are isolated, is the effect of the occasions organized by some business consultants infected by Machiavellianism which doubtless confirm among 'ordinary people' the view that *many businesses show a lack of ethical responsibility*; that most firms unscrupulously pursue their profit at the expense of the environment or the safety and health of consumers, untroubled about society as a whole. Those who know the scene even think that since the time of Reaganomics and Thatcherism a new style of profit-oriented, go-ahead young men (in this case, happily few women) who do not always act morally ('Yuppies') is climbing the top levels of American and European business. An attitude of *opportunism* is said to be widespread generally: on the one hand there is an orientation on material success, and on the other a readiness to use even dishonest means to achieve success and to affirm rules of life which point in a similar direction.[36] Indeed, it is often possible to detect a tendency towards the opportunist separation of legality and morality, a high degree of individualistic orientation and a less than average readiness for practical commitment to third parties. The existence of universal criteria is denied by such opportunists, and the ethical distinction between good and evil is often termed 'a mere matter of feelings'.

Unfortunately this tendency is to be found in particular among some of the *business consultants* who are so influential behind the scenes, though they often only popularize the ideas of academics and journalists at management levels and adjust their views to the trends. It seems suspicious that to generate sales, an 'adviser on personal development and manager training' by the name of *Reinhard K. Sprenger* has reminted the title of the famous book by the German American philosopher Hans Jonas, *The Imperative of Responsibility*, into *The Imperative of Self-Responsibility*.[37] And it is even more suspicious when, for his 'philosophy' of self-responsibility ('commitment'), he refers to a remark of Martin Heidegger, which Heidegger is supposed to have 'made to his students at the end of the 1920s': 'We must see clearly that at the present time we have no support from an objective generally binding knowledge or power; the only support which remains for us today is attitude.'[38] The author does not seem to be aware that statements like these (in reality from the famous/notorious speech which Heidegger gave as Rector in 1933, immediately after Hitler's seizure of power) made it possible for Heidegger and his students, who objectively had no 'support', to 'find support' in the 'attitude' of National Socialism. Anyone who propagates 'attitude' as mere form must not be surprised if one day it comes to be given content by ideology.

However, it is most suspicious of all when in 1995 this same business consultant – doubtless having given his readers much helpful advice – makes his remarks on the 'principle of self-responsibility' (the 'central idea which shapes business') lead up to a no less fatal epitome of the '*credibility*' of management: in a business with self-responsibility 'you are credible as management only on one condition: not because it is morally good or is recognized by others, but because you have *chosen* it. For no other reason.'[39] Is this cynicism or stupidity? According to such a subjective definition of credibility beyond good and evil it seems that any law-breaker, financial cheat, drug dealer or Mafia boss can claim credibility: because he has 'chosen' it, 'for no other reason'!

In all this there is one consolation: most recently some self-criticism has become evident even within the guild of the 'supermen' and 'saviours' of business in a disastrous time. In his *Consulting Report*,[40] the business consultant *Jörg Staute* analyses the many arrogant business advisers who, with empty talk and manipulated statistics, are masters of the art of self-presentation but, constantly surfing on the fashionable waves of management literature, and despite juicy fees (in Germany alone these supposedly amount to 15 billion DM per year), in practice produce little that is helpful. The book ends with the statement: 'There is less substance than is often assumed behind the great consulting bluff.'[41] Here of course ethical questions often come up, but even in this self-critical book, the ethic of business consultants nowhere becomes a topic; indeed, key words like morality and ethics do not appear in the wretched index. However, there are of course many serious business consultants to whom this criticism does not apply.

But contrary to my expectations, the question of ethics is also not a topic in the most recent book by the American management guru *Peter F. Drucker*, whom I much admire; with his Japanese colleague *Isao Nakauchi* he makes some interesting points in the section 'toward a new personality' but does not move on to state clear ethical requirements.[42]

The contribution to the discussion by *Joanne B. Ciulla*, professor of leadership and ethics at the Jepson School of Leadership Studies in the University of Richmond, is quite different. Basing herself on the observation that in the past ten years there has been a strong and increasing interest in questions of business ethics (documented by the numerous 'business ethics conferences and forums all over the world, from Moscow to Caracas'), she comes to the conclusion: 'It was no longer good enough for a business leader to be ethical; he or she had to make sure that moral values were inculcated into the organization.'[43] But do business leaders normally also do this?

(d) Financial and political scandals

There is no overlooking the fact that where values and clear standards have been dismissed, and where a religious orientation can no longer command a majority, the Kantian ethic of duty and orientation on a common good unfortunately does not get very far. Be this as it may, anyone who at a university has kept coming into contact with young people, and still does, could report at length the doubts, particularly among the most intelligent of our young generation, about the credibility of our leaders. These are purely subjective impressions. In a representative opinion poll[44] among Germans aged between 14 and 29 as to which organizations and personalities they thought credible, the following figures emerged: Greenpeace 64 per cent, Amnesty International 50 per cent, trade unions 17 per cent, Churches 15 per cent, business 8 per cent, political parties 5 per cent.

Older observers of the contemporary scene sometimes get the impression that in the banking world and credit system, as in economics and politics, whereas formerly petty offences were more usual, nowadays offences have become possible to a degree which people formerly, two, three decades ago, would have thought impossible in our civilized countries. Never before in the history of German business, it is claimed, 'have so many top managers been convicted of fraud, corruption, self-enrichment and status-seeking at the expense of their firms and shareholders as in recent years'.[45] It is not only due to the influence of the mass media, which are often ignorant, malicious and one-sided, that businessmen and politicians are increasingly represented in films and literature as greedy, self-seeking persons.

One thing at any rate is clear: *the credibility of the institutions, their representatives and experts, has declined.* And the *protest potential* of alternative movements, civil initiatives, groups, subcultures and also the 'potential for opting out' has increased, as has the resultant pressure for legitimation on the institutions and their representatives. So too have mass protests. And unfortunately this applies to the representatives of politics, as well as those of business and the trade unions (not to mention the representatives of the Church and the Vatican Bank). In fact nowadays those who have long been accustomed to taking the public statements of these representatives at their word cannot do other than put a sceptical question mark against any public statement.

Obviously today's financial and political scandals are not just fortuitous; they are not just individual failures and mistakes, but part of the 'system' and 'method'. This compromises the great majority of respectable people. Blatant abuses are often officially tolerated, concealed and excused for years, and quite often the political parties bear a special responsibility. It would be worth making a closer investigation of the degree to which the great bank, stock exchange and corruption scandals first utilized the same mechanisms, secondly showed a similar character, and thirdly had similarly devastating results. Here I mean above all a discrediting of the political and business elite who so often forfeit all credibility by their trivialization of actual dangers, by helpless or deceitful reactions, and finally by disarming assertions of innocence.

However, happily we do not have to wait for counter-measures to the great many scandals. I was able to discover current developments and trends in questions of business ethics not only through reports in the media but above all also at first hand through personal conversations and hard information about business ethics at the Tokyo Conference, *The First World Congress of Business, Economics and Ethics* in July 1996. In addition to the individual ethos of top management and its responsibility for a business ethic, especially in the USA, which generally dominates the market for management innovations, for some years (after a whole series of serious scandals) a tendency has become evident for business to seek to influence the behaviour of employees and begin to prevent offences which damage business through *ethical programmes* aimed at establishing codes of behaviour and wider values. With the US Sentencing Guidelines established in 1991, a clever system of incentives at the legislative level is ensuring that: first, businesses are being required to set up ethical programmes; and secondly, if they scorn or offend against ethical guidelines they are faced with significant penal measures and sanctions.[46]

These ethical measures are also being accompanied and supported by the way in which numerous *business schools* have made the dimension of business ethics a firm element of their teaching programmes. By way of example I might refer to the ethics programme of the Harvard Business School in Boston, which was initiated as early as the end of the 1980s by Thomas R. Piper; then to the Graduate School of Business under the direction of Kenneth Goodpaster at the University of St Thomas, Minnesota; and finally to the Council for Ethics in Economics in Columbus, Ohio, with Paul M. Minus as the director of the International Conferences for Business Leaders. At almost the same time a network of business ethics has formed in Europe, the European Business Ethics Network (EBEN), which has as members such prominent experts in business ethics as Horst Steinmann, Peter Ulrich and Henk van Luijk.

Individual defects and institutional failings in the realm of ethics, the disappearance of values, criteria and finally also the credibility of people in leading positions in business on the one hand, and the way in which scandals will not go away on the other, direct our attention to the heart of these problems and make us ask directly:

3. Has Ethics a Chance in Business?

In view of the many crises and scandals, one cannot avoid the impression that the god to whom tribute is paid in the most different shapes and forms is the great god of modernity *par excellence*, the god progress, the god success! That means efficiency instead of transcendence; *profit*, career, prestige and success at any price instead of openness to another dimension.

(a) Beyond good and evil?

In all the well known scandals, from Germany and Italy to America and Japan, the obvious presupposition was that *success sanctifies, justifies all means*. For success one may lie, steal, bribe, break promises, whatever. If the matter unintentionally becomes notorious, then first of all one disputes everything and where possible goes over to the counter-attack. The media which uncover the scandal are normally to blame for it (and here unfortunately the media all too often go for the principle of success and an increase in circulation). As for the guilty ones, only what can be demonstrated without providing openings for legal action is then given out, bit by bit. Then a terrifying degree of blindness to reality manifests itself, an extreme loss of confidence and a complete lack of the culture of public shame and repentance. Finally, should all honourable declarations and words prove false, it can happen that someone as a last resort commits suicide or, as in the case of Calvi, the church and Vatican banker, is done away with; Calvi was found hanged under a bridge on the Thames near to the London Opus Dei bank. No, even the early prophet of contemporary nihilism, Friedrich Nietzsche, did not imagine 'beyond good and evil' and the new 'superman', without religion and morality and committed only to the 'will to power', as being so primitive, banal, trivial.

But wait. Fortunately this is not the whole picture. Surprisingly, the questionnaire among leading business figures quoted above also shows *trends in the opposite direction*. Many people still believe in God, the true God, and even more appeal to their conscience, though in concrete terms the contours of this authority remain vague. In general, Christianity (as opposed to the Church) is seen in a positive light, though the content of Christianity, for example the commandment to love, evidently has little influence on management decisions. And if at the same time the biblical revelation or the social teaching of the Church plays hardly any role in this group, conversely many executives regard openness to transcendence as an important element in moral decisions.

Yes, one has to choose, doubtless time and again, and executives often find that their decisions are a difficult choice between what is required by business within the sphere of calculating success and what their conscience prescribes. Various empirical investigations into business ethics[47] have time and again brought out the following ways of thinking:

- those who are asked, regard their own ethical standards more optimistically than those of their colleagues;
- ethical codes of behaviour are welcomed, but are regarded as ineffective by themselves; but also
- responsibility towards customers is put above responsibility towards the shareholders.

In the matter of establishing ethical standards in business, a considerable number of the executives questioned look to help from outside: improved legislation, harsher punishment, external audits, greater watchfulness on the part of consumers and the media. But even more executives put their trust in *solutions from within*: an improved ethical training and above all an improved business culture.

Negative and positive aspects, taken together, show a tension in relation to religion on the part of many executives.[48] They are convinced that 'people' need religion, that Christianity should be preserved at least 'for the others', 'for the people'. But they themselves often believe that they can do without such a religious connection. Ethical conflicts between one's profession and religion, commerce and Christian faith, profit and confession, politics and ethics, are hardly perceived in these terms. Such perception is most likely when particular people with whom one is confronted are affected by commercial decisions, say in the harsh competitive struggle, in mass redundancies, in competition, or when because of professional dedication the executive's own marriage is destroyed and the family breaks up. By contrast, it is more difficult to perceive the conflict when more wide-ranging, more impersonal, more complex and more abstract situations have to be considered: say in business relationships with the developing countries or in dealing with nature.

All this shows that the question of ethics or religion cannot easily be settled in the sphere of business executives. In many ways it seems to be latent and diffuse. But people all too rarely give an account of themselves – either of their public status or their private attitude. However, it would help to reflect consciously on the ethical and the religious question. In principle, what is an appropriate ethic for present-day executives (and not just for them)?

(b) The chances of doing business morally

Throughout this second part, which is about the world economy, between welfare state and neo-capitalism (considered globally, nationally and locally), it has become clear that no uncritical economism was to be presented here, nor any moralism alien to the subject: no ethic imposed upon economics, but *an ethic arising out of economic processes.* Economics and ethics are not mutually exclusive, no matter how often this is asserted.

But particularly in the age of globalization the problem is becoming acute: 'Competition is getting harder. Has ethics still a chance in business?' I was asked this at the German Management Congress in Munich in 1994. My answer was that *a moral way of doing business has more chances.* Only those who themselves have an ethic can give clear *orientation* to others, which is what *strong leadership* requires. They can give this orientation by pointing to all the values to which there must be an obligation, presenting aims, observing standards consistently and adopting a quite specific attitude in practice. Or, as the businessman whom I quoted in the introduction said: a business may be run in the style of a large family, a strictly rational organization or a monarchical hierarchy,[49] but the decisive presupposition for survival and long-term success is integrity. One must always be able to rely on the firm, never have the wool pulled over one's eyes, never be lied to, never be hauled over the coals, but always be treated and served with respect and honesty.[50]

In the long term an immoral way of doing business does not pay. Why?

(1) Sooner or later a conflict with the criminal law threatens even those who think that they can always get by unscathed.

189

(2) Where offences are repeated there is always a cry for legal regulation, which is commonly complained about by business and is now complained about by the banks.

(3) Lenders do not like giving credit to those who are not creditworthy, and credit is often decided (according to a Swiss banker) according to the following criteria: first, character and then 2. capacity, 3. collateral, 4. capital, 5. conditions.

(4) All firms are dependent on more than merely financial credit: they need credit in the sense of credibility, and in many respects:

- for members of the business and those who are being trained, who want to work in a reputable firm;
- for those who live nearby and the local community on whose goodwill any firm is dependent;
- for the financiers, the suppliers and the customers, none of whom trusts those who have no moral credit;
- for the wider public, who in the long run will not tolerate a bad image for any firm (not even AT & T and Shell).

(5) Laws have only external sanctions, but an ethic has an internal sanction: a bad conscience cannot simply be suppressed, but makes itself felt, even if only in dreams and disturbed sleep. One hears that there are more neurotics at the top than is generally assumed.

So at the meso- and micro-levels too, ethics is not just a matter of 'moral appeals'. In business, too, the *pressure of suffering* often finally becomes the pressure to reform, and this becomes *a political force*. But can one change well-established ways of behaving? Yes, we have already seen that a change of consciousness is possible in the middle and long term. And instead of constantly just discussing and identifying problems, after mature consideration we as individuals should do better in our own world, smaller or greater. After all, ethical decisions are in the first place matters for the individual. For example, it is a quite personal ethical decision on the part of the banker who is already being asked too much of by his existing directorships, whether he refuses to take on yet more, or in the face of many scandals and deficient control structures protects himself against criticism by bland statements.

In view on the one hand of the corruption which is spreading like a cancer even in countries where officials, judges and the medical profession used largely to have integrity, and on the other of the increase in organized crime and juvenile criminality – defensive measures against corruption and organized crime are being strengthened everywhere – the question of the foundation for basic values and attitudes is being raised more clearly than before. It is being raised in a new way especially in the market economy.

Why should I unconditionally observe certain rules, moral standards, ethical norms?

(c) From creed to cash: the 'Singapore dream'

Ethics should not just apply hypothetically (if it corresponds with my interests), but categorically (as Kant stated it), unconditionally. But what is the foundation for the *unconditional validity* of particular basic ethical values and attitudes? For the authors of the Interfaith Declaration they clearly come from the religion concerned, be this Jewish, Christian or Muslim. But the Caux Declaration evidently presupposes that the basic values and attitudes which it calls for are also accessible to non-believers and doubters, agnostics and atheists. This cannot be disputed. But on the other hand a purely secular argument for particular values and attitudes easily gets into trouble over finding a foundation.

Thus people say, 'I must see how I get on in my profession, career, business, and get established; only I can help myself there.' The answer to that is that such an attitude will easily undermine any sense of responsibility and in the long run any sense of the law. But again there is the objection: why shouldn't I pursue my career and my business heedlessly and use my elbow? Make way for the bold! The answer is: if *the maximum* is always *the optimum*, and earning money (capitalism) and enjoying life (hedonism) have become the highest value, not only the harmony and stability of a community are threatened, but also the individual's sense of life and identity. Indeed democracy is endangered by a libertinism which is the modern way of taking to excess that '*liberté*' which originally helped democracy to break through.

However, there is increasing agreement that a society without rules, norms of behaviour, moral maxims, indeed a minimum of binding values, inner attitudes and binding criteria, cannot survive. Slowly our secular contemporaries are also recognizing that modernization brings not only an unavoidable secularization, but also a by no means unavoidable ideological secularism, in which all that is transcendent, trans-empirical, authoritative, indeed unconditionally normative, seems to have been *banished from life* and subsequently replaced by helplessness and an oppressive spiritual void. Is each his own measure?

But how is the individual or group to be given *criteria if man himself is* 'the *measure of all* things': not just under ethical obligation, as in the original Greek sense of the saying, but without any ties, as in the modern libertinistic or nihilistic sense? Since human beings cannot stand this emptiness (*horror vacui*), the spiritual vacuum already prognosticated by Nietzsche is being filled by substitute values: by something relative, if only money, which now becomes the pseudo-absolute, the idol, in place of the true absolute. Everything is voluntarily sacrificed to it, often with meaningless pomp and luxury to satisfy personal vanity, often even personal integrity and identity; but above all solidarity. This is a freedom without equality and brotherhood.

Can human standards ultimately be given an irrefutable foundation if man wants to be completely his own measure and recognizes no norms, no normative authority which transcends humanity? Does it make people happier if they know neither standards nor purpose and then, because they want to set their hearts on something, prescribe for themselves a modern pseudo-religion, of the kind expressed in the 'Singapore dream' (and to be truthful, it is not just dreamed there):

- Instead of the age-old five Cs of true religion, Creed, Cult, Code, Conduct, Community,
- the mundane five Cs of pseudo-religion: Cash, Credit Card, Car, Condominium, Country Club?

Will not such unconcealed materialism and egotism in time lead even in that Asian country which so far is most free from corruption to an equally unfair, polarized, split society of the privileged and the unprivileged, despite tremendous election results for the ruling party? The most recent controversy in Singapore over certain privileges of those in power suggests this. But these questions not only arise for the remote future; they also press in on us in the immediate present.

(d) Strong leadership with a basic ethical and religious attitude

Enlightenment in the name of a religion, which is not about restoration but renewal, is one of the great tasks of our time. While prosperity, progress, consumption, satisfaction or power are not bad in themselves, people may possibly damage themselves and others if they absolutize these so that they become the supreme value, the purpose and aim of life to which they are ready to subordinate, indeed to sacrifice, everything else. No, nothing 'earthly' should be denigrated here in a moralistic way, but simply put in the overall *context of human life*:

- against an ultimate horizon of meaning,
- in accordance with a scale of values,
- in accordance with basic norms, non-negotiable standards, which are unconditionally valid.

And what about religion itself? For all its failure in individual instances, it can be a help towards such an ultimate discovery of meaning, towards the preservation of personal identity, and towards legitimating a fundamentally correct action and making it concrete. This has already been shown in connection with politics: unless all the signs are deceptive, despite all the secularization, seen globally we are in the middle of a process of the rediscovery of that factor which for all too understandable reasons has been increasingly forced out, ignored and often violently suppressed in the paradigm of modernity: the rediscovery of religion. That is true above all if we do not remain imprisoned in the Eurocentric perspective but look to the Middle and Far East, to North and Latin America and to Africa. Here perhaps is the clearest symptom of a transition from modernity to post-socialist and post-capitalist, postmodernity.

Of course, as we have seen repeatedly, there are no patent religious solutions for coping with the problems of today's world and the difficulties that are bound up with them; there is no religious substitute for an understanding of economics, professional knowledge and common sense. But it is also true that religion can be of help in rediscovering a basic social consensus about *ultimate values*, without which modern pluralism will have a destructive effect.

Religion has an indirect effect, as it were *from the ground up,* through individuals, but it also extends to questions of the day and matters of technical detail. It does so by bringing into play basic convictions, basic attitudes, basic values, and by providing ultimate foundations, motivations and norms for concrete behaviour and decisions. To this degree economics and religion cannot be separated any more than can politics and religion, but have to be related to each other constructively. And for executives this means that economic political leadership and ethical religious leadership are interdependent, even if the decision about personal religion always remains with the individual.

Be this as it may, to be a '*great business personality*' today more than ever it is not enough to have a capital of millions upon millions, or hundreds of connections, or dozens of directorships. No, to be a 'great business personality', in addition to all analytical competence, power to make decisions and a will to implement them, one needs a view of reality as a whole which goes beyond technical knowledge and professional competence, a sense of basic human questions and ethical convictions which are deeply rooted and have been well thought out.

Conclusion

I hope that I have succeeded, as promised, in taking the global ethic project further and demonstrating a realistic vision, pointing towards the future in a global perspective which makes clearer the outlines of a more peaceful, just and humane world.

No one knows better than a person who with some difficulty has laboured through all the countless problems, just how many details are lacking in providing a basis for this work, shaping it and making the necessary distinctions. But it is more important for the decisive features to have been clarified. Both in the sphere of politics and in that of economics we need a new *sense of responsibility*:

- a *responsible politics* which seeks to achieve the precarious balance between ideals and realities which has to be rediscovered over and over again; and
- a responsible economics which can combine economic strategies with ethical convictions.

The change of consciousness needed here is a task for the new millennium. And it is for the young generation to realize decisively the sketch for the future presented here. As Victor Hugo says, the future has many names:

For the weak it is the unattainable.
For the fearful it is the unknown.
For the bold it is the opportunity.

Notes

1. K. Schwab and H. Kroos, *Moderne Unternehmensführung im Maschinenbau* (Frankfurt, 1971), p. 21.
2. Cf. H. Steinmann, 'Zur Lehre der "Gesellschaftlichen Verantwortung der Unternehmensführung". Zugleich elne Kritik des Davoser Manifests', in *Wirtschaftswissenschaftliches Studium* 10, October 1973, pp. 467–73 and 500. The version printed on 472f. is identical with the final version of the Davos Manifesto.
3. Thus Steinmann, 'Zur Lehre' (n.2); similarly, again with reference to M. Friedman, the economist G. Engel, 'Wirtschaftsethik als ökonomische Theorie der Moral. Ein Überblick', in *Diskussionsbeiträge aus dem volkswirtschaftlichen Seminar der Universität Göttingen* 52, April 1991 (manuscript).
4. H. Steinmann and A. Löhr, *Grundlagen der Unternehmensethik*, second revised and enlarged edition (Stuttgart, 1991), p. 97.
5. *An Interfaith Declaration, A Code of Ethics on International Business for Christians, Muslims and Jews* (London, 1993).
6. Caux Round Table, *Principles For Business* (The Hague, 1994). The preparation for this was done by the Minnesota Center for Corporate Responsibility, Minneapolis, USA.
7. Id., Preamble (subsequent quotations also come from this).
8. Id., *Principles* (n. 6), Section 2.
9. Ibid. These responsibilities are the basis for everything else: obligations

towards the foreign countries in which these firms are active, and to the world community generally, respect for the environment, support for multilateral trade.

10. Id., *Principles* (n. 6), Section 3.
11. *An Interfaith Declaration, A Code of Ethics* (n. 5), p. 16.
12. Caux Round Table, *Principles* (n. 6), Introduction.
13. Ibid., Section 2.
14. Ibid.
15. Cf. the reservations of the Deputy Foreign Minister of Singapore, K. Mahbubani, in his response to Huntington's 'Clash of Civilizations?', in *Foreign Affairs* 72, 1993, no. 4, 14.
16. Cf. W.J. Bennett, *The Book of Virtues: A Treasury of Great Moral Stories* (New York, 1994).
17. Cf. T. Koh, 'The 10 Values that Undergrid East Asian Strength and Success', *International Herald Tribune*, 12 December 1993.
18. Cf. H. Küng and J. Ching, *Christianity and Chinese Religions* (New York and London, 1989), reissued 1993.
19. Cf. L. Vandermeersch, *Le nouveau monde sinisé* (Paris, 1986).
20. Cf. Küng and Ching, *Christianity and Chinese Religions* (n. 18), Ching's remarks on Confucianism today, pp. 81–91.
21. Cf. Confucius, *Analects* XII, p. 7.
22. Han Minzhu (ed.), *Cries for Democracy: Writings and Speeches from 1989 Chinese Democracy Movement* (Princeton NJ, 1990).
23. K. Schwab and C. Smadja, 'Start Taking the Backlash Against Globalization Seriously', in *International Herald Tribune*, 1 February 1996.
24. Federal President R. Herzog, *Focus* 52/1996.
25. Cf. the article 'Globalisierung verändert die Arbeitswelt. Das St. Galler Management-Symposium zeigt die Problematik des Wachstums auf', *Süddeutsche Zeitung*, 24 May 1996.
26. M. Camedessus, report on the conference 'Economic Growth for What Kind of Future?', Rome, 30 November–2 December 1995.
27. Cf. the almost 1,000-page volume edited by M. Stackhouse, D.P. McCann and S.J. Roels, *On Moral Business: Classical and Contemporary Resources for Ethics in Economic Life* (Grand Rapids MI, 1996).
28. Cf. K.O. Feldt, 'What happened to the Swedish Welfare Paradise?', in The Report. SOMFY International Symposium Enlightenment in Stockholm 15–19 Mai 1996, S. 66–72: 71.
29. I am grateful for this information to K. Leisinger, the Basel Professor for the Sociology of Development and head of the Novartis Foundation for Sustainable Development. Cf. his forthcoming book *Unternehmensethik. Globale Verantwortung und modernes Management* (Munich 1997).
30. Cf. ibid., p. 19f.

31. Cf. G. Gerken, interview in *Stern*, 10 November 1988.
32. Cf. A. Jay, *Management and Machiavelli* (London, 1967).
33. Ibid., p. 36.
34. Cf. A. Riklin, *Die Führungslehre von Niccolò Machiavelli* (Bern, 1996), pp. 10–21: 'Renaissance des Machiavellismus'.
35. Ibid., p. 84.
36. Cf. F.X. Kaufmann, W. Kerber and P.M. Zulehner, Ethos and Religion bei Fuhrungskräften. Eine Studie im Auftrag des Arbeitskreises für Führungskäfte in der Wirtschaft (München), Munich 1986, above all Part IV: 'Bewusstseins-Anpassung: Religiöse Indifferenz and Opportunismus'.
37. R.K. Sprenger, *Das Prinzip Selbstverantwortung. Wege zur Motivation* (Frankfurt, 1995).
38. Ibid., p. 38.
39. Ibid., p. 242.
40. Cf. J. Staute, *Der Consulting-Report. Vom Versagen der Manager zum Reibach der Berater* (Frankfurt, 1996).
41. Ibid., p. 235.
42. Cf. P.F. Drucker and I. Nakauchi, *The Time of Challenges/The Time of Reinventing* (Tokyo, 1996).
43. J.B. Ciulla, 'Business Leadership and Moral Imagination in the Twenty-First Century', in Andrew R. Cecil (ed.), *Moral Values: The Challenge of the Twenty-First Century* (Dallas Tx, 1996), p. 155f. Cf. also T.R. Piper, M.C. Gentile and S.D. Parks, *Can Ethics be Taught? Perspectives, Challenges, and Approaches at Harvard Business School* (Boston, 1993). W.D. Hitt, who also emphasizes the ethical dimension in a variety of publications on management consultancy, has very recently written a book on a global ethic: *A Global Ethic. The Leadership Challenge* (Columbus/Ohio, 1996). R.E. Allinson, *Global Disasters: Inquiries into Management Ethics* (Hong Kong, 1996), analyses moral responsibility in business in the light of the serious business catastrophes of the past decade.
44. Cf. the Emnid Institute study, in *Der Spiegel* 38/1994.
45. Cf. the book by two economic journalists, F. Bräuninger and M. Hasenbeck, *Die Abzocker. Selbstbedienung in Politik and Wirtschaft* (Düsseldorf, 1994), p. 14: 'the deeper causes are a universal loss of values, the lack of moral principles and suitable models' (368).
46. Cf. M. Frechen, 'Geschenke sind tabu', *Die Zeit*, 6 October 1995.
47. Cf. T.M. Jones and F.H. Gautschi, 'Will the Ethics of Business Change? A Survey of Future Executives', *Journal of Business Ethics* 7, 1988, p. 232f.
48. Cf. W. Kerber, 'Bewusstseins-Orientierung: Zur Begründung ethischer Normen in einer säkularisierten Gesellschaft', in Kaufmann, Kerber and Zulehner, *Ethos und Religion* (n. 36), pp. 121–214: 182.

49. Cf. the interesting typology of understandings of business responsibility (instrumentalist, paternalist, legalist, idealist . . .) in P. Ulrich and U. Thidemann, *Ethik und Erfolg. Unternehmensethische Denkmuster von Fuhrungskräften – eine empirische Studie* (Bern, 1992).

50. The author of *The End of History and the Last Man*, F. Fukuyama, discusses the significance of trust – distinguishing between 'low-trust societies' and 'high-trust societies' – in his extensive study *Trust: The Social Virtues and the Creation of Prosperity* (New York, 1995). For a basic treatment of trust see H. Sautter, *Was glaubt der 'homo oeconomicus'?* (Marburg, 1994).

Chapter 11

Rights of the Child

Jim Richards

There is much confusion and disagreement concerning children's[1] rights within a Christian context. Some will point to the example set by Jesus (Mk 10.16) which places children in the centre, recognizing them as individuals in their own right. Other Christians, though, suggest *that children's rights are being pursued to the detriment of family life in general and parental authority in particular, separating child from parents.*

This chapter argues that giving clear rights to children is the best way of protecting them. However, rights in this regard must not be considered as a free-standing entity and in their application, rights for children must always be considered within the context of a child's life, that is, as a member of a family.

The UN Convention on the Rights of the Child

Before giving consideration to a Catholic perspective of children's rights it will be helpful to outline briefly what has been described as the most speedily ratified convention in international law – the UN Convention on the Rights of the Child.[2] It was passed unanimously in 1989, but, as with all such documents, it did not spring out of thin air. Its origins can be seen in the Declaration on the Rights of the Child passed by the League of Nations in 1924, which was subsequently expanded by the UN in 1948 and 1959.

The groundbreaking aspect of the 1989 Convention, which distinguishes it from the earlier documents, was that it sees children as active participants. Thus we can analyse the Convention on the basis of the three Ps of Protection, Provision and Participation, with this last being the one that involves input from children themselves.[3] The Preamble to the Convention explains why children need special care and protection: 'the child, by reasons of his physical and mental immaturity, needs special safeguards and care . . . before as well as after birth'.[4] Thus, for instance, although the Preamble does not forbid abortion, it does recognize that the unborn child should receive certain protection.

Those who suggest that rights for children drive a wedge between child and parents will find no support for that proposition in the Convention, which states clearly that the family is 'the fundamental group of society' and that children grow up best within their birth family. However, it is recognized that for various reasons this may not always be possible and that it is only via the exercise of lawful authority that children should be forcibly separated from their parents.

The Convention has within it four basic principles: non-discrimination, best interests of the child, the right to survival and development, and the right for children to have their views heard.[5]

With regard to the first, non-discrimination, this embraces not being discriminated against 'irrespective of . . . race, colour, sex, language, religion . . . national, ethnic or social origin, disability, birth or other status' (Article 2).[6] Article 3 highlights best interests and places a duty on 'public or private social welfare institutions' and all government organizations, whether local or national, as well as all legislature bodies, to make the best interests of the child their primary consideration.[7] The third principle is seen in Article 6 which is stark in its basic simplicity: '. . . every child has the inherent right to life' and governments 'shall ensure to the maximum extent possible the survival and development of the child'.[8] The fourth principle concerns the contribution children should be able to make in decision making. Article 12 makes reference to a child 'capable of forming his or her own views, (having) the right to express those views freely in all matters affecting the child', and states that these views should be given 'due weight in accordance with the age and maturity of the child'.[9] The practical ramifications of this last will be considered more fully below.

There is also a debate to be had on the interplay between rights and duties. Children have a right to free school education in the UK. Is there then a duty on children to attend school and do what they can to develop their own potential? A child also has a right to family life. Does it follow from this that that child should take an active contributory part in family life? More clearly, given that children have a right to school education, central and local government have the duty to provide it. By operating society, at both an individual, family and institutional level, on the basis of rights and responsibilities, we form the foundation for a just society, through an understanding of our mutual obligations to each other. However, there needs to be a caveat inserted here.

Rights are not earned by carrying out duties. A child has the right to receive education no matter how naughty he or she is in class, or how much he or she truants. Or, perhaps on a more appealing note, babies have rights yet cannot possibly 'earn' them. Consideration of the position of babies in relation to rights also helps inform an understanding of the importance of rights in protecting the weak and vulnerable. A rights framework enables those with little or no voice to what their specific rights may be, together with having a system to ensure that they receive these rights. It must never be forgotten that rights, particularly the ones in question, have not been plucked from thin air. The Convention, in particular, has moral, religious and legal foundations and authority. This enables the following statement to be made: 'Rights are the power to insist on the implementation of responsibilities and to counteract the worst consequences of lack of virtue.'[10] Such a statement has added urgency and import in societies where great inequalities exist.

Care, though, has to be exercised when the almost automatic reaction from some quarters, when rights are discussed, is to insist that people, in this case children, carry out duties in order to be accorded their rights. Such an approach may well lead to a dilution of rights, making them conditional on future behaviour. Rights thus run the risk of not being intrinsic to the person.

In discussing rights it may be helpful to distinguish between different sources of rights. There are, thus, moral rights. For instance one may talk about the right to life of an unborn child. However, there is legislation which very much circumscribes that moral call. Then there are rights which spring from an officially recognized body such as the UN and the Convention in question, but whose articles may not be fully enshrined in domestic law. Lastly, there are rights which have the full backing of domestic law.

The Convention and the Catholic Church

The views of religious denominations to the Convention illuminate some of the tensions shared in the wider community about children's rights. For instance, the Holy See of the Roman Catholic Church, although amongst the first to ratify the Convention as well as being heavily involved in its drafting, entered certain reservations.[11] One of these reservations concerned parents and stated that it interpreted: 'the articles of the Convention in a way which safeguards the primary and inalienable right of parents, in particular insofar as these rights concern education (Arts 13 and 28), religion (Art. 14), association with others (Art. 15) and privacy (Art. 16)'.[12]

The Holy See makes clear that the source of children's rights comes from their inherent dignity as human beings. It does, though, in expanding on these reservations, express concern that some of the articles may be interpreted as giving children the right to make choices which may well be against their own best interests and that therefore their rights should only be exercised 'in the light of the rights/duties of parents and the family'.[13] Indeed, it is the Holy See's views of the place of the family and what it describes as the 'inalienable rights of parents' that have made apparent the sharpest differences between the UN Scrutiny Committee on Children's Rights and the Holy See. That committee felt there was an inherent conflict between the Holy See's position and the rights of the child expressed in the Charter.

The conflict may be best illustrated by a closer examination of the word 'inalienability'. There does, it seems, have to be some sort of qualification attached to it. 'Inalienability' has about it a sense of being able to exercise complete authority without external control. In the UK such a position does not hold, not least because of our child protection legislation, which enables local authorities which manage the child protection system and the courts to override 'inalienable' parental rights. In addition, though, there are the duties placed directly on parents by the Convention, which means they have to promote the care of their children, not on the basis of their own, perhaps, narrow focus, but in relation to the parameters set by the Convention. In applying rights it needs to be recognized that there is an inherent conflict between the right to respect private family life and the State's duty to protect a child. The resolution of such a conflict needs sensitive examination and adequate resources in order to reach a resolution.

As well as ratifying the Convention, the Church has lent weight to its contents by pronouncements of its own. For instance, Pope John Paul II drew up a list of rights pertaining to family life: the right of a child to develop in the mother's womb; the right to live within a family in an atmosphere conducive to moral growth; the right to learn and to seek and know the truth; and the right to have the wherewithal to raise a family in reasonable economic circumstances.[14] The Church has also declared that parents should not be placed in a situation where they have to work such long hours that they are unable to carry out all their parental duties,[15] and that discrimination against women in the workplace should be eradicated.[16] There is a need for workers to receive a decent living wage[17] and ways should also be found to subsidize families where necessary. This should include financial recognition for housework. The family is also seen as being hugely important not least because it is the cradle within which we learn about truth, goodness and love.[18] Families are a positive good for society and strong families are needed to build strong communities.[19] It has also pronounced on the wide-ranging role of parenthood, which includes having responsibility for both the physical care and the spiritual life of a child.[20] The family has a completely original and irreplaceable role in raising children. Moreover, a primary role for parents is the duty and right to impart religious education and moral formation.[21] However, parents, although they are the first educators of their children, are not the only ones.[22] These are complex and comprehensive tasks for parents. They will need help: 'The family, then, does not exist for society or the State, but society and the State exists for the family.'[23]

The Operation of the Convention in the UK

Given the UK's ratification of the Convention, consideration will now be given to a closer examination of aspects of the Convention, to assess the extent to which the UK falls short of its intentions. This will be followed by a short discussion on how the Church might advance the Convention's full implementation.

The Convention's Preamble declares that the family is the 'fundamental group of society' and Article 7 states that a child has 'the right to know and be cared for by his or her parents'. First, let us consider the implications of both quotes in relation to aspects of family life, starting with the impact that our changing patterns of employment have had. It is becoming clear that the demands of the economy are adversely impacting on family life. That this is so can be seen in the following. It has been reported[24] that, in families where both parents worked, only 12 per cent worked typical hours (8.30am to 5.30pm). Thus the likelihood of evening work, night work and working at the weekends is more typical than the standard 9 to 5. The financial pressures that make this necessary are understandable, as is the flexibility it produces to ensure one parent is at home for the children. However, the net overall effect can too often be that the opportunities for a family to do things together are becoming rarer. Nor must we assume these hours are always worked through choice. Demands from employers, not least those following the Sunday opening of shops, can leave parents with little choice but to operate what some of us may see as unsocial hours. This even extends to some workers taking laptops on holidays and allowing themselves to be contacted whilst away. Actual hours worked are also high. In the UK, 40 per cent of fathers work more than 48 hours a week. The comparable figure in Holland and Sweden is only 20 per cent of fathers. Put another way, the French, on average, work eight weeks less than us per year, this difference being accounted for by way of shorter hours and longer holidays. The above suggests that families have to mould to the needs of commerce rather than the other way round.

In this context there is a need to examine what amounts to a revolution in the way babies are cared for, which has taken place within the space of one generation. In 1982, 24 per cent of women returned to work within a year of childbirth. By 2001 that figure was 67 per cent and it is still rising.[25] In those countries with more generous parental leave this figure is much lower. This may indicate that when there is a real choice, mothers on the whole prefer to care for their very young children themselves. This is a controversial area, involving wishes mothers have to continue to pursue a career. However, we do need to ask questions about the impact on babies and toddlers of placing them for long periods of the day with strangers. There is, for instance, worrying evidence that there is a growing number of children starting school without the expected basic building-block skills, and there is concern about the relationship this may have with changing patterns of childcare.[26]

Such social changes, both in respect of employment and consequential childcare arrangements, are in danger of dismantling the relationships of care within families. Added to this is the UK Government's drive to have, as one of its main planks for the relief of family poverty, more parents, including mothers, in work. There are obvious dangers in having children, especially if they are young children, for long periods of time on their own at home, whilst their main carer is at work. In fact it can be argued that the pendulum has swung too far towards employment, rather than regarding time caring for children as a positive good.

Articles 26 and 27 deal with social security and standards of living. Governments should, insofar as means allow, help those in poverty. The UK is one of the richest countries in the world, but levels of poverty are still unacceptably high and inequalities of wealth continue to widen.

With regard to the latter, the gap between the richest and poorest groups has widened in the UK since 1997[27] and the UK Government does not appear to be concerned to redress this. One can sometimes be accused of pursuing the politics of envy when talking about disparities of wealth, but the question has to be posed as to whether it should be possible for someone to 'earn' £11,456,210 as the head of BSkyB did in 2004. This, moreover, is not an isolated incident. Over the last ten years average earnings have risen by 45 per cent, whilst for leading executives in the FTSE 100 companies, the figure is 288 per cent.[28]

Such excesses produce a polarized society which creates its own corrosiveness. It also matters because the most egalitarian societies have the highest rate of social mobility. In the UK there is, in contrast, less mobility. It is as if the very polarization of society causes it to solidify and make movement within it, particularly for those at the very bottom of the pile, more difficult than it was in the 1950s. Moreover, high rates of inequality can also lead to mental health difficulties for the poorest, perhaps because there is a sense of them not being full members of society.[29] There is also a link between countries with high levels of income inequality and high rates of teenage pregnancy.[30] Again the UK, with regard to this last, has the highest rate in the EU, eight times that of the Netherlands and Sweden, and three times that of France. A UNICEF report suggests that amongst the reasons for this are poor sex education coupled with a loss of traditional values.[31]

The UK also has the worst problems of long-term poverty within the EU, with 6.1 per cent of the population affected, as opposed, for instance, to the Netherlands' 1 per cent. The UK is also in the top group of EU countries with the highest proportion of children living in poverty. This was not always so. In 1979 only one in ten children lived in poverty. Although it is now slowly edging downwards from the historically high figure of one in three, the comparable figure is still one in four. One of the things we know about people living in this condition is that they very often experience multi-deprivation: that is, they live in a deprived physical environment, because they do not own a car, transport is expensive, they are often socially isolated and are in poor housing.[32]

Article 18 makes it clear that Government has a responsibility to help parents 'in the performance of their child-rearing responsibilities'. Article 19 then goes on to outline Government's duties to protect children and to take 'all appropriate, legislative, administrative, social and educational measures' to achieve this. The need to supply health services adequate to the needs presented by children is outlined in Article 24.

If we consider the help parents need, some thoughts of the Archbishop of Canterbury are instructive. He has spoken about hurried childhoods.[33] What he meant by this was that all too quickly far too many children are becoming consumerized and sexualized, placing emotional and other demands on them for which they are grossly ill-equipped. Children, he suggests, need to spend time as children, to use what is called the latency period in their middle school years as a time to adjust within themselves and to prepare for what is to come. For this they need stability, within both the family and the outside world. In this atmosphere they are better able to learn to trust. He was particularly critical of the pressures of advertising on children. He suggested that the pressure was unjust and that the implications of the rights of children to justice mean we must challenge Government and advertisers to reduce the volume and type of advertising aimed at children and thereby better protect children. It has been reported that companies spend £300 million every year on advertisements that specifically target children,[34] with focus groups being organized for children as young as two and three years of age. One executive of Burger King was quoted as saying children 'have an incredible influence on what fast food restaurant their parents will choose'. Moreover, with over half the children under 16 in the UK having a TV in their bedroom, much is watched unsupervised by a caring adult.

As well as some of the broad social changes there are also specific government policies that adversely impact on children and have been the subject of criticism by the Children's Rights Alliance for England.[35] Three of these will be discussed here. The first deals with the children of refugees and asylum seekers, the second concerns children in the juvenile justice system, with the last linked to this, namely Anti Social Behaviour Orders.

Arguably, the way some children whose parents are asylum seekers or refugees are treated is by not having their welfare needs considered paramount. This is especially so when such children are detained with their parents for considerable lengths of time in detention centres. Figures are difficult to obtain, and indeed the lack of adequate statistics has in itself been the subject of criticism. That stated, Save the Children UK has estimated that approximately 2,000 children a year are detained for a length of time of between seven and 268 days.[36] The conditions in which they are held place great strain on normal family life, and there are often adverse effects on children's mental health even after they have left the centres. Moreover, educational facilities are well below the standards of those in schools, largely because the expectation, which defies the reality, is that children will only stay in centres for a few days. It is not surprising, therefore, that there have been calls for there to be judicial authority and oversight of children placed in centres.

With regard to juvenile offending, the UK has one of the highest rates of custody in the EU, and between 1994 and 2004 there has been an increase of 90 per cent in the number of children sentenced to a period of custody: this despite the fact that recorded offending has been in decline. Then, of those in custody, children from black minority ethnic groups are disproportionately represented at 22 per cent of the total in young offender institutions.[37]

The above references to children in asylum centres and in custody may be seen as examples where two principles of the Convention have not been met, namely the paramountcy of the child and non-discrimination. Furthermore, Anti Social Behaviour Orders (ASBOs) might be categorized as not meeting the principle of child involvement. The reasoning behind this view is that ASBOs are civil, not criminal, proceedings, although breach may lead to a custodial sentence. Although adults may be subjected to them, they seem to be disproportionately impacting on children. For instance, of those imposed in 2003, 40.2 per cent were in respect of those under 18 years of age. Furthermore, certain local authorities employ ASBOs with more vigour. This geographical injustice can be seen in that Lincolnshire and Wiltshire recorded only 21 ASBOs between 1999 and 2005, whereas Greater Manchester at 816 and Greater London at 560 topped the league table.[38]

Other concerns have been voiced about ASBOs with evidence that they have been imposed on children suffering from such conditions as Aspergers and Tourettes Syndromes[39] and that 35 per cent of children given this order were diagnosed with a mental health disorder or a learning difficulty.[40] Furthermore, there has been criticism of ASBOs by the Council of Europe's Human Rights Commissioner. He recommends that no child under 16 should be imprisoned for breach of an order and that the public naming of the children involved should cease. Naming can cause further difficulties because the children named may well then be taunted by their peers at school, making rehabilitation even more difficult.[41] Chris Stanley of Nacro (the crime reduction charity) has stated that ASBOs 'are purely enforcement and do nothing to address offending patterns'.[42]

There is clearly much to be done with regard to children's rights both at a structural societal level, and by central and local government. This is not to suggest that there have not been some signs of progress. The reduction in child poverty may be cited, but this notwithstanding, there is still a long way to go before levels return to those of the mid-1970s and the UK becomes more on a par with many of its EU colleagues. There has also been the appointment of the Children's Commissioner for England, who, though he has to report to the Secretary of State rather than directly to Parliament, as is the case in Scotland, is at least now in post.

A Child's Right to a Spiritual Life

Before moving on to a discussion of the responsibility of the Church in the pursuit of children's rights there is a further right to examine, which, interestingly, is seldom discussed. It is the right of a child to their spirituality, as opposed to the practice of a particular religious belief. This important aspect of a child's life is all too often hidden in our increasingly secularized culture but spiritual awareness for children (and adults) has been described as 'biologically natural'.[43] Spiritual awareness makes people more conscious of their wider responsibilities, such as to social justice or the environment. One should also make a distinction between spirituality and organized religion. Someone can, of course, be involved in the latter with its accompanying spiritual life. There are many, though, who seem to manage successfully without such structural support and yet who are very much spiritually alive.

Specifically in relation to children, a negation of their spirituality means a denial of their natural desire and need to express themselves spiritually. Without this, they are less able to create within themselves a sense of wonder, awe, imagination, delight, goodness and meaning. A child's spiritual life is closely related to their individuality. In turn a healthy spirituality extends beyond oneself to the family and the world. If this is crushed, rather than nurtured, a child can be alienated from their own consciousness, with an obvious adverse impact on their mental health.

The Catholic Church in the UK – Embracing Children's Rights

However, extending rights to children is not something where the community at large should shrug its shoulders and leave matters to Government. What is broadly described as civic society has a responsibility in this regard and this clearly includes the Catholic Church. In the last few years the Church in the UK has had to confront and deal with some notorious cases of clergy abuse of children. In a radical departure from previous responses, Cardinal Cormac Murphy-O'Connor asked Lord Nolan to head an enquiry into how the Church should respond. All of his recommendations were accepted and this led to the formation of a national coordinating body, the Catholic Office for the Protection of Children and Vulnerable Adults, with child protection commissions in every diocese, now chaired by people independent of the Church, and child protection representatives in every parish. This has, I believe, led to a heightened awareness in every level of the Church of the needs and rights of a child. It has meant, for instance, that every parish priest and a growing number of volunteers have now had training in child protection, a key element of which is taking what a child says seriously and treating children with respect and courtesy, whilst recognizing the duty to care and their vulnerability.

In addition, other groups within the Church that have been advocates for children's rights are now listened to more carefully. The support of Caritas-social action (the umbrella group for Catholic social welfare organizations across England and Wales) for the 'Children are Unbeatable' campaign, which, if successful, will outlaw the legal concept of 'reasonable chastise-ment' of children by parents, may be instanced. In a similar vein, so too can the support of Catholic child care agencies for the campaign to end child poverty. Likewise there are the vigorous campaigns of support for those legitimately seeking asylum and for a living wage to be extended to all, not least low-paid migrant workers. There are therefore clear signs within the Church, from both Rome and the UK, that the need to support the exten-sion of children's rights is firmly on the Church's agenda – not least because true respect, care and recognition of children implies support for the importance of family life.

Notes

1. The author uses 'children' in the context of this chapter to refer to all children and young people under 18 years of age.
2. Kathleen Marshall and Paul Parvis, *Honouring Children: The Human Rights of the Child in Christian Perspective* (Edinburgh: Saint Andrew Press, 2004), p. 12.
3. Ibid., p. 13.
4. Office of the United Nations High Commissioner for Human Rights, Convention on the Rights of the Child: entry into force 2 September 1990, together with two optional protocols (1) A/RES/54/263, adopted 25 May 2000 and entered into force on 12 February 2002 (2) A/RES/ 54/263, adopted 25 May 2000 and entered into force on 18 January 2002 Preamble.
5. As cited in Kathleen Marshall and Paul Parvis, op. cit., p. 18.
6. Office of the United Nations High Commissioner for Human Rights, Convention on the Rights of the Child, see note 4.
7. Ibid.
8. Ibid.

9. Ibid.
10. Kathleen Marshall and Paul Parvis, op. cit., p. 143.
11. Ibid., p. 31.
12. United Nations Document CRC/C/2/Rev. 8 of 7 December 1999.
13. As cited in Kathleen Marshall and Paul Parvis, op. cit., p. 33.
14. John Paul II, encyclical letter *Centesimus Annus*, §47: AAS 83 (1991), pp. 851–2.
15. Holy See, *Charter of the Rights of the Family* (Vatican City: Vatican Polyglot Press, 1983), Art. 10, pp. 13–14.
16. John Paul II, *Letter to Women*, §3: AAS 87 (1995), p. 804.
17. Puis XI, encyclical letter *Quadragesimo Anno*: AAS 23 (1931), p. 200; Second Vatican Ecumenical Council, Pastoral Constitution *Gaudium et Spes*, §67.
18. John Paul II, encyclical letter *Centesimus Annus*, §39: AAS 83 (1991), p. 841.
19. *Catechism of the Catholic Church* §2224.
20. John Paul II, *Letters to Families*, Gratissimam Sane, §10: AAS 86 (1994), p. 881.
21. Second Vatican Ecumenical Council, Declaration *Dignitatis Humanae*, §5: AAS 58 (1966), p. 933; John Paul II, *Message for the 1994 World Day of Peace*, §5: AAS 86 (1994), pp. 159–60.
22. John Paul II, Apostolic Exhortation. *Familiaris Consortio*, 40: AAS 74 (1982), p. 131.
23. Holy See, *Charter of the Rights of the Family*, Preamble, p. 6.
24. 'From Here to Paternity', leading article, *The Guardian*, London, 27 December 2002.
25. Mary Riddell, 'Listen to mother', *Observer* newspaper, London, 19 October 2003.
26. Luck Ward, 'Hidden Stress of Nursery Age', in *The Guardian*, 19 September 2005, and Michael Shayer, in *Education Guardian*, 24 January 2006.
27. Aloysius Rocastle, 'Time to Act as UK Poverty Gap Widens', in *Catholic Times*, 8 May 2005.
28. First leader, 'Playing Robin Hood', in *The Guardian*, 19 March 2006.
29. R. Wilkinson, *The Impact of Inequality* (London: Routledge, 2005).
30. UNICEF, *A League Table of Teenage Births in Rich Nations*, Report Card No. 3. (Florence: Innocenti Research Centre, 2001).
31. UNICEF, *A League Table of Teenage Births in Rich Nations*, Report Card No. 3. (Florence: Innocenti Research Centre, 2001).
32. Jonathan Bradshaw, 'Child Poverty and Child Outcomes', in *Children and Society*, vol. 16 (2002), pp. 131–40.
33. Archbishop Rowan Williams, 'Formation: Who's Bringing up Our Children?', from a talk given at Mile End, London, 11 April 2006.

34. Eric Schlorser, 'Stuff the Kids', in *The Guardian 2*, 24 May 2006.
35. CRAE, *State of Children's Rights in England* (London: CRAE, 2005).
36. H. Crawley and T. Lester, *No Place for a Child: Children in UK Immigration Detention: Impacts, Alternatives and Safeguards* (London: Save the Children Fund, 2005).
37. CRAE, op. cit., p. 52.
38. https:// www.crimereduction.gov.uk/asbos2.htm (accessed 24 August 2006).
39. *Hansard*, House of Commons written answer, 14 July 2005, Column 1212 W.
40. Yvonne Roberts, 'Feral Youths Make an Easy Political Target', *Community Care*, 10–16 November 2005.
41. Barnardos, Child Line, NCB and NCH, 'Children's Charities Condemn Decisions to "Name and Shame" Children given ASBOs', press release issued by these charities on 18 August 2005.
42. NACRO, 'Nacro Responds to the Government's Respect Action Plan', press release issued on 10 January 2006.
43. D. Hay and R. Nye, *The Spirit of the Child* (London: Jessica Kingsley, 2005), p. 22.

Chapter 12

Social Justice and the Open Family

Philomena Cullen

This chapter argues that if, in this postmodern era, we can accept the relationality and historicity of who we are, we will also acknowledge that our family[1] life and forms are not fixed but open to change and development. We all hold different interpretative frameworks or ideologies of the family, and if the Church can reach outside its own ideology of the idealized family, it can play a powerful role in helping people move beyond whichever ideology of the family that they occupy, towards a more gospel way of living out our family lives. A gospel vision of family life is articulated as an open family ideology rooted in a feminist perspective. This entails firstly a challenge to avoid the 'idolatry of the family' whereby we find within our biological families our ultimate loyalty and identity at the expense of belonging to God's family where all are 'brother' and 'sister'; and secondly, a rejection of a construction of the family as a private arena that is blind to the injustices that, in particular, women and children have often found within the familial embrace. By contrast, the open family ideology rooted in a feminist perspective, seeks to build diverse and fluid families that are a 'genuine community of persons' where unselfish self-love is legitimatized and where familial relationships are founded on equality and mutuality. Such families contribute to the development of a just society.

Acknowledging Our Family Ideologies

Like the wrinkles on our face or the way we walk, each of us acquires, unwittingly, an ideology. Partly by growing up in our particular social grouping, and partly by our reactions and responses to that grouping, we acquire a particular way of seeing things, an interpretation of the world.[2]

In this postmodern era, many have come to understand that we are all located within our particular historical, cultural and psychological contexts such that there is no 'view from nowhere' from which to shape our existence and relationships. Likewise our theology is always contextual and is insufficient alone to explain reality without interaction with other

210

dialogue partners (relying as it does on theoretical interpretative frameworks of the world or what the Benedictine monk Thomas Cullinan calls an ideology). This postmodern shift in consciousness invites us to see our experience and understanding as perspectival and limited and thereby encourages us to remain open to a range of alternative viewpoints that we can dialogue with on our way to a more complete grasp of reality.

Within this postmodern context, one of the most powerful ideologies that we form is our construction of 'family', at both individual and collective levels. Although there are some who might wish to treat the family as a natural given, standing independent of any force of history, for most of us, we can acknowledge that our attitudes towards, and concepts of, family are shaped by a myriad of external, context-specific forces. We can see that the history of families is a history of diversity of family form, shape and function. Even if we might wish to disagree with Engel's specific story of the evolution of the family from its feudal to bourgeois forms,[3] the Marxist critique that the family cannot but be seen as an evolving historical entity, shaped and conditioned by wider social and political forces (including who owns the means of production), is as valid an insight now as then, irrespective of whatever particular ideology of the family we may now hold. Such diversity of family ideologies has been mirrored in the Christian tradition, where, as we shall see in this chapter, even a brief foray into the tradition reveals just how radically ambivalent and developmental the Christian tradition has been in evolving in its own understanding of 'family'.

To provide just one practical example of how our ideologies of family have shifted and evolved over time, let us consider the dramatic development in our changing social interpretative concepts of the child. In the late nineteenth century, children were widely understood to be the property of adults, capable of 'hard graft' in the mines and textile mills of industrial England. Today most people would now reject such an ideology of the child as outdated and unethical. However, this is not to say that we no longer have other equally disturbing paradigms that commodify children in other ways. For example, what of the discourse in genetics which often seems to characterize children as little more than the vehicles of genetic material, valued by being judged against a template of idealized characteristics? Indeed, with the various practices nowadays of the donation of gametes, complex ethical questions arise as to how we even define who the parents and families of such children are.[4] Suffice to say that the point of this example is that, whichever of the variety of constructions of family available to us that we unwittingly or actively choose to apply, they all have implications for how we view, value and devalue families today.

This rest of this chapter will explore some of our current constructions of family in the West. In particular, it is keen to examine the evolving Catholic tradition about families and suggests that the Church has positive resources from its collective Christian narrative of the family, developed over two millennia, that it can offer to our postmodern world. It identifies current historical and social forces that are changing our families and argues that it is only when the Church actively relates to today's actual families (plural and diverse) rather than to a non-existent idealized version (always singular) that it becomes the inclusive universal family of God that the gospel directs us to be.

Continuity and Change for Families

In the UK at the dawn of the twenty-first century there is, again, considerable interest in the family, and it has been placed under the spotlight of public and academic debates with a renewed enthusiasm. This is largely due to the enormous and rapid social changes that have taken place in the last three decades in UK society, and these have been paralleled in most other Western societies. Such changes have had a significant and, in many cases, a detrimental effect on the institutions of family and marriage. Socio-economic trends in the UK such as the growth of families living in poverty, parents working long hours, overstretched and under-resourced social support services, the fragmentation of local communities and extended families, to name but a few, have all contributed to domestic instability. Such change has often generated in its wake widespread unease and anxiety about the future of the Western nuclear family – and this despite the fact that many of the family trends that seem to cause such anxiety today, such as cohabitation, births outside marriage, stepfamilies and lone parents, have been as commonplace in early centuries as they are today.

A snapshot of family life in England and Wales derived from the latest census data of 2001 shows that although there has been a decline in families with children that are headed by a heterosexual married couple (down from 90 per cent in 1971 to 64 per cent in 2001), married heterosexual families are still in the majority. The alarmist Christian rhetoric that one can so often hear about 'traditional' (meaning nuclear) families being in a state of collapse is therefore not sustained by the facts. Yet, that said, it is equally beyond doubt that families with children are changing:

- there is more parental separation (around 40 per cent of children will experience parental divorce by their sixteenth birthday);
- greater diversity of parenting arrangements (23 per cent of families are now headed by a lone parent);
- smaller families (on average families have 1.6 children); and
- more working mothers (65 per cent of women with dependent children are in employment).

In addition, there has been a steep rise in the overall number of one-person households (30 per cent) and cohabiting couple households (8 per cent, but this figure does not reflect that 70 per cent of marriages are now preceded by a period of cohabitation).[5] Yet despite this rapidity of social change in the UK, as Barton[6] has pointed out, this has not been matched by a proportionate amount of theological interest in the family. Given that social change is creating new challenges for our families, we must question what accounts for this silence and ask, how should the Church respond?

The Choice for the Church – Silence or Reaching Beyond Certainty

The challenge concerning our families comes at a time when the Church itself is going through a period of immense change and uncertainty. Within the slow emptying of Catholic pews across England and Wales,[7] we can witness a form of the theological silence identified by Barton, in the common reaction of many Catholics who wish to cope with the rapidity of the enormous social change of the last 30 years by avoiding or limiting engagement with the diverse family forms that we see around us today. Instead, blind to their own ideology of the nuclear family which is treated as a non-contextual given rather than a relatively new historical construction, they seek to annihilate the differences by pursuing a mythical bygone golden age of family stability and uniformity. As Mette writes: 'the imprisonment in romanticizing exaggerations and the inability to perceive relationships as they really exist . . . all too obviously favours an attitude which interprets any deviation from the ideal as collapse and condemns it morally.'[8]

Yet, probing below the worst of the noisy rhetoric of the 'recovery of family values', one often finds a form of Christianity that is deeply con-nected to capitalism. Here the association of 'traditional' families with financial as well as spiritual flourishing is made and in one swift construc-tion an entire capitalist economic system is also vindicated. Families that deviate from this construction become subject to an unjust, and indeed abusive, pillorying as social parasites responsible for such societal evils as benefit dependency and anti-social behaviour and crime. While the debate about what types of family provide the 'best' environment for human flourishing, especially the nurturing of children, is legitimate, what is not is the refusal to accept that 'traditional families' are themselves a construction and one that more often than not conceals an opaque political ideology.

But if the Church as a whole follows either of these two patterns and retreats into either a holy silence or becomes afraid to reach outside its own interpretative concepts of the ideal traditional family, it will trap itself in a self-fulfilling prophecy, where the less it ventures out, the more irrelevant it will become to postmodern society at large. There is too much at stake for families today, especially for those families that are most marginalized and vulnerable in our societies, for a ghettoized retreat from the complexity and relativism of postmodern society to be legitimate. Perhaps given the magnitude of contemporary social and cultural change, part of the Church's relating to the reality of diverse family lives is that it must now be prepared to entertain a discourse of family that is not dependent on a prior theology of marriage.

In contrast to an exclusivist response to postmodernity, this chapter suggests that it is those Christians who are seeking a fundamental rethinking of our family relationships, and in particular the foundations of sexuality and gender that they are built upon, who are clearing a positive way forward. By interpreting recent societal change as an opportunity rather than a catastrophe, they locate rich insights in a seeking after new possibilities for family life as old certainties evaporate. As the Church of England's Board of Social Responsibility put it in its examination of the future of the family, '*reflecting on family life today seems to require us to put aside some of our desire for certainty*'.[9]

Of course, putting aside the certainties of our past assumptions about families is not to abandon our critical faculties. The point is to discern, from emerging contemporary paradigms and from our evolving Christian tradition, what the Church has to offer family life in the twenty-first century, both in support and in resistance. We must discern, as Wheeler puts it, 'what is essence and what accident in the patterns of thought and conduct we inherit from our shared texts and traditions'.[10] We must discern how far socio-cultural change may be a source for theological vision and how far has it to be resisted because of the gospel. The Catholic Bishops of England and Wales seemed implicitly to acknowledge this in their 2004 qualitative research report that attempted to take stock of the reality of family life in the UK. Their theological enquiry began by choosing a methodology that engaged with where families 'were at' and in a year-long 'listening' exercise they heard from families directly about what they were experiencing. The title of their resulting report, *Not Easy but full of Meaning*,[11] reflects perhaps both the shift in certainties we have observed and a continued Catholic hope for the rich possibilities of family life.

Towards an Open Ideology of Family

With the postmodern context outlined, the rest of this chapter will aim to sketch from our evolving Catholic tradition an interpretative concept of family that may prove helpful for all postmodern families today. This is described as an *open family ideology rooted in a feminist perspective*. The first dimension of this gospel-derived ideology is encompassed in the concept of an 'open family', and it is here that we begin. My argument is that there has been in Catholic tradition concerning the family, from the very beginning, a significant and subversive strand that cautions against the danger of over-investment in the biological family, irrespective of its form. It is this notion of a fluid or 'open' family form that continues to expose uncritical allegiance to the idealized model of the nuclear family as an unhelpful ideology to be locked into. This is a tendency which the British theologian Linda Woodhead describes as 'one of the most pervasive idolatries of the modern church: family worship'.[12]

In Catholic teaching the family is indeed valued as 'the primordial and, in a certain sense sovereign society',[13] since it is here above everywhere else that the essential contours of a person's character are moulded. But there is too within the tradition the counterbalance that cautions against investing everything into the family, since to do so is to ignore the fundamental Christian vocation of adoption into the family of God. As the Catholic moral theologian N. Peter Harvey explains, 'for most of its history, Christianity has called people out of their families into quite different forms of identity and self-definition'.[14] This means that we need to call into question ways of organising our families that do not have God as their primary focus, hence both the Church's positive evaluation of celibacy throughout its history and its profound ambivalence towards the family.

The redefinition of who is, or who is not, part of our family begins in the Gospel stories. Let us consider, for instance, the complexity reflected in the Gospel stories of Jesus' own family background. This we shall see is starkly contrasted with the Church's idealized notions of the 'holy family' (a paradigm that closely mirrors our preoccupation with the modern Western ideal of the nuclear family, and that can often intensify the pressure on the Christian families today who are most exposed to its sentimental influence). As David McLoughlin writes: 'Jesus comes from a difficult family background. His birth has a shadow over it that, for all the stories of angels, wise men, shepherds and dreams and dramatic escapes, also includes the suspicion of illegitimacy and the expectation of divorce.'[15] Mark's Gospel goes on to record that Jesus' family seemed to consist of both stepbrothers and -sisters (Mk 6.31) whose initial reactions to his public ministry were far from favourable – they 'came to take charge of him; they said: "he is out of his mind" ' (Mk 3.21) and 'they would not accept him' (Mk 6.3) (although admittedly members of Jesus' family would later come to play a leading role in the early Christian community). Divided and unhappy families were probably not alien to Jesus or to the early Church; indeed perhaps some of the so-called breakdown of the family in Western society today would not look out of place in the worlds of the Old or New Testament.

Jesus appears to distance himself from his own 'biological' family and goes on to redefine the very concept of family itself: 'Whoever does the will of God is my brother and my sister and my mother' (Mk 3.35). This subversive statement, that cuts across the assumed norm of biological family belonging and loyalty, is echoed in other Gospel accounts where Jesus warns that the demands of discipleship will lead to conflicts within families: 'For I have come to set a man against his father, a daughter against her mother, a daughter-in-law against her mother-in-law, and one's enemies will be those of his household' (Mt. 10.34–36; Lk. 12.53). And in an even more scandalous attack on biological family loyalties which pale in significance when set against the demands of discipleship: 'Another of the disciples said to him, "Lord permit me first to go bury my father." Jesus said to him, "Follow me and leave the dead to bury their dead." ' (Mt. 8.21–22). The much-ignored message about the primacy of discipleship over biological family identity is consistent and clear: 'Anyone who comes to me without hating father, mother, wife, children, brothers, sisters . . . cannot be my disciple.' (Lk. 14.26). In return, the reward of discipleship in Mk 10.28–30 implies that anyone who leaves house and family behind will find a new home with brothers and sisters in faith, in a new non-hierarchical, universal family. So the Gospel subverts one form of family for another – kinship in the family of God. As McLoughlin writes again: 'The symbol of this new family was Jesus' open table fellowship with prostitutes and sinners.'[16] No wonder, as far as the pagans were concerned, early Christians were deemed to be anti-family.[17]

Now let us compare Jesus' paradigm of the open family of God with how people more usually experience family life today. The Western ideal of the nuclear family is very clear about its boundaries of belonging, and, while at best the nuclear family can occasionally find space for a misfit aunt or lonely grandfather, it is a long way from Jesus' open fellowship where all become sister and brother and where hospitality for the poor and marginalized takes precedence. As Woodhead writes again:

> the family can easily become no more than a licensed form of selfishness. Real hardness of heart may not be all that easy for an individual to sustain, but it can be very easy for a family to fall into. Too many families pull up the drawbridge on the 'heartless world' and refuse to open their hearts to anyone outside the family circle . . . to allow love to be limited by the limits of blood relation in this way is to fail to understand the real implications of the gospel.[18]

But imagine the potential for a more just society if we could, as gospel-living Christians, extend our sympathies beyond our blood ties and feel the same strength of attachment to, and identity with, those who are most in need of the care, nurturing and affirmation that we can find in the best of familial relationships. Imagine, for instance, what it would mean for the 59,000 children languishing in the public 'care' system in the UK. We know that the care system falters largely due to a chronic shortage of respite, fostering and adoptive families. If, as a Christian community, we lived the gospel ideology of an open family, then we would open our hearts and our homes to these most vulnerable of children and make good the failings of the system that so badly lets our children down.

This 'open family' ideology implicitly contains the hope that the 'gap' between doctrinal church teaching on the one hand, and the need for 'pastoral realism' on the other that can address today's postmodern world of families, can indeed be bridged. Indeed such a creative bridging of the gap between the normative family (what the family should look like) and what families are often like in reality, has already taken place in the work of Catholic charities which daily provide family support services to some of the most marginalized and diverse families in the UK. It is their professional praxis, which in the case of many diocesan children's societies constitutes over 100 years of careful reflection and discernment in this area, which often seems to have gone ahead of official teaching. Rather than pulling these charities back into service that reflects allegiance to an ideology of the traditional family, instead the Church would do well to learn from their trailblazing praxis and allow this to set the standard for how the institutional Church constructs its family theology today. Far from building a family theology which helps address this gap being a capitulation to our liberal secular culture, instead we see that it is fully consistent with the subversive strand of the open family ideology found in the New Testament onwards, and which continues to inspire us beyond the limits of our biology and exclusivist idealized family ideologies today.

In this way, the shifting patterns of family life and the diversity of family forms that we see in evidence today are perhaps less threatening than some would have us believe. As a recent study at the University of Leeds into changing family forms found, though people are less dependent on blood or marriage ties and their commitments extend across a range of networks, none of this suggests a loss of commitment itself. There is no indication that the traditional rules of nurture and care have been abandoned. The ethic of care remains resilient and simply expresses itself through a changing variety of family groups, where, for instance, friendship has become a key metaphor invoking the quality of a relationship marked by intimacy and mutuality, whether with children or non-kin.[19]

The Need for a Feminist Perspective in Family Theology

Following on from this articulation of the open family construct, I would now like to extend this model to include a related second dimension, namely the need for the Church to incorporate a feminist perspective in its gospel-inspired ideology of the open family. The open family construct encouraged us to look beyond our biological families to build a more just society; a feminist perspective goes further still by provoking us to make the link between a just society and how just and equal our relationships are within our families.

Part of our idolatry of the idealized family has been a romanticization of it, where the family is deemed to be so sacred that no outside 'interference' is welcomed. The family becomes solely a private arena wherein the injustices that, in particular, women and children have found within the familial embrace have too often gone unacknowledged and the father's authority and rule is supreme. A feminist ideology of the family continues to understand that our families are part of a particular social construction rather than divinely willed and so it is comfortable with a constructive critiquing of family systems that have, especially in the past, been organized on overtly patriarchal lines. So a feminist perspective is not simply a negative deconstruction of the family that leaves nothing at the end. Rather, it seeks to offer from amongst the ruins of romanticized idolatrous family worship a framework of gender justice within which the diversity of families that flourish in postmodern Britain today can be challenged and changed. Family in this usage becomes a verb, describing what families are like in their relationships with each other, rather than a noun, signifying what relationships they should be constituted by.

At heart, a feminist open family ideology is a reading of the family that understands that families are, in large part, a reading about power in relation, specifically about how people historically have or have not embodied their capacities for mutually empowering relationships within the context of their family lives. Such a feminist perspective cuts across the Western liberal ideology that the family is a solely private or personal set of relationships. Instead, families, as Catholic social teaching reminds us, are 'the foundation of society',[20] that is, they are public goods that should mirror the life of the wider Church and the loving trinity of persons-in-relation. Our ability to build just societies resides therefore primarily in our ability to build just families. The recognition that the personal is political, in other words, is one of the insights highlighted by the feminist perspective where the areas of sexuality, domesticity, childcare and family responsibilities are exposed as deeply political concerns.

To choose to embed a feminist perspective in our construction of an open family ideology means first and foremost that postmodern families cannot be comprehended or evaluated without taking into account a sustained engagement with the actual experiences of women. Women's experience is not affirmed as an afterthought to our understanding of families and family life, but as central to it. This entails an active counter to certain sections of the vocal Christian lobby that views all forms of feminism as an attack on 'family values', and that often pinpoints the emancipation of women into the workforce during and beyond the 1940s as the cataclysmic moment where it all started to go wrong for family life. In contrast to this attitude, the feminist open family ideology commended here might even identify, within official church documents themselves, an acknowledgement of the corrosive effect that patriarchy has had upon families (though official documents often seem to speak with a forked tongue in this regard). For example, the Congregation for the Doctrine of the Faith describes distorted familial relationships to be a direct result of original sin which changed the way in which the first man and the first woman related:

> God's decisive words to the woman after the first sin express the kind of relationship which has now been introduced between man and woman: 'your desire shall be for your husband, and he shall rule over you' (Gen. 3.16). It will be a relationship in which love will frequently be debased into pure self-seeking, in a relationship which ignores and kills love and replaces it with the yoke of domination of one sex over the other. In this tragic situation, the equality, respect and love that are required in the relationship of man and woman according to God's original plan, are lost.[21]

And yet, this said, I would suggest it is a sophisticated liberationist feminist perspective which needs to be selected, which, while centred in women's experience, is also capable of understanding that systems of domination do not operate along absolutely fixed gender lines – that all men do not dominate equally and not all women are equally dominated within families – indeed, that all dominant ideologies entailing the misuse of power, whether manifested as sexism, racism, disabilism, ageism, heterosexism and so on, that operate across personal, cultural and institutional levels, are invariably part and parcel of each one of us; that just as there is nothing essential about being a woman that means that one will adopt a feminist perspective, so too there is nothing essential about being a man that entails that one will oppose it. The liberationist feminist perspective commended here is therefore committed to the dismantling of all oppressive structures and dynamics operating within families and to the fostering of dignity and equality for all persons, female and male alike.[22]

An example of oppressive dynamics operating within our families today is derived from certain recent data from social surveys that suggest, for example, that married men are physically and psychologically healthier than their unmarried counterparts, while the opposite is true for women.[23] In our living out of our family lives, both individually and collectively, we should be reflecting seriously upon why this may be the case. What is it about how we structure our family relationships and responsibilities that seems to be having a detrimental effect on women? Interpreting this social data through our feminist perspective, we are called to make good the deficit within much of our current church discourse where there is often little said about the realities of family life beyond a characteristically sickly sweet eulogizing about Christian marriage. Indeed, beyond this routine level of daily injustice, we know that, within the UK alone, one in four women and one in six men will experience domestic violence at some point in their lives and that in 90 per cent of incidents children are in the same or next room.[24] Given these disturbing official statistics, as Alison Webster writes, our family discourse must also acknowledge that for too many people the home is far from being a place of security, love and justice:

> there is little recognition within the churches of the immense suffering to which women and children have been subjected within families. Physical, sexual, emotional, psychological and economic violence against women and children have had little coverage in church reports which glorify and romanticize married life.[25]

In seeking to unmask the realities of what family life has all too often entailed for women, certain schools of Christian feminism, contrary to their critics, are not seeking to be either anti-men, anti-marriage or anti-motherhood. Of course, other schools within Christian feminism are guilty, to varying degrees, of many such faults. The broader liberationist form of feminism commended in this chapter and exemplified by Catholic feminist theologians like Mary Grey, Tina Beattie and Lisa Cahill rather attempts to build a family theology which is knowledgeable about power, its structures and dynamics within family life, and understands how women really experience family life. It wants to move away from a practice of family life that has too often been an institution of structured inequality into a vision of partnership between mature and loving persons. It aims to be both realistic about the limitations that we often find there while also offering hope that these can be transcended. At heart, a Christian liberationist feminist perspective of family believes that all relationships, and most especially our intimate family relationships, should be built on equality and mutuality and not on one-way sacrifice.

As Elizabeth Moltmann-Wendel[26] in her pivotal work on Christian feminism in the 1980s explained, patriarchal love depends on subjugation and self-destruction of the self to the demands of the father who embodies a family or wider group. It does not create mutuality between the father and child but teaches conformity to the principles and laws established by the father and upon which faithful obedience produces conditional love. This model of patriarchal family relationships, she claims, is a far cry from the love experienced by the prodigal son that has yet to be appropriated as a pedagogical possibility in our families in the Christian West. At best this is what our families can be and do. They can be places of unconditional mutual love where we are forgiven when we least deserve to be.

In acting as the bearer of this pedagogical possibility for how we could live our family lives, the Church should be guiding all, but especially women, into experiences of familial intimacy where one is not drawn more and more into a non-reciprocal giving away of oneself in the constant service of others' needs and desires. That love of self and love of others, though undoubtedly not free from what should act as a creative tension in family life, are at root not diametrically opposed, but complementary. The search for unselfish self-love and the building of a just family dynamic are in reality part of the same struggle. Yet the lack of emphasis on proper self-love that is found in the Catholic tradition's over-emphasis on self-sacrifice and self-abnegation, which in the context of a historical patriarchal family tradition has been promoted disproportionably between the sexes, has proved damaging to healthy, flourishing family life. Even within Pope Benedict's first encyclical *Deus Caritas Est,* an extended meditation on the nature of Christian love, there is no attention to love of *self* as a Christian obligation, and this is indicative of a broader pastoral failing of the Church in this area. As Kurt Remele reflects on this: 'the command to love one's neighbour as oneself is too frequently interpreted to imply that self-love is a given, and that other-love follows in its train. Yet in practice it is as likely to be the other way around and therefore real, non-narcissistic self love can be as challenging as other-love.'[27]

For those who think feminism has already succeeded in defeating the rule of the father and conquered patriarchal tendencies within families today, and so remain unconvinced of the continued relevance and legitimacy of a feminist perspective in any Christian conception of family, an illuminating report that examined equality in heterosexual relationships among 16–21-year-olds in Manchester and London makes for sober reading. Among the grim findings of the WARP Report[28] was a sense overall that young women seem to experience their sexuality as disembodied, that they are passive objects who find it frightening to make their desires known. They use language that is about pleasing, not pleasure, and rigorously observe the 'social mechanisms of sexual reputation'. Although the young women interviewed were aware of the double standards they experienced in the sexual arena, they were resigned to this. The argument is that heterosexuality is about much more than a set of sexual practices. Although sexuality has become one commodity amongst others for both men and women in our Western consumer society, the argument is that for young women, hetero-sexuality represents and makes manifest in their lives a set of gender relations, which in turn underpin patriarchal family forms and society at large. The feminist theologian, Lisa Isherwood, who is concerned to promote a positive theology of the body, reflecting theologically on the WARP Report, concludes that 'women are encouraged to gain control over the surfaces of their bodies but to give away all control in social relations, intercourse and pleasure'.[29] For Isherwood the report highlights what sex is like in our Western society that is itself constructed on institutional inequality and domination. For the purpose of the feminist open family ideology that we have been suggesting the Church can offer to the postmodern world of families, it will therefore need to encompass an alertness to how our private sexualities are lived out in our range of family structures and be quick to critique how these function as litmus tests for our wider societal values.

Towards Inclusive Ideologies of Families

To conclude, this chapter has argued that the history of families has always been one of diversity of family form and shape. Such diversity has been mirrored in church tradition that has itself evolved in its understanding of 'family'. Rather than trying to reconcile the disparate and often conflicting voices of Catholic tradition on the family that we find, this chapter has argued that an acknowledgement of the development of doctrine that seeks to engage with the signs of the times would seem a more helpful way forward than an enforced allegiance to a romanticized ideology of 'the family'. It is when the Church relates to actual diverse families rather than to the non-existent idealized version that it becomes the inclusive universal family of God that Jesus directed us to be. This is especially important in this post-modern era where the challenges facing our diverse families are significant and demand a guiding response from the Church.

By looking at our ideologies of family and by examining the collective narrative of the family we have shared over two millennia, we can find positive resources for the journey towards gospel living. This is not to suggest that we can simply read off from the tradition the answers to our current family challenges. Rather we discover in our Catholic tradition an ongoing exhortation and, at times, even a provocation to examine the ideologies that we nurture today, to see if they cohere with a gospel vision of familial relationships where there is fluidity in how we choose to see those who belong to our family, and where justice provides the framework within which our families are challenged and changed. In trusting the revelatory power of our personal and collective family stories, we take our incarnation and redemption seriously, and, from the messiness of our family lives today, dare to find the action of a liberatory God. This God, I believe, calls on us to theologize about our diverse experiences of family and to build an inclusive theology of the family that is based on justice, mutuality and reciprocal love. The task now facing the Church is to encourage us to throw off our lingering idealism of 'the family', pursue a healthy Christian realism in examining family life and open the past limitations of our ideologies of the biological family so that those who are most alienated in our society can come home.

Notes

1. For reasons that will become clear in this chapter, the author uses the term 'family' in an inclusive sense to include any grouping of people, whether related by blood or not, who collectively self-define as family.

2. Thomas Cullinan OSB, *Mine and Thine, Ours and Theirs: An Anthology on Ownership in the Christian Tradition*, privately published pamphlet available from the author at Ince Benet, Ince Blundell, Liverpool, p. 1.

3. Friedrich Engels, *Origin of the Family, Private Property and the State* (Middlesex: Penguin Classics, Penguin Books Ltd, 1986).

4. For an illuminating discussion of some of the complex ethical dilemmas for families posed by current genetic practices, see Michael Banner, ' "Who are My Mother and My Brothers?" Marx, Bonhoeffer and Benedict and the Redemption of the Family', *Studies in Christian Ethics* (London: T&T Clark 1992), pp. 1–22.

5. All figures obtained from Office of National Statistics, *Census 2001: National Report for England and Wales* (London: HMSO, 2003).

6. Stephen C. Barton (ed.), *The Family – In Theological Perspective* (Edinburgh: T&T Clark Ltd, 1996).

7. The Catholic Bishops' Conference of England and Wales website contains annual statistics of Mass attendance. These show a slow but steady decline in numbers attending Mass on a given Sunday, from 1,385,408 Mass attendees in 1988 to 958,541 Mass attendees in 2003 (latest data available), http://www.catholic-ew.org.uk/cathstats/population.htm.

8. Norbert Mette, 'The Family in the Teaching of the Magisterium', in Lisa Sowle Cahill and Dietmar Mieth (eds), *The Family, Concilium*, 1995, no. 4, p. 79, as cited in Gerard Mannion, *The Family (from 1960 to present day)* (London: Caritas-social action, 2005), p. 30.

9. Church of England Board of Social Responsibility, *Something to Celebrate – Valuing Families in Church and Society* (London: Church House Publishing, 1995), p. 7.

10. S. Wheeler, 'Christians and Family', in G. Meilaender and W. Werpehowski (eds), *The Oxford Handbook of Theological Ethics* (Oxford: Oxford University Press, 2005), p. 355.

11. Catholic Bishops' Conference of England and Wales, *'Not Easy but full of Meaning': Catholic Family Life in 2004* (London: Redemptorist Publications, 2005).

12. Linda Woodhead, 'Christianity Against and For the Family: A Response to Nicholas Peter Harvey', *Studies in Christian Ethics* (London: T&T Clark, 1992), p. 40.

13. John Paul II, *Letter to Families* (2 February 1994), §17: *AAS* 86 (1994), p. 906.

14. Nicholas Peter Harvey, 'Christianity Against and For the Family', *Studies in Christian Ethics* (London: T&T Clark, 1992), p. 34.
15. David McLoughlin, *Jesus, the Family and Children* (London: Caritas-social action, 2005), p. 8. I am indebted to David for his work in this area.
16. Ibid, p. 13.
17. See Sara Parvis, *The Open Family: Kinship in the Bible and the Pre-Reformation Church* (London: Caritas-social action, 2005), p. 25.
18. Linda Woodhead, op. cit., p. 41.
19. Fiona Williams (ESRC CAVA Research Group), *Rethinking Families* (London: Calouste Gulbenkian Foundation, 2004).
20. *Gaudium et Spes*, §52.
21. Congregation for the Doctrine of the Faith, *Letter to the Bishops of the Catholic Church on the Collaboration of Men and Women in the Church and in the World* (31 May 2004), §7.
22. For an accessible introduction to reading through a feminist lens, see ch. 1 of F. Scott Spencer, *Dancing Girls, Loose Ladies and Women of the Cloth: The Women in Jesus' Life* (London: Continuum, 2004).
23. Office of National Statistics, *Social Trends 32* (London: HMSO, 2002).
24. Home Office, *Safety and Justice* (London: HMSO, 2003).
25. Alison Webster, *Found Wanting: Women, Christianity and Sexuality* (London: Cassell, 1995), p. 15.
26. Elizabeth Moltmann-Wendel, *A Land Flowing with Milk and Honey* (London: SCM Press, 1986), p. 177.
27. Kurt Remele, 'Is Theological Ethics in Need of Psychotherapy? Self-love, Self-Realisation and the Common Good', paper presented to a meeting of the Association of Teachers of Moral Theology at Hinsley Hall, Leeds, UK, May 2006.
28. J. Holland, C. Ramazanoglu, S. Sharpe and R. Thomson, *The Male in the Head: Young People, Heterosexuality and Power* (London: The Tufnell Press, 1998).
29. Lisa Isherwood, 'Learning to be a Woman: Feminist Theological Reflections on Sex Education in Church Schools', in *Sex Education*, vol. 4, no. 3, October 2004, p. 278.

Chapter 13

The Key is Empathy

Sheila Cassidy

The author sees empathy as the key to pastoral care in many different settings. 'The ability to enter the other's world as if it were your own' (Carl Rogers) leads to a depth of understanding and compassion which makes loving-kindness a necessity rather than an option. The author writes openly of her own failure to respond adequately to the suffering of her dying father and of how the experience of torture and solitary confinement in Pinochet's Chile gave her an insight into the world of the frightened and powerless. Working empathetically with those who suffer is a costly business and this chapter is based upon 20 years of the author being along- side terminally ill cancer patients and their grieving families. Survival in such work depends not upon external defences and refusal to 'become involved', but rather upon clarity of internal boundaries, teamwork and adequate time out. The importance of active listening is discussed using the Chinese symbol for the word; a composite of attending to another with the ears, eyes, undivided attention and with the heart.

If someone were to ask me what I believe to be the key to Christian pastoral ministry, I think I would say that it is empathy: what American psycho- therapist Carl Rogers defined as the ability to enter the other's world *as if* it were your own, without losing the 'as if' quality. In fact, I would go further and say that empathy is the key to living a Christian life, which is, of course, a life in which social justice is not just a theory but a way of being. The notion of empathy has been around for a long, long time and there are all sorts of wise sayings which incorporate it. My favourite is the American Indian prayer which goes: 'Grant O Lord that I may not criticize my neigh- bour until I have walked a mile in his moccasins.'

I have become acutely aware of the need for empathy over the past 20 years or so, during which time I have been working with men and women with cancer and, more recently, as a psychotherapist, with adults afflicted with depression, anxiety, stress and grief. My work in teaching nurses how to care psychologically and spiritually for the terminally ill has given me the opportunity to articulate what was originally only an intuition: that you cannot accompany the suffering without sharing some of the pain. As hospital chaplain Peter Speck taught me many years ago, you cannot watch

225

through binoculars from a hundred yards away, but if you want to help people, you must get 'Gethsemane' close. It is interesting in this context to think of the word 'compassion', which comes from the Latin for 'suffering with'. Compassion, of course, has a very 'Jesus' quality: he was always having compassion on the lame, the lepers and those possessed by grief or demons.

Although I like to think of myself as an empathic person now, I have not always exercised this gift, far from it. When I was in my mid-thirties and had been qualified as a doctor for about ten years, my father, with whom I had a very difficult relationship, fell ill with cancer of the bowel. He had surgery in the August of 1974, recovered for a while but deteriorated steadily and died in early December. During those months I visited him in hospital and in his home but I have no recollection whatsoever of talking to him about how he was feeling in his spirits. I have no idea if he knew that he had cancer or if he knew that he was going to die. It just didn't occur to me to talk to him in such an intimate way. His last weeks were very difficult: we placed him in a nursing home but he kept running away and was picked up by the police on more than one occasion. Eventually we paid for him to be cared for in his own home and he died peacefully.

As I look back I feel deeply ashamed of my lack of care for him. The trouble was that I had no empathy: I did not bother to use my imagination to understand how it *felt* to be old and ill and confused. It simply did not occur to me that he might be frightened or might wish to know that his life was drawing to its close.

The problem was that, although I was a competent and kindly young doctor, I had been trained to care for the diseased body, not for the failing mind or the frightened soul. The other problem, of course, was that this was my father, not an 'ordinary' patient, and there were enormously powerful and complex bonds of emotion both binding us together and keeping us apart. My father and I were very close when I was a child, but as I grew older, I found his love possessive and I resented the power that he held over me. I suspect that he tried to live his life through mine and I wanted to live my own life free from him. These emotions unfortunately came between us at a time when he was most needy.

In 1980, around six years after my father died, I came to work in the radiotherapy department in Plymouth. New to the city, I had very few friends and spent my evenings drifting round the wards talking to the patients. In particular, I spent time with the terminally ill and learned from them what it was like to be facing death. This was the beginning of my education in empathy: I took the time and the trouble to sit with these men and women and listened to what they had to say.

I should perhaps explain that something had happened to me in the six years between my father's death and the beginning of my work with the dying, and that was that I had been forced to face my own death. In 1975

I was working as a doctor in Chile, at a time when the country was under the military dictatorship of General Augusto Pinochet. People were frequently abducted by the secret police and held in hidden detention centres where they were routinely tortured and sometimes killed. One day in mid-October in 1975, I was asked by a priest if I would treat a man who was in hiding from the security forces. I had no hesitation in agreeing to the request when they explained to me that he was a high-ranking member of the underground resistance and would quite certainly be killed if apprehended. I treated him in the convent where he was sheltering but, unfortunately, someone informed on me and I too was arrested a few days later.

I spent the next three days in a secret torture centre where I was interrogated with electric shocks until I divulged the names of the priests involved in sheltering the man I had treated. I was then transferred to another detention centre where I spent three weeks in solitary confinement. The last five weeks of my detention I spent in a more open prison where there were around 80 women and 500 men.

This was, as you can imagine, a completely terrifying experience and I believe that I suffered from the symptoms of post-traumatic stress for a number of years. More important than that, however, was that during this time I gained first-hand experience of what it was like to be powerless, to experience great pain and to be very, very frightened. The Chileans talk of experiencing something '*in carne propria*', in one's own flesh, and this, of course, is what happened to me. It was not until I resumed my medical work, however, that I realized how important the Chilean experience had been. When I began my work with cancer sufferers in July 1980 I found that I was completely at ease with the patients, especially those who were most afraid.

In practice, this meant that, most of the time, I knew what to say, when to speak and when to be silent. It has, of course, taken me many years to refine my sensitivity, to hone my communication skills, but even at the beginning of this work I was at home with patients with whom my colleagues were often ill at ease.

The reason that I was 'at home' with the terminally ill, of course, was that I could intuit or imagine how they felt because I knew how *I* had felt when I was helpless, humiliated and in pain. I could, in Carl Rogers' language, enter into their world *as if* it were my own. It is important to make clear at this point that, however highly developed our intuition, that alone is not enough. We must use our knowledge of emotional processes to ask the right questions so that our empathy may be *accurate*. Let me give you an example of what I mean.

Many years ago, when I was working at St Luke's Hospice in Plymouth, I met a man in his fifties with secondary liver cancer. He had come to visit the anaesthetist from the pain clinic to see if he would be helped by a special injection to control the pain in his liver. It soon became clear that his pain could be controlled by tablets, so we sent for the next patient. I was struck,

however, by the man's facial expression because he looked absolutely terri-
fied. When he left, therefore, I excused myself and took him to a room where
we could talk. I asked him if he was afraid and he said yes: it was not, as I had
imagined, a fear of death which troubled him but the terrifying dreams
which disturbed his sleep each night. He explained to me that during
the Second World War, when he was eight years old, his home had been
bombed and he had been buried alive in the air-raid shelter. He had vivid
memories of trying to dig his way out with his bare hands and now these
memories came back to haunt him in nightmares. It was not just the bomb
incident but he also dreamed of his mother screaming and of a time much
later, when a friend who had been shot, died in his arms.

I admitted him to the hospice for a few days and took advice from a
psychiatrist colleague as to how I could blot out his nightmares. I often think
that, if I had not asked him why he was afraid, he might never have told
anyone about his problem.

During ten years of work at the hospice I developed my skills of empathy
with the patients, but absurdly, I never exercised it with my colleagues. As
my lecturing invitations increased I spent more and more time away from
Plymouth and I never gave a thought as to what it was like for my colleagues
to have me come and go in this fashion. I knew I was a good lecturer and it
seemed important to spread the gospel of care of the dying. I had no idea
that my assistant doctors were getting angrier with me; although I did know
that the hospice council was concerned at my trips away. Eventually, in
1992, I was asked to leave and in January 1993 I was lucky enough to be
appointed to work as a palliative care doctor in Derriford Hospital in
Plymouth.

With hindsight, this was the best thing that could have happened to
me because I was able to sow the seeds of hospice philosophy within the
hospital, but at the time I was completely devastated. The moral of this story
is that it's all very well to have accurate empathy with your patients, but if
you don't bother to practise the same skills with your colleagues, things can
go badly wrong.

In my work as a psychotherapist, I listen for a couple of hours each day to
the difficulties of my patients and I am increasingly aware that so many of
their relationship difficulties occur because either they or their partners are
not able to walk in each other's moccasins. The severely depressed woman,
whose husband never mentions her illness, longs to be affirmed and hugged
and told that she is loved, but alas he is the strong silent type and doesn't
'do' emotions.

It is listening to the stories of abusive childhoods, however, which both
saddens and enrages me: the mothers who never hugged their children, the
fathers whose only communication was criticism and outright denigration.
I encounter women in their fifties and sixties who have lived good lives but
who still believe that they are worthless.

All this is ordinary, commonplace psychological abuse, but what of physical and sexual abuse? If only stepfathers and grandfathers and kindly parish priests who sexually molest little boys and girls could stop and think what it must be like to be five or ten years old and to have a grown man push his penis into your vagina or rectum. If only they were able to think of the fear, the guilt, the shame and the confusion that they produce in their victims, perhaps they would think twice before kidding themselves that they do no harm. Likewise, some of the Catholic bishops in England, who only a few years ago moved their erring priests to another parish, should have imagined the confusion and distress of the children concerned and the risks involved in placing a paedophile where he had easy access to children. Happily the situation is now much better, with any priest involved in abuse dealt with according to carefully defined protocols that emerged out of a thorough enquiry into how the Church should better respond. It is hoped that, while abuse may still occur in the future (it is impossible to ensure that this can never be the case), the cover-ups of past years have stopped, and the Catholic bishops across England and Wales have convened a national coordinating body of child protection specialists to advise on all such issues (the Catholic Office for the Protection of Children and Vulnerable Adults). Sometimes I think we should have a yearly service of penitence in Westminster Cathedral in London, for all the victims of abuse. Enough of the Church Triumphant: how about a day for the Church Penitent?

There are so many aspects of our lives where justice is merely a dream. One which has forced its way into my own awareness is the 'problem' of asylum seekers and refugees. I am not thinking of the British National Party or those who believe that the asylum seekers are taking 'our benefits', 'our jobs' and 'our houses', but rather of the clever people in housing, education and benefit departments, who rarely bother to imagine what it must be like to watch your wife and child be raped and killed, or to spend your life savings on a horrific journey hidden in the back of a lorry and then find yourself poor, unemployed, despised, reviled and unwanted in a country whose language you cannot understand and whose culture is completely alien to you.

The opposite, of course, is true: those of us who can imagine what it is like to be a refugee or asylum seeker must also try to walk in the shoes of those frightened by the influx of foreigners into what they understood to be their street, their town and their country.

The eternal social justice problems of global poverty, conflict and natural disasters call daily upon our reserves of generosity and empathy, and the charity fundraisers get more and more creative in helping us enter their 'clients'' world. How then are we to live with the constant demands for our money and attention which drop through our letterboxes each morning?[1] The television daily beams pictures of the suffering and dying into our living-rooms and we wrestle with compassion fatigue with each new flood or earthquake that reaches our screens. My most vivid memory of the year is seeing a girl of about 12 shivering in the Himalayas as winter descended upon her isolated village. I wanted to give her my coat there and then.

As St Basil taught, to the starving belongs the bread in your larder, to the naked the cloak in your wardrobe. From time to time I give some clothes to my friend Helen who distributes them to the asylum seekers she works with and I support events for Jeremiah's Journey, my local charity for bereaved children. But I still have my lovely flat overlooking the ocean and my two pedigree dogs, not to mention the sparrows who eat me out of house and home, and the dormice that have moved into the garden to feast upon the dropped seeds! Empathy may well be the key to an authentic Christian life that incarnates social justice in our daily lives, but you and I must work out our balance of giving and survival. I don't have the answer: if you have, let me know.

The second part of Rogers' definition of empathy contains the caveat that although we should enter the other's world as if it were our own we must do this without losing the 'as if' quality. This of course is easier said than done and medical students and nurses in training are frequently warned not to get 'involved' with their patients lest they become overwhelmed by the patient's suffering and 'burn out'. Although I understand the rationale behind this admonition, it makes me sad because it is often interpreted as an instruction to be 'professional', to keep their distance or assume a sort of Teflon coating to which the pain and dirt of the world will not stick. As I have grown older and more experienced in the care of vulnerable and suffering people, I realize that, somewhere along the way, I have dropped my protective barrier of formality and am able to trust in a system of internal boundaries which protect my emotional core. What I mean by this is that I know quite clearly in my own mind that the people I work with are neither friend nor family but patient or client. It is this clarity which enables me to expose myself to the pain of others, 'holding' them metaphorically and often physically in my arms. It's not that I do not grieve for my patient's suffering, but this grief moves me to action rather than to impotent distress.

When, on the other hand, it is a friend or family member who is sick or hurting, I am much more vulnerable and it is harder to be patient and loving. It's almost as if sickness in my family makes me feel guilty – as if I have not protected them as I should. I find myself easily irritated by the frail and elderly members of my family in a way which doesn't happen when I am dealing with my patients. I admit this readily because I suspect that many professional carers feel guilty that they are not able to be as loving as they think they should be to their families.

I have recently offered to provide supervision and support to a group of nurses who care for terminally ill men and women in their own homes. Their manager worries that they are becoming overwhelmed by their contact with the dying and wants me to teach them 'coping skills' so that they can be more resilient. The trouble is, I'm not sure if my own coping skills are 'transferable'. What I can offer is a listening ear, an experienced and hopefully constructive response. I was taught many years ago about the 'rules of feedback' in role play which insist that the observer must always comment upon what was done well before mentioning that which could have been done better. I look forward to starting this work because I enjoy teaching nurses and I believe that providing support for those at the coalface is enormously important. The fact is that talking about one's difficulties is a human need and this applies to carers as well as to patients, to clergy as well as to their penitents. It follows that attentive listening is a pastoral work which as many people as possible should learn to provide. Attentive or 'active' listening is quite costly in terms of emotional energy and is very different from the way most of us listen in ordinary social exchange. When attempting to teach this, I use the Chinese symbol for listening which is said to be a composite of the symbols for the eye, the ear, the undivided attention and the heart.

Ears

Eyes

Undivided attention

Heart

When we listen with the eye we note not only the person's facial expression but his or her body language: whether it is 'open' and trusting or tense and defensive. As a doctor I automatically take in a patient's complexion, stance, gait and physique, while, as a woman, I am particularly aware of whether another woman has dressed with care or with little or no attention to the way she looks.

Listening with the ear means that we take in not only the content of what the other is saying but also the unspoken feelings which we pick up from use of language and tone of voice. We are consciously or unconsciously screening for painful emotions such as fear, anger, bitterness or guilt. Counsellors and therapists learn to be alert to what is called 'counter-transference' – the way the person talking is making us feel.

Many years ago I gave regular supportive psychotherapy to a young woman whose father had sexually abused her from aged four until her teens. 'B' was a pitiful sufferer from insecurity, low self-esteem, agoraphobia, bulimia and self-harm. For an hour each week she talked about her feelings and somehow 'transferred' them to me so that at the end of the session she walked away cheerfully while I felt totally drained. One of the physical therapists in the unit where I was working used to give me a ten-minute foot massage as a way of restoring my spirits and energy.

Listening with undivided attention is often the most healing thing we can do for an individual because it, of its nature, affirms the worth of the person speaking. Carl Rogers speaks of the 'core conditions' in the therapeutic relationship as being transparency, empathy and unconditional positive regard. By this he means that we should not assume a professional front because it scares people and that we should accept each person without judgement, whatever he or she may reveal to us. It seems to me that this unconditional loving and acceptance lies at the very heart of Jesus' message.

Lastly the symbol tells us that we should listen with the heart, something which I interpret as an exhortation to love, empathy and compassion (from *com-passio* – to suffer with).

All of this brings me full circle to the question of survival of the carer, social justice activist or pastoral minister in his or her work with the suffering. My intuition is that survival is a question of honesty, humility and teamwork. Those who listen, comfort and guide must in turn be listened to, comforted and guided. Carers must listen to (be aware of) their own feelings and signs of stress so that they may know when to take time out. This is where humility comes in: we are all of us human and this means that we all need rest, nourishment, time out and fun. To believe that one is 'special' or extra holy and can therefore work around the clock as a routine is, alas, a pious and arrogant delusion. As Jesus said on that last and dreadful night: 'My little children, love one another as I have loved you – it is by this that people shall recognize you as my disciples.'[2]

Notes

1. I have spent a working lifetime contributing to Oxfam, CAFOD and Christian Aid and years of feeling guilty when I have sent five pounds instead of fifty. In my retirement when I have much less money than before, the requests still come and I pocket the coins sellotaped to the letters (a new marketing tool) and bin letter after letter requesting aid for prisoners, donkeys, whales and homeless mothers. I send two pounds a month, or sometimes five, to a random group of charities and feel guilty about the rest. What else can we do? Each of us must choose who to support and who to leave to others richer or more generous than ourselves: a sort of hideous financial triage.
2. Author's paraphrase from the Last Supper discourse, Jn 13.33–35.

Chapter 14

Discerning the Signs of the Times: Who Owns Catholic Social Teaching and Who Should Own Up to It?

Noel Timms

This chapter, noting the strong papal grip throughout the course of modern Catholic social teaching (CST), raises questions about the reception and the development of this teaching. How are the sources of any such teaching to be excavated – either in natural law or the Bible or in some yet to be achieved integration of the two – and how can the signs of the times be unambiguously discerned? Can and should CST be developed?

Introduction

It could be said that the Church's foundational teaching – say on the Trinity – has profound social significance. It might also be suggested that it is eccentric even to suggest the possibility of any teaching that was somehow *not* social. However, a teaching specified distinctively as social is usually considered to make its debut with the publication in 1891 of *Rerum Novarum*. This was the first in what turned out to be a series of papal encyclicals and pronouncements. The high point of confidence in their problem-solving capacity was possibly reached in *Menti Nostrae* (1950): 'the teaching that the Church gives in social matters . . . alone can offer a remedy to the present evils'.[1] It is worth noting the idea of teaching as simple bestowal on passive recipients. It is ironic that a Church preoccupied with the office of teaching should for so long have failed to appreciate teaching as an activity distinct from 'taming, ruling, restoring to health, conditioning or commanding'.[2] In this regard it is significant that Dorr welcomes *Laborem Exercens* (1981) as 'far more like teaching in the ordinary sense of the word, namely, explaining and helping people to understand why things are the way they are – and how they might be changed'.[3] The idea of praxis, now fitfully received into CST, would suggest that people may have their own understanding of their predicament and the way in which it might be changed, but the object of understanding is still papal teaching, rather than the thinking of the Church as a whole, to use a distinction made by O'Connell.

O'Connell argues that papal ownership of CST has resulted in an impoverishment of the potential contribution of local episcopates. This has coincided with a growing realization that the central authority was facing an increasingly complex world in which 'it was difficult to utter a unified message and to put forward a solution which has universal validity'.[4] Local Episcopal conferences have recently started to issue statements on a range of social issues. The American bishops, for example, have published on peace, economic justice, the American economy and the role of women, though not without experiencing pressure from the Vatican. In 1996 the bishops of England and Wales published *The Common Good and the Catholic Church's Social Teaching* (hereafter CG). This is largely based on a repetition of papal teaching, but it also welcomes discussion and collaboration in the application and development of CST (CG, p. 4).[5] This welcome is directed to experts and to those in positions of influence – presumably an exercise of the option for such groupings. Dorr has noted that the Vatican has come to consult more frequently with lay experts, but he argues that 'Many Catholics would like to be actively involved in the formation' of CST (p. 377).[6] Taking this possibility seriously – which is the intent of this chapter – involves making and sustaining at least three important moves at a conceptual level. First, from claim rights – to be given teaching, as in the above quotation – to liberties or the right to do certain things. Second, from treating the social question as an undifferentiated question to which simple answers can be delivered from on high, to an appreciation of the complexities and ambiguities involved. Third, from the assumption that teaching belongs exclusively to the clerical office, to von Hugel's denial of a strict demarcation of roles and his view that 'The Church is, thus, ever and everywhere, both progressive and conservative; both reverently free-lance and official; both daring to the verge of presumption, and prudent to the verge of despair.'[7]

With these considerations in mind this chapter discusses the status and purpose of CST. It then considers ambiguities in three of the key concepts in CST – option for the poor, human rights and the common good. Such ambiguities are not easily resolved, but, as the conclusion suggests, they can be made more intelligible if viewed in the context of political thinking, not so much about the legitimate basis of political authority but about manners of governance. This context will enable a wider ownership of CST and also provide a framework for its necessary development.

Status and Purpose

Questions about the status and purpose of CST have been raised in relation to its doctrinal status, its coherence and unbroken continuity as a body of teaching, and the extent to which it represents a compromise between two opposing forces or ideological interests and a set of ideas legitimate in their own independent light.

CG asserts a strong sense of doctrine in describing CST as more relevant than it has ever been, and no 'less important than other branches of the Church's moral teaching'.[8] This appreciation of a doctrinal gold standard is not shared by everyone. McCabe, for example, did not believe that CST was on a par with accepted Catholic teaching about, for example, the Trinity or the Eucharist. He argued that the social encyclicals should be judged as responses 'to concrete circumstances rather than the handing down of already traditional doctrine. It was simply a matter of preaching the gospel as best you can in a certain time and place'.[9] This suggests a comparison between, as it were, sound Nicean tweed and material that is somewhat off the peg. More importantly it raises the issue of particularity of time and place; how particular can CST become? For example, the warning that labour unions should not be too closely linked to political parties may make sense in the light of the particular experience of a pope's previous life in Poland. The simple repetition of the warning in CG[10] in a different context is scarcely intelligible.

CG also adopted a strong view of the inner coherence of CST. The preface refers to 'a set of consistent and complementary principles, values, and goals', and argues with some historical licence that 'The fashioning of social teaching is a task the Church has undertaken down the ages'.[11] Cornwell has remarked that *Centesimus Annus* (1991) 'proclaimed the encyclical's continuity with previous papal teaching, as if to give the impression that he [John Paul II] was engaged with his predecessors in the weaving of a seamless doctrinal tapestry'[12] Celebration of coherence and continuity can also be found in *Populorum Progressio*, p. 12: 'the Church has never failed to foster the human progress of the nations'. CST does appear to be self-congratulatory, acknowledging neither flaw nor ambivalence in its always evolving, never-changing teaching. Two examples may assist.

An example of flaw can be found in Ruston's use of Maxwell's 1975 history of Catholic teaching on slavery.[13] Maxwell questions the claim in *In Plurimis* that popes before Leo XIII had made every effort to ensure that the institution of slavery was abolished. He argued that the contribution of church leadership on this crucial social issue was minimal and came too late. Moreover, it should be critically assessed in the light of previous papal authorizations of the practice of slavery and the failure to question the moral legitimacy of the institution of slavery which continued throughout the nineteenth century.

To illustrate ambivalence we may note Dorr's opinion that between *Rerum Novarum* and *Quadragesimo Anno* there is both continuity and significant change. He senses that it is possible to find in the latter the beginning of a spirituality of justice, but this does not emerge with sufficient clarity. 'On some occasions it almost seems as though concern for justice is little more than a means to the end of bringing workers into the church, or ensuring that they are not led astray.'[14]

Much of the papal tradition of social teaching was concerned with naming the evils that threatened the established positions of Church and State which, it was assumed, had interests in common in social stability. So, *Inscrutabile* of 1878 looks to state rulers to join with the Church 'as the source of authority and salvation . . . considering that their own peace and safety, as well as that of their own people, is bound up with the safety of the Church and the reverence due to her . . .'. In *Auspicato Concessum* religion was deemed to be the most effective way to root out violence, class envy and the desire for a new social order. Conflict between rich and poor could lead to revolution and anarchy, so the Church warned the rich with eternal punishment should they fail to give from their superfluity, whilst it comforted the poor with the hope of rewards in heaven. Concern with the effects of violence is not simply a historical residue. The former Cardinal Ratzinger in an Instruction on Certain Aspects of the Theology of Liberation accused such thinking of reducing the whole essence of salvation to the struggle for social justice and advocating the overthrow of unjust social structures. 'To put one's trust in violent means in the hope of restoring more justice is to become the victim of a fatal illusion: violence begets violence . . .'[15] Reliance on such homespun wisdom illustrates one of the basic failings of CST, the failure to deal analytically with conflict. It should at least confront the kind of philosophical analysis presented for example in the work of Honderich.[16]

The balancing character of CST was questioned implicitly in *Quadragesimo Anno* and rejected in *Centesimus Annus*. The former stated that 'The aim of social policy must . . . be the re-establishment of vocational groups',[17] but this romantic harking back to a supposed era of social cohesion is not taken up in later encyclicals. John Paul II rejected the view that social doctrine should be envisaged as some kind of compromise between liberal capitalism and Marxist collectivism. It emerges from a distinctive theologizing on human nature which appears at once highly abstract and also concerned with the way in which man conducts himself. (A drawback in the consideration of an ungendered notion of human nature will be noted below.)

The history of CST suggests that it may not be wise to rely on a freestanding clerical theology. There is more than one strand to CST. CG points to 'an oral tradition as well as a written one . . .' (p. 28).[18] Some have argued that 'unofficial' social teaching has always exercised the greater influence, pointing to the work of philosophers like Jacques Maritain and the vitality of movements for social justice, such as Pax Christi. Yet, the official and the unofficial do not sit easily together, and the problem cannot be solved by simply stating that 'Many Catholics whose lives are dedicated to the service and welfare of others make this teaching present, even if they have never read a social encyclical.'[19] It has been argued that for much of the period 1891–1965 Catholics were in fact engaged in a subterranean dialogue with liberal and with Marxist thought.[20] Retrieving such dialogue, for instance in the case of Slant,[21] would contribute to a greater understanding of conflict in ideas, interests and goods which eludes CST. It would also constitute a sounding board against which recent alliances between CST and liberalism, albeit of a communitarian kind,[22] may be tested.

Some Key Notions in CST

Option for the poor

This idea has made a relatively recent appearance in CST, and as initially received it marked a considerable departure. Contrast its positive intent with the comment by Benedict XV in *Ad Beatissimi*: 'And so the poor who strive against the rich as though they had taken part of the goods of others, not merely act contrary to justice and charity but also act irrationally, particularly as they themselves by honest industry can improve their fortunes if they choose' (Dorr, 1992, p. 65).[23] The idea of solidarity with the poor entailed the abandonment of attempts to divide the labour movement into Catholic and non-Catholic sectors, which were according to Chenu (cited Boswell, 2000, p. 271), based on a misunderstanding of the gospel: the Church should build the workers' movement as it existed.[24] The option for the poor suggested at least a beginning response to critics of previous encyclicals who detected little by way of analysis of the structural causes of poverty. It also indicated a shift away from concern about the poor and concern for the poor towards concern with the poor. Use of the idea of praxis, of change arising from considered actual experience, contributed to a change in the stance of CST which relied less on exhortation addressed to the world from outside the world.

The force of these changes has been blunted, however, by the ways in which 'option' and 'poor' have been interpreted. CG refers to the avoidance of an option against the poor and treats as equivalent 'the preferential option' and the special place in Catholic teaching of people who are poor. The Vatican uses the notion of a 'preferential but not exclusive option'.[25] What seems to be required is some framework within which different options can be identified and placed. As Barry has noted: 'To choose between options sensibly, you need to understand the nature of the options. There will normally be a range of possible outcomes arising from each choice.'[26]

Different understandings of 'the poor' have also emerged. Tripole,[27] reviewing Moltmann's ecclesiology, which tends to subordinate the Church to the world, argues that Jesus was partisan not for the poor as such, but rather for the alienated and dehumanized. 'Ultimately, to be on the side of the alienated means to be working for the amelioration of the structure of society as a whole, so that no one might be indigent or excessively well-possessed.' It is worth observing that CST uses structural ideas in a weak and a strong sense; for example, structural sin is sometimes viewed as inherent in societal structures, and sometimes as the outcome of many personal sins. This ambivalence seems striking in the way in which 'anti-Semitism' has been constructed recently in the Church. Dorr[28] has recently revisited the question of who are to be considered as poor. He argues that the option for the poor should include beside the intransigent those subject to racism, sexism, ageism, homophobia, and also those who subject people to these conditions. This begins to resemble an option for most of us.

Human rights

'Human rights, which have now been incorporated into Catholic thinking on social questions, are also not plain sailing.'[29] It is not clear from CG which are the shores between which we voyage – there is, for instance, no reference to the uncertain reception of the idea of individual rights in relation to members of the Church. One of the strongest statements of the problems arising from the use of natural human rights in CST can be found in Fortin.[30] He argued that the notion of individual rights is alien to CST and that it was introduced initially through the emphasis in *Rerum Novarum* on the natural right to property. 'Never before had the notion of natural rights figured so prominently and so massively in a pontifical document. The phenomenon is all the more remarkable as natural rights are totally foreign to the literature of the premodern period. The Bible certainly knows nothing of them.' Rather than calling for any bill of rights we should, according to Fortin, be obeying a bill of duties. CG does not go this far, though it does stress duties as well as inalienable rights and the value of the principle of human rights. However, its general treatment of the idea of human rights moves between seeing them as a direct means towards a substantive form of human flourishing and regarding them as a protective framework which enables respect for the rights of others and for their freedom.

Ruston, in marked contrast to Fortin, has welcomed the incorporation of human rights into CST, but he raises three considerations of critical import. First, unlike CG, he does question the extent to which the Church has fully accepted the practice of human rights, by observing that, according to canon law, 'Ecclesiastical authority is entitled to regulate in view of the common good, the exercise of rights which are proper to Christ's faithful.'[31] Second, he examines the connection between ideas of human rights and the particular conception of humankind as made in the image of God. He usefully draws attention to two different ways in which 'image of God' can be used. Humankind can be understood in this way in a passive sense. This would refer to how men and women should or should not be treated. The active sense refers to the human intellect which, according to Augustine, God gave humankind and in accordance with which humans should lead a good life. (Ruston argues that the assertion in *Rerum Novarum* that the soul carries the image and likeness of God seriously misinterprets the Augustinian and Thomist tradition in which the mind is the locus of the image of God.) Identifying the two senses of image is significant in view of David Tracy's assertion that 'image of God' is one of the key ideas indicating that CST has become a fully theological enterprise without loss of appeals to reason.[32]

Finally, Ruston discusses MacIntyre's criticism of the use of rights-talk in a statement made by the American bishops in 1986. MacIntyre was not in disagreement with the substance of the statement, but was anxious that talk in terms of individual rights could lead to the unconscious acceptance by Christians of the presupposition of the stark, unsituated individual asserting his or her individual interest over and against all others. The significance of shared meanings and a particular societal context in the formation of the individual has been recently explored in the work of Walzer, for example, though Plant[33] has pointed out that ideas of community to combat sub-jectivism and social atomism can be traced back to Hegel, T.H Green, Bosanquet, Tawney and others. Plant argues that those favouring what may be called a strongly communitarian notion of self 'are very ambiguous when it comes to specifying the relation between self and society, qualifying these formulations in crucial ways'.[34] CST requires likewise to analyse any relation between what is supposedly given foundationally as human nature and the view, for example, that 'Men and women do indeed have rights beyond life and liberty, but these do not follow from our common humanity, they follow from shared conceptions of social goods; they are local and particular in character.'[35] A strong version of the communitarian self has its attraction for Christians, but it needs to be assessed in the light of a gendered human nature. 'Men may need to sensitise themselves to the social construction of their identities, but women need to do exactly the opposite – to realise some degree of autonomy and assert some independence from social definition.'[36]

The common good

The common good is cited frequently in *Pacem in Terris*, and is given a central place in CG: 'The British have always had a feeling for the common good even if they have not expressed it in these terms.'[37] At times the idea is treated as an uncomplicated call not to be selfish or, as Stiltner puts it, 'an imperative to put the welfare of the whole ahead of our own narrow interests'.[38] Unselfishness is not as simple a notion as it appears. Jencks, for instance,[39] helpfully distinguishes between complete, partial and extreme unselfishness and between three sources of unselfishness in empathy, morality and community. In complex, modern society this last source assumes particular importance, since we can be said to identify, at least in part, with more than one collectivity and so experience conflict between the claims and goods inherent in different collectivities. Conflict, as already noted, is not extensively explored in CST and this applies particularly to expositions of the 'common good'. This provides one reason for supporting Boswell's belief that what he significantly describes as 'the retrieval of the concept of the common good in contemporary society . . . is more fraught with peril than Catholics usually acknowledge'.[40]

Some of the problems become apparent if we return to Stiltner's definition which continues by referring to 'an imperative for a national embrace of responsibility and sacrifice, of compassion and caring as building blocks for meaningful lives and for a healthy society'. This suggests that the common good can somehow be engineered, that the unit of commonality is in fact the nation-state, and that individual and common goods can be achieved simultaneously. CG discusses the common good at a supranational level as well as at the level of individual families. The question of the reach of commonality is significant in the context of discerning the signs of the times. It is difficult to see how the good of the whole human family can be knowingly realized. We may not always choose goods at the level of the family wisely, but the chances of unwise decisions increase the wider the range of 'the common'.

This issue of specifying the boundaries within which any warrant for the common good runs can also be illustrated by raising the question of the possibility of a common good for Christians. Ward, noting that there are now 30,000 Christian denominations, considers it unlikely that for Christians there is a single, all-embracing purpose that subsumes all others. 'There may be many goals, realized in many developing traditions, all of which have distinctive value . . . there may be many diverse goals, none of them realized unambiguously.'[41] So, we should not consider the common good as simply consisting in the achievement of all the goods which might be thought to have a bearing on that flourishing that is designated as human. As Berlin has argued:

> The notion of the perfect whole, the ultimate solution, in which all good things co-exist, seems to me to be not merely unattainable – that is a truism – but conceptually incoherent; I do not know what is meant by a harmony of this kind. Some among the Great Goods cannot live

together . . . We are doomed to choose, and every choice may entail irreparable loss' (1997, p. 11).[42]

Cornwell is of the view that 'the failure of John Paul II to espouse pluralism as a crucial *Christian* legacy may well prove the greatest failing of his papacy'.[43]

In a chapter on Berlin's treatment of pluralism, Grey[44] indicates that it has application at three levels and that at each level the problem Berlin crucially identified as incommensurability arises. First, in any system of morality conflicts are bound to surface between goods recognized as intrinsic to that morality. As an example he cites the goods intrinsic to a liberal morality, but these, such as liberty and equality, are inherently rivals and their rivalry cannot be settled by appeal to some superior standard that acts a referee. Second, each of the goods within that morality is of considerable complexity, and so inherently pluralistic. Berlin's well-known discussion of negative and positive freedom would be a case in point. Third, different cultural forms may present features that overlap, but also specify virtues and conceptions of the good that are different and incommensurable. An example can be found in Berlin's description of the value placed by Herder on membership of a particular nation: 'to be a member of a group is to think and act in a certain way: and to think and act so is to belong to a group'.[45] 'No writer has stressed so vividly the damage done to human beings by being torn from the only conditions in which their history has made it possible for them to live full lives.'[46]

CG does not seem to recognize problems of pluralism and incommensurability at any of these levels. At a cultural level it attempts to accumulate into a single whole body of material deriving from Scripture, the early Fathers, the writings of numerous Christian thinkers down the ages, the documents of Vatican II, the statements of local and regional Episcopal conferences, and the social encyclicals.[47] It refers to the principles of subsidiarity and solidarity without reflecting on their internal complexity or how conflicts between the two may be resolved. Mansbridge may well be correct in contending that 'we must learn to live with, even welcome a concept of public good that remains continually in contest' (quoted in Boswell, p. 289).[48] The contention may become more intelligible if we consider less the high levels of thought about society and attend more to ways in which as individuals we somehow or other manage to keep afloat in the troubled sea of daily life. As Midgley has written:

> Conflict of goods is the heart of our problems. Love clashes with honour, order with freedom, art with friendship, justice with prudence, kindness with honesty – and not just in the rare, melodramatic cases of major decision, but in the constant, quiet grind of everyday

living. Somehow we manage to balance their claims, by bargain, compromise, sublimation, partial combination and sacrifice.[49]

These means of managing would repay careful consideration.

Conclusion

The impact of CST has been variously assessed at different times. Lesch, for example, in a work significantly titled *Catholic Social Thought: Twilight or Renaissance,* argues that CST has been buried and revitalized several times and for many different reasons in recent decades.[50] When strength has been recognized it has frequently been found in unofficial action. O'Connell, for example, argued that 'the activities of Western and Central democratic parties owed less to papal teaching and more to the faith and moral and practical principles of sensible middle class politicians'.[51] He goes on to support a teaching role for the Church as specifically a brokering agent, but 'this is not separate from its learning role; and neither role is carried out without considerable discussion with the church as well as with contemporaries, Christians and others . . .'. This positive attitude can also be found in CG which seems eager to listen to anyone wishing to contribute and appears to endorse a notion of development as applied to CST. If development is to be taken seriously certain obstacles need to be removed. The role of lay people in helping to discern the signs of the times, whether they are considered experts or simply those experiencing particular forms of oppression, should be actively supported by the hierarchy. The long tradition of reliance on the Bible, the Church Fathers and quotations from previous popes should be questioned. Preston has remarked on the recent use of references to United Nations documents, whilst calling attention to the complete absence of empirical material.[52] Markham has also called attention to a failure to recognize 'the revelatory significance of complexity and ambiguity'.[53] It is the purpose of this chapter to suggest that complexity and ambiguity are best understood in the terms of political thinking rather than in a politicized theology.

A recent edition of Oakeshott's Muirhead Lectures[54] accepts that ambiguity is to be found in all political language. 'Rights bear a double meaning; and there is scarcely need to pause in order to draw attention to the double-entendre in "democracy" . . . And the current dilemma in respect of "toleration" springs largely from the ambiguity in the word.'[55] Such ambiguities cannot be resolved through simple, stipulated definitions, but they can be rendered intelligible if they are placed within the continuous movement in the activity of governing between two poles, the politics of faith and the politics of scepticism. According to the former the governing body decides the one direction in which it is best to proceed. 'In the politics of faith, political decision and enterprise may be understood as an inspired perception of what the common good is, or it may be understood as the conclusion which follows a rational argument; what it can never be understood as is a temporary expedient or just something to keep things going.'[56] The attraction to this pole can be seen in the assumption that 'The social order requires constant improvement' (*Gaudium et Spes*, p. 26)[57] or in the assertion that 'we are today witnessing a widening of the role of the common good, which is the sum total of social conditions which allow people, either as groups or individuals, to reach their fulfilment more fully and more easily'.[58] It can also be glimpsed in the frequent references in CG to healthy society and healthy democracies.

In contrast the politics of scepticism are somewhat embarrassed by power. As a style of governance it declines the comprehensive purpose of the pursuit of the common good, and sees its chief office in lessening the severity of human conflict. In this perspective what has to be improved are not human beings or even human conduct but the existing system of rights, duties and the means of redress. The attraction of this pole is visible in the notion of subsidiarity and in certain ambivalences over the idea of structural sin and the value of single solutions to global problems. Thinking in terms of movement between the two poles may help to avoid acceptance of an assumption of perpetual progress to be found in certain readings of church teaching both at the level of CST and also in a theology that speaks of an ever-deepening, always growing relationship with the divine.

Notes

1. J. O'Connell, 'Is There a Catholic Social Doctrine? The Problem of Content and the Ambivalence of History, Analysis and Authority', in P. Furlong and D. Curtis (eds), *The Church Faces the Modern World* (Scunthorpe: Earlsgate Press, 1994), p. 80.
2. M. Oakeshott, 'Learning and Teaching', in T. Fuller (ed.), *The Voice of Liberal Learning* (New Haven and London: Yale University Press 1989), p. 44.
3. D. Dorr, *Option for the Poor* (Dublin: Gill and Macmillan, 1992), p. 288.
4. Paul VI, Apostolic Letter *Octogesima adveniens*, 1971, p. 4. Quoted in J. Boswell, F. McHugh and J. Verstraeten (eds), *Catholic Social Thought: Twilight or Renaissance?* (Leuven: Leuven University Press, 2000), p. 283.
5. Catholic Bishops' Conference of England and Wales, *The Common Good and the Catholic Church's Social Teaching*, 1996, p. 4.
6. Dorr, op. cit., p. 377.
7. J. Heaney, *The Modernist Crisis: von Hugel* (London: Geoffrey Chapman, 1968), p. 153.

8. *The Common Good*, p. 42.
9. H. McCabe, *God Still Matters* (London: Continuum, 2002), p. 86.
10. *The Common Good*, p. 94.
11. Ibid., 24.
12. J. Cornwell, *The Pope in Winter* (London: Penguin, 2004), p. 116.
13. R. Ruston, *Human Rights and the Image of God* (London: SCM, 2004), p. 289.
14. Dorr, op. cit., p. 78.
15. Quoted in S. Thakur, *Religion and Social Justice* (London: Macmillan, 1996), p. 58.
16. T. Honderich, *Terrorism for Humanity* (London: Pluto, 2003).
17. Pius XI, encyclical letter *Quadragesimo Anno*, 1931, p. 82.
18. *The Common Good*, p. 28.
19. Ibid.
20. *Catholic Social Thought*, p. 266.
21. B. Wicker, 'Justice, Peace and Dominicans 1216–1999: VIII – Slant, Marxism and the English Dominicans', in *New Blackfriars*, vol. 80, no. 944 (October 1999), pp. 436–43.
22. C. Insole, *The Politics of Human Frailty* (London: SCM, 2004).
23. Quoted in Dorr, op. cit., p. 65.
24. Cited in *Catholic Social Thought*, p. 271.
25. *Catholic Social Thought*, p. 255.
26. D. Barry, *Theories of Justice* (Cambridge: Polity, 2005), p. 137.
27. M. Tripole, 'A Church for the Poor in the World: At Issue with Moltmann's Ecclesiology', in *Theological Studies* 42 (1981), pp. 645–59.
28. *Catholic Social Thought*, p. 255.
29. *The Common Good*, p. 3.
30. E. Fortin, 'Sacred and Inviolable: Rerum Novarum on Natural Rights', in *Theological Studies* 53 (1992), pp. 203–33.
31. R. Ruston, *Human Rights and the Image of God* (London: SCM, 2004).
32. R. Douglass and D. Hollenbach (eds), *Catholicism and Liberalism* (Cambridge: Cambridge University Press, 1994).
33. R. Plant, *Modern Political Thought* (Oxford: Blackwell, 1991), p. 325.
34. Ibid., p. 373.
35. M. Walzer, *Spheres of Justice* (Oxford: Martin Robertson, 1983), p. xv.
36. M. Segers, 'Feminism, Liberalism and Catholic Social Teaching', in *Catholicism and Liberalism*, op. cit., p. 247.
37. *The Common Good*, p. 116.
38. R. Stiltner, *Religion and the Common Good* (Oxford: Rowman and Littlefield, 1999).
39. C. Jencks, 'Varieties of Altruism', in J. Mansbridge (ed.), *Beyond Self-Interest* (Chicago: University of Chicago Press, 1990), pp. 53–67.
40. *Catholic Social Thought*, p. 289.
41. K. Ward, *Religion and Community* (Oxford: Clarendon, 2000), p. 323.

42. I. Berlin, *The Proper Study of Mankind*, ed. H. Hardy and R. Hausheer (London: Chatto and Windus, 1997), p. 11.
43. Cornwell, op. cit., p. 124 (my italics).
44. J. Grey, *Isaiah Berlin* (London: HarperCollins, 1995).
45. Op. cit., p. 413.
46. Ibid., p. 415.
47. *The Common Good*, p. 3.
48. Quoted in *Catholic Social Thought*, p. 289.
49. M. Midgley, *Beast and Man: The Roots of Human Nature* (Brighton: Harvester, 1979), p. 190.
50. W. Lesch, *Catholic Social Thought: Twilight or Renaissance* (Leuven: Leuven University Press, 2000).
51. O'Connell, op. cit., p. 72.
52. Quoted in C. Longley, *The Worlock Archive* (London: Geoffrey Chapman, 2000), p. 327.
53. Ibid.
54. M. Oakeshott, *The Politics of Faith and the Politics of Scepticism* (Newhaven: Yale University Press, 1996).
55. Ibid., p. 14.
56. Ibid., p. 27.
57. *Gaudium et Spes*, p. 26.
58. Ibid.

Index